YALE CLASSICAL STUDIES

YALE CLASSICAL STUDIES

EDITED FOR THE DEPARTMENT OF CLASSICS

by

THOMAS COLE
AND
DAVID ROSS

VOLUME XXIII
STUDIES IN LATIN LANGUAGE
AND LITERATURE

CAMBRIDGE
AT THE UNIVERSITY PRESS
1973

Published by the Syndics of the Cambridge University Press
Bentley House, 200 Euston Road, London NW1 2DB
American Branch: 32 East 57th Street, New York, N.Y. 10022

© Cambridge University Press 1973

Library of Congress Catalogue Card Number: 72–80595

ISBN: 0 521 08683 3

Typeset in Great Britain
at the University Printing House, Cambridge
(Brooke Crutchley, University Printer)
Printed in the United States of America

Contents

Clarence Whittlesey Mendell
1883-1970

PROFESSOR MENDELL came to Yale as an undergraduate from the Boston Latin School in the autumn of 1900 and thereafter – except for the periods of two world wars – was either in the center of or scarcely separable from Yale concerns and interests for virtually seventy years.

This notice will be confined to a brief review of Professor Mendell's published work, which speaks for itself. It should be remembered, however, that his eight books, thirty articles and a score of review and minor papers were the fruit of tranquil intervals in an extremely active life which the very diversity of his native gifts made inescapable. It was a life filled with teaching, administrative responsibilities (including eleven years as dean of Yale College), chairmanships and directorships of organizations, service to the nation in two world wars, and the answering of incessant calls to speak to academic and alumni groups. Of his services to classical education outside Yale particular mention should be made of his years devoted to the Classical Committee of the American Academy in Rome. He was unique in his days at Yale in that each circle with which he was associated felt that Dean Mendell was primarily one of them. His forte was the inspirational teaching of undergraduates, generations of whom can never forget him.

Professor Mendell's scholarly production was concentrated in the field of Augustan and post-Augustan Latin literature, Tacitus in particular being the object of a life-long interest. Particularly noteworthy was his contribution to the study of the manuscript tradition of this author, and in 1966 he had the satisfaction of seeing the publication of Sijthoff's facsimile of the Leidensis ('praefatus est C. W. Mendell') that he had been instrumental in rescuing from oblivion. The titles that have been listed below contain what Professor Mendell regarded as his serious contributions to classical studies. Any attempt to collect the reviews, translations, addresses and minor papers in the field would result in a list of equal length. A charming conclusion of a life whose leisure was given to the study of letters is a privately circulated volume of verse translations, imitations of favorite Greek and Latin poets and original pieces, filled with the richness that a rare spirit had acquired from seventy years' or more association with his beloved classics.

SELECTED BIBLIOGRAPHY OF THE WRITINGS OF C. W. MENDELL

Sentence Connection in Tacitus (New Haven 1911)

Latin Sentence Connection (New Haven 1917)

Prometheus Bound and Prometheus Unbound (New Haven 1926)

Livy, xxx–xxxiii, edited with introduction and notes (New York 1928)

Tacitus, the Man and his Work (New Haven 1957)

Latin Poetry: the New Poets and the Augustans (New Haven 1965)

Latin Poetry: the Age of Rhetoric and Satire (Hamden 1968)

'Petronius and the Greek Novel', *CP* (1917), 158–72

'Satire as Popular Philosophy', *CP* (1920), 138–57

'Literary Reminiscences in the *Agricola*', *TAPA* (1921), 53–68

'Martial and the Satiric Epigram', *CP* (1922), 1–20

'*Nec cithara carentem*', *CJ* (1924), 369–79

'Silius the Reactionary', *Philological Quarterly* (1924), 92–106

'*Ut* Clauses', *AJP* (1925 and 1926), 293–316 and 124–52

'The Epic of Asinius Pollio', *YCS* (1928), 195–207

'Catullan Echoes in the Odes of Horace', *CP* (1935), 289–301

'The Discovery of the Minor Works of Tacitus', *AJP* (1935), 113–30

'The Dramatic Construction of Tacitus' *Annales*', *YCS* (1935), 1–54

'Horace, Odes i 14', *CP* (1938), 145–56

'Vergil's Workmanship', *CJ* (1938), 9–22

'Manuscripts of Tacitus xi–xxi', *YCS* (1939), 39–70

'Lucan's Rivers', *YCS* (1942), 1–22

'Manuscripts of Tacitus' Minor Works', *Mem. Am. Ac. Rome* (1949), 135–45

'Horace, Odes II 18', *YCS* (1950), 279–92

'The Influence of the Epyllion on the *Aeneid*', *YCS* (1951),
203–26

'Ryck's Manuscript of Tacitus', *AJP* (1951), 337–45

'Leid. BPL 16. B. Tacitus XI–XXI', *AJP* (1954), 250–70

Particularum quarundam uarietas: prae and pro

E. D. FRANCIS

AUGUSTUS' chief concern as a stylist was clarity of expression. To achieve that end he was willing to employ prepositions where their use might, strictly speaking, have seemed redundant.[1] In 50 B.C. Cicero had self-consciously apologized to Atticus for a similar practice.[2] Seven years earlier, among the regulations governing a temple of Jupiter, prepositional phrases occur in place of the expected dative case.[3] The increasing prominence of prepositions in marking syntactic relations previously expressed by case inflection represents one of the most important grammatical developments in the history of Latin.

In addition to presiding over the demise of the inherited case system, Latin prepositional usage has special interest for its exemplification of diverse syntactic and semantic change.[4] Pre-

1. Suetonius, *Aug.* LXXXVI. The following works are cited by author and short title: B. Kranz, *De particularum 'pro' et 'prae' in prisca latinitate vi atque usu* (Dissertation, Breslau 1907); E. Benveniste, 'Le système sublogique des prépositions en latin', *Travaux du Cercle linguistique de Copenhague*, 5 (1949), 177–84 (reprinted in *Problèmes de linguistique générale* (Paris 1966), pp. 132–9); J. André, 'Les adjectifs et adverbes à valeur intensive', *RÉL* 29 (1951), 121–54; by author only: Kühner–Stegmann, *Lateinische Grammatik* II. 1⁴ (Hannover 1962); M. Leumann, *Lateinische Grammatik* [= Stolz–Schmalz, *Lateinische Grammatik* 1⁵] (Munich 1926); J. B. Hofmann, *Lateinische Syntax und Stilistik* (= Stolz–Schmalz, *Lateinische Grammatik* II), new ed. A. Szantyr (Munich 1965) (abbreviated Hofmann–Szantyr); Walde–Hofmann, *Lateinisches etymologisches Wörterbuch*³ (Heidelberg 1938–56); Ernout–Meillet, *Dictionnaire étymologique de la langue latine*⁴ (Paris 1960). I thank A. T. Cole and Eric Laughton for their helpful comments during the preparation of this paper.

2. *Ad Att.* VII. 3. 10, a passage in which Cicero invokes the precedent of Caecilius and Terence for his use of the phrase *in Piraeea* at id. VI. 9. 1 (cf. *postquam hinc in Ephesum abiui*, Pl. *Bacch.* 171, beside *uenit Ephesum, MG* 975). For further discussion, see Hofmann–Szantyr, pp. 49–50, and P. G. Walsh, *Livy* (Cambridge 1961), p. 263.

3. *CIL* IX. 3513: *si pecunia ad id templum data erit...Quod ad eam aedem donum datum erit....*

4. The 'adverbial' origin of Latin prepositions has often been discussed; cf. Meillet–Vendryes, *Traité de grammaire comparée des langues classiques*² (Paris

[1]

positions reflect the expression of time–space relations in the Roman world and play a central role in the construction of idioms. Notable semantic realignments have been occasioned by the interaction between prepositional and prefixational uses of the same form, or of different forms with similar or opposite meanings.

Like other Latin prepositions, *prae* and *pro* are commonly discussed in one of two ways. Traditional lexicographers distinguish between 'literal' and 'figurative' usage, isolating a basic meaning to which all other meanings are presumably subordinate. Thus, according to Lewis and Short, *prae* is used 'literally' when it refers to place, but 'figuratively' in comparisons. Yet while locative *prae* may claim historical priority over comparative *prae*, it is unclear from a descriptive standpoint in what sense the Ciceronian phrase *prae nobis beatus* 'fortunate by comparison with us' (*ad Fam.* iv. 4. 2) contains a 'figurative' use of the preposition. Benveniste,[5] on the other hand, has attempted to reconcile all uses of *pro* and *prae* under a single rubric: *pro* 'ne signifie pas tant "devant" que "au dehors"', while *prae* 'indique la position non pas "devant", mais "à l'avant" d'un objet'. The potential shortcomings of both methods are obvious. Neither adequately expresses the relationship among the various meanings of each

1948), p. 524 (cf. pp. 573 f.): '[prepositions were originally derived from] un élément adverbial autonome dont la place n'était nullement fixée ni par rapport au nom ni par rapport au verbe. Quand la rection s'est constituée, la préposition a été souvent placée après son régime' (cf. Hofmann–Szantyr, pp. 494 f., J. Wackernagel, *Vorlesungen über Syntax* ii² (Basel 1928), pp. 153f. and the bibliography there cited). The syntactic status of these 'éléments adverbiaux' in Proto-Indo-European deserves thorough re-evaluation in view of the widely divergent opinions held by many scholars (cf. B. Delbrück, *Vergleichende Syntax der idg. Sprachen* i (Strasburg 1893), pp. 643f.; contrast O. Behaghel, *Deutsche Syntax* ii (Heidelberg 1925), pp. 21f., especially p. 34). De Saussure's categorical statement that 'l'indo-européen ne connaissait pas les prépositions; les rapports qu'elles indiquent étaient marqués par des cas nombreux et pourvus d'une grande force significative' (*Cours de linguistique générale*⁴ (Paris 1949), p. 247) raises many serious questions of definition and, in terms of current grammatical theory, is at least misleading. (On the inadequacy of the term 'preposition' see Wackernagel, *Vorlesungen über Syntax*, ii², 153.)

5. 'Le système sublogique'; Benveniste's argument is conducted according to the terms of Louis Hjelmslev's theory of 'sublogical systems' (*La catégorie des cas* [= *Acta Jutlandica* 7. 1, 1935], pp. 127f.; cf. V. Brøndal, *Praepositionernes Theori* (Copenhagen 1940)).

form. Both approaches tend to obscure the productivity or obsolescence of different uses across the history of Latin. It is obviously
important to define, for example, the grammatical and chronological circumstances under which *prae* means 'in front of', 'on
account of', or 'by comparison with'. Attention must also be
given to the ways in which specific synonymic conflicts are
resolved and a balance maintained among the uses of different
prepositions so that each is fully and uniquely effective. In the
present article the history of Latin *prae* and *pro*, as adverb,
preposition, and prefix, will be discussed in the light of these
general considerations, and with particular reference to the ways
in which the productive functions of each form were successively
reorganized until, at the end of the Latin period, they finally
converged.[6]

ADVERBIAL *PRAE* AND *PRO*

Adverbial *prae* and *pro* are only attested in highly restricted
contexts, and did not survive the second century B.C. Nevertheless
their respective uses can be clearly distinguished. Adverbial *prae*
is characteristically constructed with imperative forms of *ire* and
its compounds: *abi prae, Sosia; iam ego sequar* (Pl. *Amph.* 543–4),
eamus nunciam intro: i prae, sequor (Ter. *Andr.* 171).[7] The exclamatory
use of *pro* throughout the history of Latin is well-known.[8] Exclama-

6. Cf. Hofmann–Szantyr, p. 241 Zus. *a*, p. 269 Zus. *c*, R. A. Latham,
Revised Medieval Latin Word-list (London 1965), p. x. *Prae* and *pro* have
frequently been discussed together for both etymological and semantic reasons
(cf. Kühner–Stegmann, pp. 512f., Kranz, *'Pro' et 'prae'*, and Benveniste,
'Le système sublogique'; note also O. Kuebler, *De differentia inter particulas
'ante' et 'prae' intercedente* (Dissertation, Breslau 1850). For further bibliography
see Hofmann–Szantyr, pp. 268–71. A full-scale investigation of Latin time–
space prepositions and their relation to other categories expressing tense and
aspect, cause and effect, is obviously an important *desideratum* but lies beyond
the scope of this article which represents merely a preliminary contribution
to such a study.

7. Cf. Pl. *Cist.* 773, *Pseud.* 170, 241, Ter. *Eun.* 499, 908, *Ad.* 167. Other relics
of adverbial *prae* (e.g., *prae* at Pl. *Stich.* 362, *praefiscini*) will be discussed below.
Note also *praeter*, *praequam*, and *praeut* (on which *pro quam* (Lucr. ii. 1137) and
prout (Titin. *com.* 59, Cic. etc.) are analogically based, Hofmann–Szantyr,
p. 270).

8. Cf. *pro fidem, Thebani ciues* (Pl. *Amph.* 376), *pro Iuppiter* (ibid. 1074, cf.
Verg. *Aen.* iv. 590), *pro, di immortales* (Cic. *Leg. Man.* xii. 33), *tantum, pro!
degeneramus a patribus* (Livy xxii. 14. 6).

tory *pro* probably first developed in construction with verbs of command and entreaty, but was then generalized to other contexts. Its adverbial origin may still be perceived in a passage from Caecilius:

pro deum popularium omnium omnium adulescentium
clamo postulo obsecro oro ploro atque imploro fidem (fr. 211–12 (R²))

in which *pro...clamo* can be plausibly rendered 'I call forth.'[9] Even if Caecilius' use of *pro* is merely exclamatory, the passage illustrates a context from which adverbial *pro*, originally meaning 'forth, forwards', could have developed its attested function.

The contrast between adverbial *pro* and *prae* can be drawn as follows: *i prae* means 'you go in front, you go first', without necessarily specifying a distinction between time and place.[10] In this example, *prae* indicates a relation between speaker and interlocutor, or, secondarily, a relation between two positions occupied by the interlocutor, in either case without reference to motion. (At a pre-Plautine stage of the language, *prae* was doubtless used more generally with reference to the relation between any two persons or objects). Adverbial *pro*, on the other hand, not only implies an exclusive reference to place, but designates the movement of the verb subject as well as the forward direction of that movement (without necessary reference to the position of

9. Not simply 'Oh! I shout, wail and bewail' (E. H. Warmington, *Remains of Old Latin* I (London 1967), 539). Note Hofmann's convincing interpretation of this passage in the development of the attested *Beschwörungsformel* (*Lateinische Umgangssprache*³ (Heidelberg 1951), p. 28; cf. Hofmann–Szantyr, p. 271 Zus. *d*: 'zur Loslösung des *pro* vom Verbum und Zusammenstellung mit dem Vokativ vgl. *porro* in Fällen wie Laber. mim. 125 *porro Quirites, libertatem perdimus*'). (The archaic use of *pro...clamo...* may be reflected in the legal expression *proclamare ad libertatem*, on which see *RE* 45, pp. 69f.). Other possible evidence for adverbial *pro* meaning 'forth' will be discussed in connection with the development of prepositional *pro* on p. 45. Wagenvoort (*Mnemosyne* IV Ser. 2 (1949), 319f.) suggests that an exclamatory use of *pro* underlies the adjective *profanus* (from **pro fano* 'weg vom Heiligtum'). A prepositional origin is, however, at least equally possible (from *pro fano* 'in front of the *fanum*' as opposed to 'inside the *fanum*, initiated'; for the construction compare *praegnas* and *proconsul*). On *profanus*, see also E. Benveniste, '*Profanus et profanare*', *Hommages à G. Dumézil, Coll. Latomus* 45 (1960), 46f.

10. The etymologically related forms *prior* and *primus* exhibit a similar ambivalence. Their corresponding adverbs, *prius* and *primum*, however, refer exclusively to time.

the speaker).[11] Adverbial *ante*, as a partial synonym of both *pro* and *prae*, is still attested in the Augustan period.[12] Its temporal reference, like that of *antea* and preverbal *prae-*, was, however, extended at the expense of its reference to place. While *ante* survived as an adverb, especially with reference to time, it took little part in verb prefixation. On the other hand, *pro* and *prae*, obsolete as adverbs at an early date, became highly productive as verb prefixes. Indeed the obsolescence of adverbial *pro* and *prae* is closely connected with the increasing productivity of these forms as verb prefixes, which resulted from analyzing the construction of 'verb modifier + verb' as a single lexical unit. The relationship between the development of adverbial *prae*, *pro*, and *ante* will be discussed again at the end of this article.

PREPOSITIONAL *PRAE*

Three functions are traditionally attributed to prepositional *prae*: locative, causal,[13] and comparative. Comparative *prae* is well-attested from the beginning of the literary tradition and, in its restricted contexts, causal *prae* is also relatively common. On the other hand the prepositional use of locative *prae* is virtually non-existent and no direct evidence exists for its temporal use.[14]

The first and last example of the prepositional use of locative *prae* before late Latin occurs in the phrase *prae tet tremonti*, com-

11. Cf. Benveniste, 'Le système sublogique', p. 178: 'c'est en quelque sorte une nécessité interne qui fait surgir *sequi* à la suite de *prae*: une fois énoncé *prae*, l'objet est figuré comme continu, et le reste doit "suivre", ne peut pas ne pas suivre, étant continu.' While this statement clarifies some of the implications of *prae(-)*, it overemphasizes 'consequence' at the expense of 'state'.

12. The following passage illustrates a context in which this ambivalence could readily develop: *saeuit et in lucem Stygiis emissa tenebris | pallida Tisiphone morbos agit ante metumque* (Verg. *G.* iii. 551–2). A similar semantic merger is also exemplified by adverbial *prae se* (see below, pp. 6f.).

13. *Prae* characteristically denotes cause in contexts such as *neque miser me commouere possum prae formidine* (Pl. *Amph.* 337, cf. n. 23). Because this use of *prae* most frequently occurs in negative sentences, it has also been termed privative *prae*, or *prae* of hindrance.

14. *Praegnas*, however, may continue an earlier temporal use of prepositional *prae* (pp. 26–7). Note that both temporal and locative uses of the forms corresponding to *prae* are attested in Oscan and Umbrian: Oscan *prai mamerttiais* (= Latin *ante Martias*, temp.), Umbrian *preveres* (= Latin *ante portam*, loc.).

monly attributed to the *Carmen Saliare*.[15] It survives, albeit un-
productively, in adverbial idioms like *prae manu* and *prae se*.
The idiom *prae manu* 'ready to hand' (originally 'in front of the
hand, within reach', cf. German *vorhanden*) is already attested in
Roman comedy (cf. Pl. *Bacch.* 624, Ter. *Ad.* 980) and persists
into Medieval Latin in the form *pre manibus* 'in advance, cash
down'.[16]

Prae se is more interesting than *prae manu*, not merely because
of the greater frequency and variety of its use, but because it
provides a complex illustration of idiomatic development. In
some instances *prae se* seems to mean 'ahead, in front' (e.g.,
singulos prae[17] *se inermos mittere*, Sall. *Iug.* XCIV. 2), in others it
functions as a synonym of *palam, aperte* (e.g., *nil me fatalia terrent,* |
si qua Phryges prae se iactant, responsa deorum 'however brazenly the
Trojans boast', Verg. *Aen.* IX. 133–4). Furthermore, *prae se ferre*,
an idiom meaning 'reveal', must be considered in relation to
these other uses of *prae se*. Some contexts are ambiguous: does
prae se at Cic. *Phil.* II. 12. 30 (*ille* [sc. *Brutus*] *qui stillantem prae se
pugionem tulit*) mean that Brutus held the dagger dripping 'in
front of him' or that he held it 'for all to see'? The distinction is,
at most, one of emphasis.

15. Ap. Terent. Scaur. VII. 28. 11, Fest. 222. 28 (ed. W. M. Lindsay
(Leipzig 1913)). Given the uncertainty regarding the text of the *Carmen
Saliare*, even in Classical times (cf. Hor. *Ep.* II. 1. 86, Quint. 1. 6. 40), this
quotation is relatively insecure. On the other hand, since adequate evidence
exists which suggests that the prepositional use of locative *prae* not only
occurred in Old Latin (cf. *prae manu, praecordia* etc.) but was etymologically
original, the construction of *prae tet tremonti* appears to be entirely regular.
Prae at Petronius XXXIX. 12 and XLVI. 1 does not mean 'before, in front of', as
Lewis and Short (*prae* II init.) imply, but is causal (cf. Hofmann–Szantyr,
p. 269 Zus. *b*, and n. 25 below).

16. Latham, *Medieval Latin Word-list*, p. 363. (For the plural, see Gell.
XIX. 8. 6). A financial context is already apparent in the comic uses of *prae
manu* (but not in Gellius, loc. cit.): *qui patri reddidi omne aurum amans,* | *quod
fuit prae manu* (Pl. *Bacch.* 623–4), *siquidem...huic aliquid paulum prae manu* |
dederis, unde utatur (Ter. *Ad.* 979–81); cf. *petenti mutuam pecuniam creditori, cum
prae manu debitor non haberet, species auri dedit, ut pignori poneret* (Ulpian ap.
Dig. XII. 7. 27).

17. I accept the reading of KTs (P¹ *pro*, cett. *per*, cf. Kurfess ad loc.): *per se*,
immediately following *singulos*, is redundant and easier to understand as a
corruption than as Sallust's intention. *Pro* makes good enough sense but since
the idiom *prae se* meaning 'ahead' also occurs in Livy, the reading of KTs is
entirely supportable. A change of *prae* to *pro* can be explained as an attempt
to replace a relatively rare usage by a more common one (on the medieval

Plautus attests constructions of the type *i prae* (adverb), *ego sequar*, but not **i prae* (preposition) *me, ego sequar*, which would presumably be synonymous, or **it prae me, ego sequar*. In the Plautine contexts, adverbial *prae* ambiguously specified either the relation between the speaker and the verb subject or the relation between two positions occupied by the verb subject (p. 4). In the latter case, although *prae* still signified position and not, like obsolescent *pro*, directional movement, the distinction between the two was doubtless blurred. Construction of the lingering prepositional *prae* with the reflexive pronoun appropriately clarified that distinction. In other words, *prae se*, as a specialized idiom – etymologically prepositional *prae* of place + reflexive pronoun – continued the function of the obsolescent adverb *prae*. Sallust's *prae se mittere* therefore closely paralleled *praemittere* (Pl. +), but specified position more emphatically (cf. n. 17); compare Sallust's use of *praemittere* in *dum legatus ad flumen, quo praemissus erat, festinans pergit... (Iug. LII. 5)*.

It has often been observed that this use of *prae se* in the wholly locative sense of 'in front, ahead' was characteristically restricted to archaizing writers (cf. Hofmann–Szantyr, p. 268). A stricter *latinitas* may indeed be exemplified by the following passage from Caesar: *equitatumque omnem ante se mittit. P. Considius...cum exploratoribus praemittitur (BG I. 21. 3–4; cf. prae se agere* at Livy III. 66. 6 but *ante se...agebat* at Nep. *Dat.* III. 2). 'Archaism' may, however, be too normative a term to apply to the presence of *prae se* in Sallust and Livy by contrast with Caesar and Nepos. The temporal and locative use of Osco-Umbrian equivalents of Latin *prae* was cited in n. 14. The use of locative *prae* may have still been regular in non-Roman dialects of Latin during the first century B.C. and the occurrence of *prae se* in Livy and Sallust

confusion between *pro* and *prae*, see Latham, *Medieval Latin Word-list*, p. x). Note also that *prae se* nicely balances *sequi* in the following clause and thus adds syntactic coherence to the sentence (cf. *prae se* beside *retro* at Livy III. 66. 6 and an implied sequence at id. I. 7. 4: [*Tiber*] *qua prae se armentum agens nando traiecerat*). Compare Columella, *RR* I. 5. 4: *cauendum erit ut* [*uilla*] *a tergo potius quam prae se flumen habeat* with *prae se* corresponding to adverbial *ante* at Livy XXVII. 18. 5: *fluuius ab tergo, ante circaque uelut ripa praeceps oram eius omnem cingebat*, in which the collocation with *circaque* and the presence of *praeceps* may have inhibited the use of *prae se*. The synonymy of *prae se* and *ante* (continuing the earlier connotations of both *pro* and *prae*) was observed in n. 12. Benveniste's comments quoted in n. 11 are particularly appropriate to the use of *prae se* in Sall. *Iug.* XCIV. 2, Livy I. 7. 4 and III. 66. 6 (cit. supr.).

possibly reflects a dialect as much as a consciously stylistic distinction.[18]

If *prae se* occurs as an archaism (or provincialism) in Sallust, its presence in the *Second Philippic* (loc. cit., listed by Lewis and Short as a 'literal' use of *prae se*) presumably cannot be explained in this way. *Prae se* is first attested in Lucilius (fr. 166f. Marx: *hi prae se portant ingentes munere pisces | triginta numero*, cf. Marx ad loc. and n. 20 below), a context which well illustrates the potential transition from prepositional phrase to adverbial idiom. Thus the characteristic collocation of *prae se* with such verbs as *agere*, *portare*, and, in particular, *ferre*, led to a semantic change whereby *prae se* 'in front' became synonymous with *palam*, *aperte* (cf. *prae se iactant* at Verg. *Aen.* IX. 134, above, p. 6). In Cicero, *ferre* is frequently used with adverbs such as *aperte* or *obscure* in the sense of 'make public', or 'conceal', for example, *cum ipsum dolorem hic tulit paulo apertius* (*Planc.* XIV. 34), *neque id obscure ferebat nec dissimulare ullo modo poterat* (*Clu.* XIX. 54), and *laetitiam apertissime tulimus omnes* (*ad Att.* XIV. 13. 2; note the co-occurrence of *apertius*, *neque...* *obscure | nec dissimulare*, and *apertissime*, respectively). It is easy to see how *prae se* + *ferre* developed in constructions of this kind from a synonymy with *ante ferre* to one with *aperte ferre*. Connotations of both place and publicity are probably exemplified in the phrase *prae se pugionem tulit*, the latter being predominant, but the choice of *prae se* (rather than *palam* or *haud clam*) partly derives from its potential locative resonance.[19] A similar allo-

18. The use of *ab* to denote cause in Livy (e.g., *ab ira* XXVI. 1. 3, cf. VII. 10. 5, XXI. 26. 7, XXIV. 30. 1, and Walsh's comments, loc. cit.), Sallust (born in Amiternum: *ab ignauia atque socordia*, *Iug.* XXXI. 3), and Cornelius Balbus (a native of Gades: *ab singulari amore*, ap. Cic. *ad Att.* IX. 7*b*) may likewise represent a non-urban provincialism. Compare Cicero's remarks on the loss of final *-s quod iam subrusticum uidetur, olim autem politius...* (*Or.* XLVIII. 161). The possibility that these facts reflect dialect distinctions within the Roman world deserves thorough consideration (regardless of what Asinius Pollio may have intended by the term *patauinitas*, on which see K. Latte, 'Livy's *patavinitas*', *CP* 35 (1940), 56f., repr. *Kleine Schriften* (Munich 1968), pp. 896f., Walsh, *Livy*, pp. 267f., and J. Whatmough, *HSCP* 44 (1933), 95f., *CP* 38 (1943), 205; cf. Väänänen's negative conclusions regarding dialect differentiation in the Empire, 'Unità del latino, realtà o illusione?', *AION* 5 (1963), 63f.).

19. *Brutus...cultrum manente cruore prae se tenens* (Livy I. 59. 1) may well represent a reminiscence of the Ciceronian passage as Livy describes the acts of a former Brutus on behalf of the restoration of liberty (cf. R. M. Ogilvie (ed.), *Livy* (Oxford 1965) ad loc.).

cation of sense is implied by the use of *prae se* at Verg. *Aen.* XI. 544–5:

> ipse sinu *prae se* portans iuga longa petebat
> solorum nemorum

where Metabus flees in haste from his angry subjects, clutching his infant daughter to his chest. Beside *sinu*, *prae se* in a wholly locative sense would be somewhat redundant, but if it means 'openly, i.e., unprotected', the precipitateness of Metabus' flight is heightened by this reference to the lack of care he was able to allow himself in concealing and protecting his child.[20] In this context, it is highly significant that sentences of the type **clam equites prae se misit* are unattested, even in those writers who also use *prae se* as a straightforward locative adverb.

Once *prae se ferre* and *aperte ferre* were considered closely comparable expressions, a further synonymy developed between *prae se ferre* and such verbs as *ostendere*.[21] In Ciceronian Latin we may perhaps distinguish *prae se + ferre* '*aperte ferre*' from *prae se ferre* '*ostendere*' by the fact that *prae se* '*aperte*' is not necessarily juxtaposed to the verb, while in the second case it is. This distribution contributed to the establishment of *prae se ferre* as an autonomous idiom, a status it had achieved in Quintilian's writings where *prae se* characteristically occurs in construction with *ferre*.[22]

20. Compare *dona ferunt prae se, declarant gaudia uultu* (Cat. LXIV. 35; Lewis and Short take *prae se* with *declarant*) and *munera praeferimus* (Verg. *Aen.* XI. 249, with prefixational *prae-*); note also *praeportans* (Cic. *Arat.* LII. 209 Traglia), *prae se portans* (ibid. 127), and *prae se...Scorpius infestus praeportans flebile acumen* (ibid. 429f., A. Traglia, *La lingua di Cicerone poeta* (Bari 1950), pp. 138–9). Ambiguous contexts inevitably remain: at Livy XXVIII. 38. 5 (*argenti prae se in aerarium tulit quattuordecim milia pondo*), did Scipio merely send his spoils ahead to the *aerarium*, or did he forward them 'openly, publicly', which, in terms of the political context, would have been a shrewd action?

21. Cf. *ceteris prae se fert et ostentat* (Cic. *ad Att.* II. 23. 3), *nec uero, cum uenit, prae se fert, aut qui sit aut unde ueniat aut etiam quid uelit* (*RP* II. 3. 6), *fortasse ceteri tectiores; ego semper me didicisse prae me tuli* (*Or.* XLII. 146). Note the use of the first person singular pronoun in *prae me tuli*. The inflection of the pronoun for person in the phrase *prae + *reflexive pronoun seems to have been restricted to the construction with *ferre* (on the use of the reflexive pronoun with comparative *prae*, see pp. 17f.).

22. Cf. *hanc uirtutem prae se ferunt* (Quint. II. 3. 11), *oratio prae se fert felicissimam facilitatem* (id. X. II. 11), and *liberalium disciplinarum prae se scientiam tulit* (id. XII. 11. 21). Note the separation of *prae se* from *tulit* in the last example, which constitutes no ambiguity since *prae se ferre* was established as an idiom.

Prae se thus developed as a prepositional phrase used adverbially (cf. *pro certo 'certe', extemplo 'subito'* etc.). As an idiom its internal grammar is fixed. At one level of grammatical analysis, adverbial *prae se* can therefore be distinguished from the otherwise homonymous use of *prae se* (i.e., comparative *prae + se*) at Cicero, *Brut.* LXXXIII. 286: *ac Charisi uult Hegesias sese similis, isque se ita putat Atticum ut ueros illos prae se paene agrestes putet.* In the latter construction, one can substitute for *se* terms like *magnitudine* (Caes. *BG* II. 30. 4), *tuis facultatibus* (Cic. *Rabir. perd.* XIV), and *diuitiis* (Livy III. 26. 7). At another level, in the idiomatic expression, such substitutions (with the qualification cited in n. 21) are by definition impossible.

Causal and comparative uses of prepositional *prae* may now be considered. The following examples illustrate the development of causal *prae*:

igitur demum Vlixi cor frixit *prae pauore* (Liv. Andr. *Od.* 18R²)
prae laetitia lacrimae prosiliunt mihi (Pl. *Stich.* 466)
neque miser me commouere possum *prae formidine* (id. *Amph.* 337)[23]
solem *prae iaculorum multitudine et sagittarum* non uidebitis (Cic. *TD* I. 42. 101)
nec diuini humaniue iuris quicquam *prae impotenti ira* est seruatum (Livy XXXI. 24. 18)
[murenae]...in summa aqua *prae pinguitudine* [al. *pinguedine*] flutentur (Varro ap. Macr. *Sat.* III. 15. 8)
prae turba occurrentium eum discrimen uitae adisse (Suet. *Cal.* IV)
N.B. scimus te *prae litteras* fatuum esse (Petr. XLVI. 1)

Before the Ciceronian period causal *prae* occurred in both positive and negative sentences, but generally with nouns connoting emotion (e.g., *amor, formido, laetitia, maeror, metus, pauor* etc., cf. n. 23). In the first century B.C., the possible collocation

23. Causal *prae* is relatively common in Roman Comedy. Plautus attests the following examples: *ego miser uix asto prae formidine* (*Capt.* 637), *prae lassitudine opus est ut lauem* (*Truc.* 328), *prae maerore adeo miser atque aegritudine | consenui* (*Stich.* 215f.), *terrore meo occidistis prae metu* (*Amph.* 1066), *prae metu ubi sim nescio* (*Cas.* 413), *prae timore in genua in undas concidit* (*Rud.* 174), *omnia corusca prae tremore fabulor* (*Rud.* 526); cf. Terence: *uide, quam iniquos sis prae studio* (*Andr.* 825) *prae amore exclusisti hunc foras* (*Eun.* 98), *domum reuortor maestus...prae aegritudine* (*Heaut.* 122–3), *prae gaudio...ubi sim, nescio* (id. 308), *prae iracundia non sum apud me* (id. 920). On *prae candoribus* at Pl. *Men.* 181, see n. 34.

of *prae* was, on the one hand, extended to include other classes of
nouns (e.g., *multitudo* Cic. *TD* loc. cit., cf. Caes. *BG* VII. 44. 1,
seditio Livy IX. 14. 5, *tenebrae* id. XXVIII. 36. 12) but, on the other,
restricted in its occurrence 'nur mit einem negativen Ausdruck
oder einem Verbum negativen Sinnes zum Ausdruck des
hinderndes Grundes.'[24] Varro's *prae pinguitudine flutentur* illustrates
that the latter restriction was not universally observed although,
even in this instance, the transformation of a negative sentence
may be distantly implied: *murenae sub aqua prae pinguitudine nare
non possunt.* (The same may also be true of pre-Ciceronian usage.)
In post-Augustan literature causal *prae* occurs again in positive
sentences with nouns of emotion, for example, in Apuleius (*prae
pudore*, *Met.* 1. 6) and Fronto (*prae amore*, p. 116. 4 van der Hout).
The more productive post-Augustan use, however, lacks any
restrictions in respect of sentence-type or noun class. Moreover,
the fact that causal *prae* came to govern the accusative case (cf.
prae litteras, Petr., loc. cit.)[25] can be explained by syntactic analogy
with *propter* which in turn implies the semantic generalization

24. Kühner–Stegmann, p. 513, list several Ciceronian uses as causal which
probably do not belong in that category: *prae salute* at *Verr.* II. 2. 156 (*qui...
omnia pericula prae salute sua leuia duxerint*), *ad Fam.* XIV. 4. 2 (*qui periculum
capitis prae mea salute neglexit*), and *Mil.* II. 3 (*qui semper genus illud hominum
clamoresque maximos prae uestra salute neglexit*). In these closely comparable
examples (where *leuia duxerint* and *neglexit* can be paraphrased as *pro nihilo
putauerint* or *putauit*, respectively, *prae* in all likelihood implies comparison.
Hofmann–Szantyr (p. 269) likewise cite Livy VI. 40. 1 as an instance of causal
prae in a positive sentence: *cum prae indignitate rerum stupor silentiumque inde
ceteros patrum defixisset.* As Lutenbacher, however, rightly observes (ad loc.), this
clause can be rephrased (with change of emphasis rather than of sense) as
cum...ceteri patrum loqui non possent. The following sentences illustrate the
convergence of comparative and causal uses of *prae*: *publicae utilitatis species
prae honestate contemnitur* (Cic. *de Off.* III. 11. 47) beside *Gallis prae magnitudine
corporum suorum breuitas nostra contemptui est* (Caes. *BG* II. 30. 4). Kühner–Stegmann
(loc. cit.) may be correct in terming the former 'causal' and the latter
'comparative', but the potential ambiguity is obvious. These questions will
be reconsidered during the discussion of comparative *prae*.

25. I.e., 'we know you're stupid because you've read so much', irony at
the expense of Agamemnon; cf. XXXIX. 12: *in capricorno aerumnosi, quibus prae
mala sua cornua nascuntur* where *prae mala sua* also means 'on account of'.
Petronius' use of *prae* has been called solecistic (cf. T. A. Key, *A Latin–English
Dictionary* (Cambridge 1888), ad loc.), but what may be plausibly explained
as a standard colloquial use is not necessarily a solecism. On the extension of
this use in later Latin, see Baehrens, *Glotta* 4 (1913), 277f. (Another possible
influence on the change of case in the construction of causal *prae* is considered
below, p. 17.)

of causal *prae*. The Varronian usage significantly demonstrates
a transitional stage in this development.

The origin of causal *prae* has often been disputed. According
to Delbrück (above, n. 4, *Vergleichende Syntax*, p. 639), 'tatsächlich
ist das *prae* der hindernden Ursache nichts anderes als das
zeitliche "vor". Denn *prae lacrimis loqui non possum* heisst eigent-
lich: "Ich kann nicht vor den Tränen zum Reden kommen, sie
kommen mir immer zuvor."' Kranz (above, n. 1, '*Pro*' *et* '*prae*',
p. 51) rightly objects to this account on the following grounds:
'huius enim generis exemplum in prisca latinitate non modo non
exstat, sed ne veram quidem vim illius usus reddit; nam *prae*
particula, ubi causalis vis exstat, semper fere cum nominibus
coniuncta invenitur, quibus animi affectiones exprimuntur' (cf.
n. 23). Brugmann proposed a locative origin,[26] but, as Benveniste
observes (above, n. 1, 'Le système sublogique', p. 181, ad Pl.
Stich. 466), 'dira-t-on que "quelque chose" se place "devant" la
joie?...l'explication de Brugmann...supposerait en latin "je
pleure *devant* la joie" pour dire "je pleure de joie".' Benveniste's
own explanation is relatively complicated (pp. 182–3):

> Indiquant le mouvement vers la partie antérieure et avancée
> d'un continu, *prae* laisse en quelque sorte le reste de l'objet
> en position d'infériorité; c'est pourquoi prédominent les
> expressions négatives [cf. Pl. *Amph*. 337]...C'est donc à tort
> qu'on parle ici d'un sens 'causal'. *Prae* ne fait pas intervenir
> une cause objective; il marque seulement une pointe extrême,
> un excès, qui a pour conséquence une certaine disposition,
> généralement négative, du sujet.

Although Benveniste's emphasis on 'le mouvement vers' may be
misplaced (cf. n. 11), reference to 'une pointe extrême' recalls
a specialized use of preadjectival and preverbal *prae-* as in *quoi
ego iam linguam praecidam* ('cut off in front' Pl. *Aul*. 189) or
praeferratus ('tipped with iron', Pl. *Pers*. 22, Cato, *Agr*. XI. 3). On
the other hand such constructions cannot strictly be compared
with that of the phrase *prae laetitia* 'à l'extrême de ma joie' and
the use of *prae-* as an intensive prefix (which might also seem to

---

26. *Grundriss der vergleichenden Grammatik der idg. Sprachen*[2], II. 2 (Strassburg
1909), p. 881, cf. Hofmann–Szantyr, pp. 268–9: 'aus lokal-temporaler
Grundlage...erwächst auch kausales *prae*.'

support Benveniste's thesis) did not become significantly productive until the Augustan period. Under these circumstances, Benveniste's definition of *prae* in terms of 'le degré extrême'[27] arises more clearly from the possibilities offered by Hjelmslev's 'système sublogique' (n. 5) than from any attested Latin usage.

Both Benveniste and Hofmann–Szantyr reject Kranz' derivation of causal *prae* from an ablative absolute construction of participial *praesente* + noun.[28] Although from a historical standpoint Kranz' proposal is unacceptable, his reference to *praesens* may be suggestive. Benveniste's own account of *praesens* depends on the view that *prae*- connotes 'imminence' ('Le système sublogique', pp. 178–80). The explanations of causal *prae*- offered by Brugmann, Delbrück, and Benveniste imply a prepositional origin. The possibility of an adverbial construction, which Kranz' theory indirectly suggests, deserves consideration.

Cause is expressed in Latin in several ways, by dependent clauses, prepositions like *propter* and *ob*, and by the ablative case. This last construction was already common in early Latin and occurs frequently (though not exclusively) with nouns expressing emotion: *lacrimo gaudio* (Ter. *Ad.* 409 beside *prae gaudio*, id. *Heaut.* 308), *delirat miser | timore* (id. *Phorm.* 997–8 beside *prae timore*, Pl. *Rud.* 174), and *terrore meo occidistis prae metu* (Pl. *Amph.* 1066, with both the causal ablative and causal *prae*).[29] The early use

27. For Benveniste's view ('Le système sublogique', p. 183) that comparative *prae* supports his analysis of causal *prae*, see n. 37.

28. Kranz ('*Pro*' et '*prae*', p. 52): 'uelut *prae metu ubi sim nescio* (Pl. *Cas.* 413) primo significauisse putauerim *prae*- (sc. -*sente*) *metu ubi sim nescio* id quod significat *praesentiā metus efficitur, ne ubi sim sciam*. Causae vis igitur non particulae *prae* inest, sed ex constructione ipsa exorta est. Postea autem, cum constructio participialis cum praepositionis usu, quoniam et simillima est, commisceretur, causae vis in *prae* particulam inferebatur' ('ce qui est l'invraisemblance même', Benveniste, 'Le système sublogique', p. 180; 'verfehlt', Hofmann–Szantyr, p. 269 Zus. *b*).

29. Note the continued use of the causal ablative in Classical Latin: *paene ille timore, ego risu conrui* (Cic. *ad Q. Fr.* II. 9 [8]. 2), *ita cupidine atque ira, pessumis consultoribus, grassari* (Sall. *Iug.* LXIV. 5), and, in particular, *ita cunctos strepitu, clamore, nullo subueniente, nostris instantibus, tumultu, formidine terror quasi uecordia ceperat* (ibid. XCIX. 3) beside *neque decretum exaudiri consulis prae strepitu et clamore poterat* (Livy II. 27. 8). Cf. Kühner–Stegmann (loc. cit.): 'aber regelrecht wird der hindernde Grund in positiven Sätzen durch den blossen Ablativ bezeichnet, der sich in negativen Sätzen nur nachklassisch vereinzelt findet: Sen. *suas.* 6. 17 *uix attollentes lacrimis oculos*. Vell. 2. 70. 2 *neque puluere signa denotari possent*.' In early Latin this restriction did not apply (cf. *quarum*

of *prae* as a causal preposition thus seems to have been somewhat pleonastic. From a descriptive standpoint *prae* might have been used to intensify an emotional cause, to make it seem more immediate (cf. *prae metu*, Pl. *Amph.*, above). Etymologically, *prae pauore, prae laetitia* etc. can be derived from expressions originally containing adverbial *prae* and meaning 'on account of *pauor, laetitia* etc. being *prae*, "imminent, present" (as in *praesens*)', reinterpreted as prepositional phrases by analogy with constructions like *propter malitiam* etc.[30] One may speculate that the attested shift of semantic emphasis on the part of causal *prae* from collocation with nouns like *amor, gaudium, laetitia, maeror,* and *timor* to occurrence in negative sentences at least partially reflects a social view, hardly unparalleled in contemporary Rome, that emotions hinder action.

The following examples illustrate the use of comparative *prae*:

clam illuc redeundum est mihi,

odore praeterire nemo pistrinum potest, Pl. *Capt.* 808, *aetate non quis obtuerier*, id. *Most.* 840). Evidence for the Classical specialization of causal *prae* in negative sentences is thus reinforced. As this specialization lost ground, the (literary?) restriction on the occurrence of the causal ablative in negative sentences became obsolete.

30.   Causal and locative uses of *propter* coexisted in Plautus:

illic habitat Daemones
in agro atque uilla proxuma *propter* mare,
senex, qui huc Athenis exul uenit, hau malus;
neque is adeo *propter* malitiam patria caret (*Rud.* 33–6)

Prepositional *prae* also may have already developed a limited causal function in such contexts as *prae tet tremonti* (*Carm. Sal.*, cf. n. 15) 'they tremble in front of you', hence 'because of you'. A merger may therefore have taken place between *prae* (adv.) *pauore* (reinterpreted as a prepositional phrase) and an otherwise obsolescent prepositional *prae*. On account of their obsolescence, locative uses of adverbial and prepositional *prae* would not have inhibited such a development, for which, however, no direct evidence exists: Ciceronian *prae nobis beatus* presumably specified comparison without ambiguity. It has also been suggested (Hofmann–Szantyr, p. 269) that a causal use of *prae* could derive from its collocation with a verb of motion (cf. Pl. *Amph.* 337: *neque...me commouere possum prae formidine* 'I cannot move in front, ahead, through fear'. While these two possibilities cannot be definitely excluded, our account of causal *prae* does not necessarily depend on either of them. Moreover, they do not help to explain the attested collocation of causal *prae* with nouns denoting emotion. The interpretation of causal *prae* as etymologically an adverb, intensifying the presence of an emotion, is particularly appropriate to such contexts and can be supported by reference to the contemporary use of *prae-* in *praesens* (below, pp. 40f.; cf. *praefiscini*, below pp. 32f.).

ne me uxorem praeuortisse dicant *prae re publica* (Pl. *Amph.* 527–8)

non sum dignus *prae te* (id. *MG* 1140)

Riemann observed[31] that 'en règle générale, le complément de *prae* désigne celui des deux termes de la comparaison qui est supérieur à l'autre [cf. *MG* loc. cit.]...; le contraire [cf. *Amph.* loc. cit.] est *rare*.' The evidence appears strongly in support of this thesis:

uideo te nihili pendere *prae Philolache* omnis homines (Pl. *Most.* 245)

nam omnium unguentum odor *prae tuo* nautea est (id. *Curc.* 99)

pithecium haec est *prae illa* et spinturnicium (id. *MG* 989)

prae illius forma quasi spernas tuam (ibid. 1170)

me minoris facio *prae illo* (id. *Epid.* 522)

hic ego illum contempsi *prae me* (Ter. *Eun.* 239)

te omnis res postputasse[32] *prae parente* intellego (id. *Hec.* 483)

omnia sibi post putarit esse *prae meo commodo* (id. *Ad.* 262)

ut cuncta opima leuia *prae illis* putet (Acc. *tr.* 146R²)

qui...omnia pericula *prae salute sua* leuia duxerint (Cic. *Verr.* II. 2. 156, cf. *Mil.* II. 3, *ad Fam.* XIV. 4. 2, and n. 24)

Romam...*prae sua Capua*...irridebunt atque contemnunt (id. *Leg. agr.* II. 96)

isque se ita putat Atticum, ut ueros illos *prae se* paene agrestes putet (id. *Brut.* LXXXIII. 286)

Gallis *prae magnitudine* corporum suorum breuitas nostra contemptui est (Caes. *BG* II. 30. 4)

qui omnia *prae diuitiis* humana spernunt (Livy III. 26. 7)

uidebant...omnes *prae illo* parui futuros (Nep. *Eum.* x. 4)

cf. immo res omnis relictas habeo *prae* quod tu uelis (Pl. *Stich.* 362)

In all these instances the complement of *prae* can indeed be regarded as 'supérieur' to its counterpart. This fact, however, is scarcely remarkable on account of the major semantic characteristic which

31. *Syntaxe latine*⁷, ed. A. Ernout (Paris 1942), p. 195 n. 1, quoted with approval by Benveniste, who uses Riemann's thesis as the basis of his own explanation (cf. n. 37).

32. The opposition of *post* and *prae* in these Terentian passages will be discussed below: note the contrast of *postputo prae* and *praeuorto prae* (*Amph.* 528).

these sentences share: in each case, the underlying comparison is expressed in negative terms. In positive comparisons, on the other hand, the complement of *prae* is 'inferior' to its counterpart, for example, at *Amph.* 528; compare:

> quae si in illo minima fuissent, tamen *prae tuis facultatibus* maxima putarentur (Cic. *Rabir. perd.* v. 14)
> at contra nobis non tu quidem uacuus molestiis [sc. uideris], sed *prae nobis* beatus (id. *ad Fam.* IV. 4. 2).

If negative comparisons are rephrased in positive terms, then the resulting complements of *prae* likewise become 'inferior' to their counterparts. In other words the relation of complement to counterpart in comparisons employing *prae* is no different from those expressed by *quam* or the ablative case. (Note, however, that in *prae*-comparisons, unlike other types, the use of comparative adjectives is exceedingly rare.)[33]

As a descriptive statement, Riemann's thesis is therefore valid only insofar as comparative *prae* most commonly occurs in negatively expressed comparisons. This distribution, however, has special significance in that it reflects the point of ambiguity between causal and comparative uses of *prae* (n. 24 ad fin.). In positive sentences this ambiguity is not attested: no confusion exists between the comparative use of *prae* in *prae re publica* at *Amph.* 528 and its causal use in *prae laetitia* at *Stich.* 466. On the other hand, in negative sentences, the distinction between these uses sometimes seems slightly blurred; for example, just as fright prevents Sosia from moving at *Amph.* 337 so thoughts of Philolaches caused Philematium (*Most.* 245) to consider all other men *comparatively* worthless. From a descriptive standpoint the constructions of *prae formidine* and *prae Philolache* might have been considered syntactically comparable (i.e., 'on account of *formido* being *prae*' beside 'on account of Philolaches being *prae*, at least

---

33. Cf. *me minoris facit prae illo* (Pl. *Epid.* 522) where either *prae* or the comparative, *minoris* (for *parui*), might appear to be pleonastic. *Prae*, however, does not necessarily depend on the comparative *minoris* since *minoris facit* may represent an idiom parallel to *nihili pendere* at *Most.* 245 or *parui futuros* at Nep. *Eum.* x. 4. The fact that a comparative adjective would be largely redundant in comparisons expressed by *prae* provides the most straightforward explanation for its characteristic absence from such constructions until the Frontonian period (or, perhaps, Tac. *Dial.* XVIII. 4, if Groslot's *prae* for codd. *pro* is genuine; cf. Hofmann–Szantyr, p. 112).

in Philematium's thoughts'). Although in no sentence is the distinction totally neutralized,[34] the underlying similarity may, however, have further influenced the specialization of the exclusively privative use of causal *prae* in Cicero, Caesar, and Livy. Causal and comparative *prae* grew more clearly distinct as soon as the former became productive in positive sentences (cf. Varro's *prae pinguitudine* and Petronius' *prae litteras*). Indeed, the colloquial collocation of causal *prae* with the accusative case may partly reflect an attempt to resolve any potential ambiguity with comparative *prae*.[35]

The history of comparative *prae* can be discussed in terms of the following passages:

ne me uxorem praeuortisse dicant *prae re publica* (Pl. *Amph*. 528)
et tamen, cum ita uiuit, neminem *prae se* ducit hominem (*ad Her*. IV. 20. 28).[36]

34. Note the implied distinction between comparison and cause at *Most*. 245–6:

uideo enim te nihili pendere *prae Philolache* omnis homines.
nunc, ne *eius caussa* uapulem, tibi potius adsentabor.

Possibly the most striking instance of ambiguity is attested at Pl. *Men*. 180–1:

oh! solem uides
satin ut occaecatust *prae huius corporis candoribus*?

which seems remarkably similar to Cicero's *solem prae iaculorum multitudine et sagittarum non uidebitis* (*TD*, loc. cit.). Benveniste ('Le système sublogique', p. 183) classifies both passages together with comparative uses of *prae* at *Curc*. 99, *MG* 989, 1170 etc. On the other hand, the Ciceronian passage is probably best interpreted as causal. The use of *prae* at *Men*. 181 depends in part on the meaning of *occaecatust*. If *occaecatust* means 'is dark', then *prae* is comparative; if it means 'is darkened (pass.)', *prae* is causal. In the context, however, comparison between Erotion's dazzling beauty and the brightness of the sun is clearly implied. Furthermore, an interpretation of *prae candoribus* as causal would be anomalous in terms of the otherwise exclusive co-occurrence of causal *prae* with words denoting emotion, at least in Roman Comedy (cf. n. 23). *Candores* and *sol* are comparable entities in a way that *sol* and *multitudo* (ap. Cic. *TD*) are not. Acceptance of *prae candoribus* as comparative does not thereby exclude the analysis of *prae iaculorum multitudine* as causal. The potential coincidence of the two constructions is, however, apparent from these examples.

35. This explanation, along with the analogical pressure from *propter* cited above, provides a more adequate account of the development of expressions like *prae litteras* than simply attributing these phrases to the solecistic collapse of the Latin case system (cf. Baehrens, loc. cit., above n. 25, and Süss, *De eo quem inesse dicunt Trimalchionis cenae sermone uulg*. [= *Acta et Comm. Univ. Dorpatensis* B ix 4] (Dorpat 1926), p. 25).

36. Cf. Cic. *Rosc. Am*. XLVI. 135; *uidetis...ut omnes despiciat, ut hominem prae se neminem putet, ut se solum beatum, solum potentem putet*. At *ad Her*. II. 22. 34, *prae ceteris* is read by BC, but Marx excludes the phrase: *ea* [sc. *stultitia*] *parit*

The basic charge which causes Jupiter's pretended anxiety at
Amph. 528 may be reconstructed as *uxorem tuam prae re publica esse
duxisti* or *uxorem tuam rei publicae praeuortisti* (cf. Pl. *Pseud.* 293). The
sentence *uxorem tuam prae re publica praeuortisti* can therefore be
regarded as a conflation of these two constructions. It is possible
to reverse the accusation by substituting for *praeuortisti* an antonym
like *posthabuisti* or *contempsisti*: *uxorem tuam posthabuisti* (cf. Ter. *Hec.*
483, *Ad.* 262) / *contempsisti* (cf. Ter. *Eun.* 239) *prae re publica.* By
this stage of the development, the comparative use of *prae* was
unambiguously established.

This account derives comparative *prae* from a locative preposition.[37] The possibility of an ancillary adverbial origin should
also be considered. At *Stich.* 362 Pinacium retorts to his mistress:

   immo res omnis relictas habeo *prae* quod tu uelis
cf. omnia sibi post putarit esse *prae meo commodo* (Ter. *Ad.* 262).

One may plausibly assume that *prae* in these contexts reflects an
adverbial function: 'since my convenience is *prae* etc.'[38] Such
an explanation not only parallels that of causal *prae* but is
particularly attractive in that it helps to account for the characteristic use of *prae* in negative comparisons. Comparative *prae*
therefore probably represents the convergence of two originally
distinct constructions, involving prepositional and adverbial uses,
respectively.

immensas cupiditates (not *ea prae ceteris*). If genuine, *prae ceteris* (literally, 'in front
of all other things') would provide a further illustration of the locative
origins of comparative *prae*. These passages are introduced to suggest the
development of comparative *prae* and the following argument is thus intended
as an historical rather than a synchronic account of their significance.
37. Benveniste ('Le système sublogique', p. 181) objects to a locative origin
on the grounds that *prae* 'ne signifie jamais "devant" au sens de "en face"
et impliquant comparaison d'un objet avec un autre, pour cette raison majeure
que, dessinant la continuité et donc l'unicité de l'objet, il ne saurait confronter
deux objets distincts'. 'Superiority' is, however, not only implied by *prae*
(cf. Benveniste, ibid., p. 183) but clearly appropriate as a starting point for
its use in comparisons. Since superiority can be derived as a metaphor of
place, Benveniste's objections to a locative etymology of comparative *prae* may
be overruled. Benveniste's own account (loc. cit.) seems unnecessarily complicated (and somewhat unhistorical). After citing Riemann's thesis, he continues:
   c'est...de la notion d''extrême' que résulte la fonction comparative de
   prae, car *prae magnitudine* [Caes. *BG* ii. 30. 4] signifie 'à l'extrême de leur
   grandeur = si haute est leur taille (que nous leurs semblons petits).' Étendant
   son emploi, *prae* pourra alors se joindre à n'importe quel genre de nom et

The comparative function of *prae* is also reflected in its pre-fixational usage (cf. *praeferre*, *praestare* etc. and *praematurus* 'over-ripe', originally 'ripe too early') and, more distantly, in the etymologically related *praeter*. The implication of hindrance in uses of causal *prae* can similarly be compared with the prefixational function of *prae-* in verbs like *praecludo*, *praestringo* etc. The obsolescence of prepositional and adverbial uses of locative *prae* is matched both by its productivity as a prefix and by the establishment of its causal and comparative functions. This latter development took place at the expense of constructions involving only case inflection (e.g., ablative of cause and comparison, *praeuortere +* dative) and thus illustrates the gradual decline of the inherited case system during the history of the Latin language (cf. Hofmann–Szantyr, pp. 111f.).

PREFIXATIONAL *PRAE-*

Prefixational *prae-* is constructed with nouns, adjectives, adverbs, and verbs in a variety of functions (locative, temporal, intensive, comparative, and preventive) which generally depend on the syntax and semantics of the underlying form. Each of these functions will be examined in some detail and major emphasis in the following discussion will generally be placed on primary compounds such as *praecordia*, *praeses*, and *praesum*. Secondary derivatives will be mentioned only insofar as they clarify the

même de pronom pour mettre en relief une supériorité [cf. Pl. *Curc.* 99, *Men.* 181, *MG* 989, 1170 etc.]...Et enfin on atteint la réalisation de l'expression comparative [ibid. 1140].

The use of locative prepositions in comparative constructions (e.g., *ab*, *ante*, *praeter*, *supra*, and, in late Latin, *super*) is attested at all stages of the language and becomes especially frequent in late Latin (cf. Hofmann–Szantyr, pp. 111–12).

38. Cf. Kranz ('*Pro*' et '*prae*', p. 45 n. 1). It was presumably the possibility of such an interpretation that led Kranz (ibid., following Skutsch) to propose a participial origin for comparative *prae* (from *praeposito*, rejected by Hofmann–Szantyr, p. 268). In any case note the antithesis of *relictas/post*: *prae* in the Plautine example. *Praequam* (cf. *praeut*) was doubtless created to clarify the descriptively adverbial function of *prae* in contexts such as *Stich.* 362. *Satin parua res est uoluptatum in uita atque in aetate agunda | praequam quod molestumst* (Pl. *Amph.* 633–4) can be analyzed, as Kranz (ibid., n. 3) rightly judges, as a pleonastic conflation of *res uoluptatum est parua prae [eo] + minor quam quod molestumst*.

function of their derivational base or contribute to the productivity of their prefixational class. It will therefore be unnecessary to discuss a form like *praescriptio* as an example of prenominal *prae-* because it not only derives unambiguously from *praescribo* but did not cause prenominal *prae-* to be re-established as a productive prefix.

Prefixational *prae-* was, at least through the Classical period, the preferred equivalent of Greek πρό. (The Greek word for 'preposition', for example, was πρόθεσις, cf. Chrysipp. *SVF* II. 45, D.T. 634. 5). If *praeuides* at *CIL* I² 585. 47 (the *lex agraria* of 111 B.C.) was calqued on Greek προέγγυος (cf. n. 42), this recognition predated the first century B.C. Cicero certainly contributed to its development, particularly in his rendering of Greek philosophical terminology: *ista... bona non dico, sed dicam graece* προηγμένα *latine autem producta – sed praeposita, aut praecipua malo, sit tolerabilius et mollius* (*de Fin.* IV. 26. 72).[39] *Praenotio* likewise renders the Epicurean term πρόληψις (*ND* I. 17. 44). At *TD* I. 40. 96, *praebibo* is calqued on Greek προπίνω; contrast Ennius, *Sat.* III. 6–7V³:

> Enni poeta salue qui mortalibus
> uersus propinas flammeos medullitus

on which Nonius (33. 4, cf. 139. 15) commented: '*propinare*' *a Graeco tractum, post potum tradere.* The occasional equivalence of Greek παρα- and Latin *prae-* has been remarked by several scholars but this relation never became productive.[40]

---

39. Cf. *de Fin.* III. 16. 52: προηγμένα, *id est, producta... quae uel ita appellamus – id erit uerbum e uerbo – uel promota et remota uel, ut dudum diximus, praeposita uel praecipua, et illa reiecta.* Other examples include *praefatio* (cf. πρόλογος), *praesultor*: ὁ ἐν τοῖς ἱεροῖς προορχούμενος (gloss ap. Cod. Paris. 7651 [Regius 5479], ed. G. Goetz and G. Gundermann, *Corpus glossariorum latinorum* II [abbreviated *CGL*] (Leipzig 1888), 157. 38), *praeiudex*: προδικαστής (gloss ap. Cod. Harl., *CGL* II 417. 13), *praefurnium* (cf. προπνιγεῖον Vitr. V. 10. 2, but see n. 42), *praeexercitamentum*: προγυμνάσματα (Priscian), and *praeseminatio* 'foetus' (Vitr. II. 9. 1), possibly based on a derivative of προφυτεύω 'engender' (cf. Soph. *El.* 198). (On *praes, praeuius*, see n. 42 and pp. 24–5, respectively.)

40. Cf. *praebeo* and παρέχω, *praemium* and παραλαμβάνω, *praestes* and παραστατεῖν (cf. Hofmann–Szantyr, p. 269 Zus. *a*). Wackernagel (*46. Jahrbuch d. Schweizer Gymnasiallehrervereins* (1919), pp. 166f.) considers *praesens* calqued on παρών (cf. Benveniste, 'Le système sublogique', pp. 179–80). The potential similarity of Greek περι- and Latin *prae-* as intensive prefixes likewise had no influence on the Latin development (on *per-* and περι- see M. Leumann, 'Lateinisches

PRENOMINAL *PRAE-*

As a noun prefix *prae-* was relatively unproductive.[41] Many of the nouns prefixed with *prae-* were already attested before 150 B.C. and remained common at all periods of the language (e.g., *praeco*, *praeda*, *praemium*, *praetor*). Other forms may be at least equally archaic but are only found in lexicographers. The evidence can be divided into two classes, depending on the derivational morphology of the unprefixed stem, denominative or deverbative.

In the denominative type, the compound means 'that which is *prae* in respect of the unprefixed noun stem', for example, *praeclauium*, *praecordia*, *praefurnium*, *praenomen*, *praeuerbium*, and, at least in terms of popular etymology, *praeputium*.[42] *Praefericulum*, a

enklitisches *-per* und steigerndes *per-*', 'Ἀντίδωρον (*Festschrift Jacob Wackernagel*) (Göttingen 1923), pp. 339f., reprinted in *Kleine Schriften* (Zürich 1959), pp. 49f.); the same is true of ὑπερ-: *super-*, at least until late Latin (cf. J. André, 'Les adjectifs et adverbes', p. 152 n. 2).

41. Cf. *praebia*, *-clauium*, *-co*, *-cordia*, *-da*, *-fericulum*, *-fica*, *-furnium*, *-metium*, *-mium*, *-nomen*, *-putium*, *-s* (from **prae-vas*, n. 42), *-stigiae*, *-sul*, *-tor*, *-uerbium*. *Praeses* and *praestes* will be discussed with other ·examples of preadjectival *prae-* (pp. 23f.).

42. *Praeclauium*, for example, designates 'the piece of cloth in front of the *clauus*'. On *praecordia*, compare Pliny (*HN* XI. 37. 197): *exta homini ab inferiore uiscerum parte seponantur membrana, quae praecordia appellant, quia cordi praetenditur, quod Graeci appellauerant* φρένας. *Praefurnium* (Cato, *Agr.* XXXVIII. 1) refers to the door in front of the *furnus* through which fuel is fed; at Vitr. V. 10. 2, *praefurnium* provides a convenient equivalent for Greek προπνιγεῖον with Latin *prae-* corresponding to Greek προ- (cf. n. 39; contrast the transliterated *propnigeum*, Vitr. V. 11. 2, Plin. *Ep.* II. 17. 11). *Praes, praedis* (from **prae-uas*, cf. O. Lat. *-uides*, *CIL* I² 585. 47) 'surety' can be plausibly explained as calqued on Greek προέγγυος, attested in Sicily from the fourth century B.C. (*Tab. Heracl.* I. 100 al., προωγγυεύω, ibid. 155; cf. Bücheler's interpretation of *praes stat* on a Tarentine inscription [*CIL* I² 590. 7, c. 90 B.C.] as a calque of ἐγγυᾶται *Rh. Mus.* 52 (1897), 397). Leumann (p. 253) cites this account, though on p. 200 he terms *praes* 'unsicher...zu **uădere*?' According to Ernout–Meillet (p. 532), the Greek form was calqued on *praes* 'au moment où ce terme était encore **praivas*'. This view is relatively implausible considering the widespread distribution of προέγγυος in the Greek world and the lack of cogent parallels for the translation of Latin *prai/prae* by Greek πρό in the fourth century B.C. The colonial origins of *praes* as a technical term may be supported by the fact that it first occurs in a passage from the *lex agraria* cited above, p. 20, where African land is being discussed, then in the Tarentine constitution (loc. cit.: *quei pro se praes stat praedes praediaque ad IIII uir det...*), and in Cicero's account of Verres' Sicilian escapades (*Verr.* II. 1. 115). *Praedium* (*RE* 43, pp. 1213f.) is derived from *praes* (not from *praeda*); note their collocation at *CIL* I² 590, loc. cit. (For a useful collection of passages where

sacrificial vessel which preceded the *ferculum* in public processions, may belong to this group, but its exact meaning remains unclear.[43] The locative use of *prae-* is evident in all these examples.

Locative *prae-* also characterized the most usual deverbative construction, namely, 'that which does something *prae*', for example, *praefica*, *praesul*, and *praetor*. The *praefica* was a hired mourner who performed her function *at the head of* the funeral procession.[44] The *praesul* was originally one who danced *in front* (specifically, the leader of the Salii; cf. *praesultor*, n. 39). As Varro perceived (*LL* v. 80), '*praetor*' dictus qui praeiret iure et exercitu; a quo ait Lucilius – ergo praetorum est ante et praeire (cf. *praeses* and *praestes*). *Praeco* 'herald' could also be understood descriptively as someone who traveled *in front*, or, perhaps secondarily, in the temporal sense of someone who made announcements *in advance* of the event.[45]

Some words, however, imply a passive construction and are somewhat ambiguous in terms of their time–space reference, for example, *praemium* from **prai-emiom* (:*emo*), 'that which is taken

praes is mentioned, see H. Nettleship, *Contributions to Latin lexicography* (Oxford 1889), pp. 556f.) The etymology of *praeputium* is disputed (cf. Walde–Hofmann, II 354–5).

43. Cf. Paul. ex Fest. 293. 11: *praefericulum uas aenium sine ansa patens summum, uelut peluis, quo ad sacrificia utebantur* (cf. Ch. Daremberg and E. Saglio, *Dictionnaire des Antiquités* IV (Paris 1907), 622).

44. On the functions of *praeficae*, see E. Fraenkel, *Plautinisches im Plautus* (Berlin 1922), pp. 21f.

45. Cf. n. 84. Most scholars derive *praeco* from **praedico* (presumably based on **prai-dik-o-s*) and invoke Plautus' *praeco praedicat* (*Bacch.* 815, *Stich.* 194f.) as support (cf. Leumann, p. 92, Walde–Hofmann II 352). On the other hand, it is somewhat hazardous to impute etymological sensitivity rather than mere *paronomasia* to this Plautine collocation. Ernout–Meillet (p. 530) suggest *praiwokōn-* (:*uox*) as a possible alternative. Perhaps the most likely explanation is that *praeco* derived from **prai-ko-*, parallel to **pro-ko-*, as in Lat. *reciprocus* (from **re-ko- + pro-ko-s*, ibid. 566); cf. *posticus*. The etymological argument, however, is not strictly relevant to an evaluation of how a Roman of the Plautine or Classical periods might have understood the word *praeco* (cf. *RE* 43, pp. 1193f.). (On *praecia*, see ibid., 1192 and Walde–Hofmann, loc. cit.) The etymology of *praestigiae* 'legerdemain' is also unclear (on *praestigiator*, see *RE* 44, pp. 1567). The form is most usually derived from **praestrigiae*, with dissimilatory loss of the second *-r-* (cf. Leumann, p. 179, Walde–Hofmann, loc. cit.). *Praestringo* 'blind' indeed occurs in Plautus. On the other hand, *praestigiae* might originally have meant 'things which disappear in front (sc. of the eyes)'; cf. Lucr. II. 827–8: *ut cernere possis | euanescere paulatim stinguique colorem* (also Cic. *Arat.* xx. 2 Traglia). In either case the construction conforms to the *praetor*-type and *prae-* is locative.

prae' (cf. *praeda* from *prai-heda:*prai-hendo*, Leumann, p. 313)[46] and *praemetium* 'that which is gathered *prae*'. Although locative *prae-* may be etymologically reflected in *praemium* (if it derives from a locative adjective *praimios, parallel to *eximius*), its descriptive interpretation would probably be temporal. Paulus (ex Fest. 267. 1 Lindsay) makes this assumption with regard to *praemetium*: *quod praelibationis causa ante praemetitur.*[47]

Praebia (neuter plural) '*amulet*' (if derived from *prai-hibia:*habeo*, Ernout–Meillet, p. 530) evidently reflects locative *prae-*, but whether the original compound meant 'that which holds something in front of one' (i.e., 'away from one'; cf. the specialization of causal *prae* with reference to hindrance, also *praecludo* etc.) or, passively, 'that which is held in front', may be open to question. In view of the apotropaic function of the *praebia* (cf. *praefiscini*), the former interpretation is preferable and seems to be reflected in Verrius' comment (ap. Fest. 276. 7): *praebia rursus Verrius uocari ait remedia...quod mala prohibeant.*[48] Note the semantic correspondence between *prae-* as noun prefix in *praebia* and *pro-* as verb prefix in *prohibeo*.

This evidence suggests the following distinction between locative and temporal *prae-* in nominal prefixation: a deverbative derivation with an underlying passive construction referred to time while other derivational types referred to place. If this distribution is not coincidental, it would support our interpretation of *praebia*.

PREADJECTIVAL *PRAE-*

Preadjectival *prae-*, already attested in early Latin,[49] became relatively productive in the Augustan and post-Augustan periods

46. The reference of *praeda* to the act of plunder is probably secondary (e.g., Livy ii. 25. 5, and Ogilvie's note ad loc., also E. J. Kenney, *CQ* 9 (1959), 242 and *RE* 43, pp. 1200f.).

47. *Praemessum*, cited by some lexicographers as a variant of *praemetium*, is presumably based on *messum*, past participle of *meto*. Its temporal interpretation is apparent in the following gloss (ap. *CGL* ii 157. 4): ἡ πρὸ θερισμοῦ Δημήτρας θυσία. For the construction, compare *praecisum* (Naev. +).

48. The connection with *praebeo* was perceived, though incorrectly interpreted, by Varro (*LL* vii. 107): *praebia 'a praebendo ut sit tutus quod si[n]t remedia in collo pueris* (cf. *RE* 43, pp. 1189f.).

49. *Praeceps, -cidaneus, -cipuus, -clarus, -cox, -feruidus, -fidens, -gnas, -grandis, -liganeus, -maturus, -pes, -potens, -ses,* and *praesepe* are all attested before 100 B.C. (On *praeualidus*, read in Lucilius by I. Dousa, see n. 63.)

as an intensive prefix.[50] In the following discussion of Old Latin
words like *praeceps, praegnas*, and *praepes*, etymological considerations
will be introduced only insofar as they clarify the function of
prefixational *prae-*.

Locative *prae-* is implicit in several forms, each of which merits
a brief explanation. *Praeses* (originally 'sitting in front') clearly
exemplifies locative *prae-* (cf. the derived substantives, *praeses*
'guardian' and *praesidium*, and also *praepes* from **prai-pet-s*).[51]
Praesepe (*-es* f., Pl. +) was probably an adjectival derivative
based on *saepes* originally meaning 'that which had a *saepes* in
front'. *Praenum* 'comb for hackling flax' (gloss ap. *CGL* II 158. 50)
was likewise derived from *prae + aenus* (cf. the meaning of *praeferratus*); for the metal implement, compare Plin. *HN* XIX. 3. 18
(describing the preparation of flax): *et ipsa tamen pectitur ferreis
aenis* [:*aculeis* Jahn] *donec omnis membrana decorticetur*. *Praeceps* is
descriptively parallel to *anceps* and Szemerényi has convincingly
revived Solmsen's argument that these forms derive by syncope
from **prai-kapu(t)-s* and **amb(i)-kapu(t)-s*, respectively.[52] Latin
thus preserved the etymological meaning of *praeceps* ('with one's
head in front, i.e., headfirst'). *Praeuius*, attributed to Cicero by
Nonius (cf. Traglia, *La lingua di Cicerone poeta*, p. 120), was probably
formed by analogy with *obuius* under the influence of locative *prae-*
in forms like *praecedo*; cf. Ov. *Met*. XI. 65: *nunc praecedentem sequitur,*

50. Adjectives which either imply a verb paradigm (e.g., *praeacutus, praepilatus*) or are descriptively associated with one (e.g., *praenuntius, praescius*)
will only be discussed if they exemplify the productive construction of
prae- + adjective or differ sharply in meaning from attested uses of the cognate
verb (e.g., *praecidaneus*).

51. *Praepes* (*RE* 44, pp. 1556f.) appears to have been specialized at an early
date as an augural term referring to good omens (opp. *infera*); compare Enn.
Ann. 91–4V³. Ennius also uses *praepes* of *ferrum* (id., 397) and *portus* (id., 488,
cf. *praepetibus…locis*, id. 94). Scholars have suggested that *praepes*, in at least
some of its uses, is etymologically connected with *pateo* (cf. Leumann, p. 200,
Norden on *Aen*. VI. 15; on p. 89, however, Leumann implies a connection with
peto). Walde–Hofmann (II 354) reject this possibility and derive *praepes* from
peto (cf. Ernout–Meillet, pp. 531–2). On the semantics of Vergilian *praepes*, see
Wackernagel, *ZVS* 33. 53f. and Norden, loc. cit. The Vergilian use probably
reflects in part the increasing productivity of intensive *prae-* during the Augustan
period (n. 63).

52. *Syncope in Greek and Indo-European* (Naples 1964), p. 380 and n. 1 (cf.
F. Solmsen, *ZVS* 34 (1897), 36). *Praecipes* (Pl. *Rud*. 671, cf. *ancipes*, ibid. 1158)
and *praecipe* (Enn. *Ann*. 399 V³) are secondarily based on the nominative
singular *praeceps* by analogy with *princeps, principis* (so Ernout–Meillet, p. 99) and
do not represent a more archaic inflection as Walde–Hofmann (I 44) suppose.

nunc praeuius anteit. It is, however, conceivable that Cicero's
praeuius was influenced by Greek πρόοδος (coupled with ἡγεμών
as an epithet of the Ram, dub. lect., Schol. ad Arat. *Phaen.* 545,
cf. n. 39). *Praeposterus*, at least in its local sense (cf. n. 65), can be
regarded as the antonym of *praeceps*. Since, however, the simplex
commonly refers to time not place, *prae-* would be liable to
descriptive interpretation as a temporal prefix (cf. Cic. *ad Att.*
VII. 16. 1). Cicero, who apparently introduced the word, typically
uses it of people who are perverse, or, at best, paradoxical, in
their behaviour (cf. *Clu.* XXVI. 71, *Pis.* XXXVIII. 92, *ad Fam.* XV. 17. 1,
also Sall. *Iug.* LXXXV. 12).[53]

Praecipuus, *praecidaneus*, and *praeliganeus* share an underlying
passive construction and thus, like *praeda*, *praemetium*, and *praemium*,
are ambiguous in their time–space reference. For example, did
praecipuus originally mean 'taken in the first place' or 'taken
first' (cf. *praemium*)? The Classical use of *praecipuus*[54] as a synonym
of *eximius* (cf. *primus*) derived from contexts such as *hic homost
omnium hominum praecipuos* (Pl. *Trin.* 1115) where a local etymology
may still be perceptible. At any rate a local interpretation of
prae- seems to be suggested by the prefixational balance between
praecipuos and *antepotens* in the following line. The development of
praecipuus parallels that of comparative *prae* and preverbal *prae-*
in *praecellere*, *praeferre*, *praestare* etc. A temporal interpretation of
praecipuus is implied by its specialized reference as a neuter
substantive to that part of the inheritance received before the
general distribution of a deceased's property (cf. Suet. *Galb.* V;
cf. its less particular use at Pl. *Rud.* 190, Ter. *Ad.* 258).[55] This
development reflects the increasing productivity of temporal
prae- at the expense of locative *prae-* in post-Augustan Latin,

53. For the assumption, widespread in ancient literature, that what is
'back-to-front, topsy-turvy' is essentially absurd, see Gow (ed)., *Theocritus* II²
(Cambridge 1952), p. 28 ad *Id.* I. 132f. The prepositional antithesis in *praeposterus* recalls Terence's use of *posthabeo prae* (p. 18).

54. It is possible that *praecipuus* specifically developed at the expense of
*praemius, assumed as a possible source of *praemium* on p. 23. Note the use of
ex- in the semantically comparable *eximius* (cf. *egregius*, *excello* etc.).

55. Cf. Paul. (ex Fest. 70. 5): *praecipuum quod ante capitur*; Festus characteristically uses adverbial *ante* with reference to time while the increasing productivity of prefixational *ante-* of place at the expense of locative *prae-* in later
Latin is illustrated by Paulus' remarks on *praestes* (ex Fest. 250. 1): *praestitem
in eadem significatione dicebant antiqui, qua nunc dicimus antistem.*

which will be discussed again. *Praecidaneus* (of a sow, Cato, *Agr.* CXXXIV, cf. *praecisum*, n. 47) also potentially emphasizes time – at least it was understood in this sense by Paulus (ex Fest. 250. 11): *praecidanea* [opp. *succidanea*, ibid. 393. 1] *agna uocabatur quae ante alias caedebatur* (cf. n. 55 and Gell. IV. 6. 7) – but, once again, a locative origin is not inconceivable. Compare *praeliganeus* (Cato, *Agr.* XXIII. 2), describing a bad wine made from unripe (or overripe?) grapes (cf. *praematurus*); here also, a locative origin ('grapes gathered from the front of the vine') cannot be categorically denied. (Note the Classical meaning of *praecido* 'cut off in front'; **praeligo*, 'pluck from the front of', is not attested.) Thus, regardless of its potentially locative etymology, prefixational *prae-* appears to have been particularly liable to a temporal interpretation in those nouns and adjectives whose stems imply a basically passive construction.

The temporal connotations of *praegnas* are much less ambiguous than those of preadjectival *prae-* in passive constructions; compare Varro, *RR* II. 4. 7 (of a sow): *quattuor...menses est praegnas et tunc parit.*[56] Its etymology, however, raises some important questions. If Ernout–Meillet (p. 531) are correct in deriving *praegnas* from a zero-grade *t*-stem formation, morphologically parallel to *comes* (:*com-i-t-*; cf. Greek ἀ-δμη-τ-) etc., then the compound could only mean 'having the birth in the future'. This proposal is, however, unattractive from a semantic standpoint since the implied reference of prefixational *prae-* to *future* time is unparalleled. Moreover a convincing explanation is readily available. According to Vaniček,[57] *praegnas* continues an old prepositional phrase **prai gnatid* meaning 'before birth'. The Varronian passage provides an excellent example of a context in which **prai gnatid* could be reinterpreted as an adjective; cf. *ouis praegnas* (from **prai gnatid*) *est diebus CL* (Varro, *RR* II. 2. 14). (The remodeling of the prepositional phrase **prai gnatid* as a declinable form is

56. Locative *prae-* would imply that *-gnāt-* referred to the embryo or the tumescent belly, for which the use of *uenter* with reference to pregnancy in the phrase *uentrem ferre* (Varro, *RR* II. 1. 19) provides at best only slight support. Moreover, *grauida* appears to have been the appropriate adjective for this condition (cf. Paul. ex Fest. 87. 1: *grauida est quae iam grauatur conceptu; praegnans uelut occupata in generando quod conceperit*).

57. *Etymologisches Wörterbuch der lateinischen Sprache*[2] (Leipzig 1881), p. 75, accepted by Leumann, p. 232; F. Müller, *Altlateinisches Wörterbuch* (Göttingen 1926), p. 358; and Walde–Hofmann II 354.

structurally comparable with the derivation of *praecordia* from
*prae corde and *proconsul* from *pro consule*.) The development of
praegnas as (participial) *praegnans* probably occurred relatively late
in the tradition[58] and was due, most specifically, to the analogy
of *inciens*, combined with the fact that, in pronunciation, *-gnās*
and *-gnans* would have been identical. (Contrast the use of *pro-*
in *procreans*.)

If we accept Vaniček's explanation, then *praegnas* represents
a unique relic of prepositional (as opposed to adverbial) *prae*
used with reference to time. It is possible that this usage derives
from a rustic, non-Roman source (cf. Oscan *prai Mamerttiais* and
nn. 14, 18). On the other hand, the evidence of *praegnas* may
suggest a functional distribution according to which prepositional
prae was temporal when its complement designated an event, but
otherwise referred exclusively to place; contrast the semantics
of *praegnas* with those of *praecordia* (from *prai corde). This temporal
use of prepositional *prae* was usurped by *ante* before the start of
the literary tradition. After further evidence has been discussed,
the questions raised by *praegnas* can be evaluated in greater
detail.

The productive use of preadjectival *prae-* as an intensive prefix
in post-Republican Latin has already been noted (pp. 23f.). Its
origin must now be considered. Besides *-potens*, *praeclarus* is the
only adjective with prefixational *prae-* which is common to all
periods of the language and occurs from the beginning of the
literary tradition beside its corresponding simplex (i.e., *clarus*).
Praeclarus (originally 'shining in front') was already used by
Plautus in a metaphorical sense: *hominem tam pulchrum et praeclarum
uirtute et forma* (*MG* 1042). Under the influence of forms in which
prefixational *prae-* connoted superiority (e.g., *praecello, praecipuus,
praesertim* etc.), it was grammatically possible to interpret *praeclarus*
as an intensive form of *clarus* (cf. *praepotentes pulchre pacisque
potentes...fuimus*, Pl. *Poen.* 1182). Due largely to the continuing
productivity of intensive *per-*, however, this possibility was not
fully implemented until the Augustan period: in Republican
Latin there is virtually no unambiguous evidence for a descriptively intensive use of *prae-*. *Praeferuidus* (of lightning, Acc. *tr.*

58. Cf. F. Sommer, *Handbuch der lateinischen Laut- und Formenlehre*[3] (Heidelberg
1948), pp. 245–6.

652R²) probably contains a locative use of *prae-* (cf. *praeacutus*) and *praegrandis* (Pacuv. *tr.* 37R²) may be a redactional error for *pergrandis* (cf. *pergrande*, Pl. *Pers.* 494, *pergrandescere*, Acc. *tr.* 440R²) due to the relative frequency of *praegrandis* beside *pergrandis* in late Latin.[59] Garnier[60] suggested that this lack of evidence reflects the continuing influence of locative *prae-*, which inhibited the productive development of intensive *prae-* on the basis of such pairs as *praeclarus:clarus* and *praepotens:potens*.

Two other potential sources for intensive *prae-* are suggested by words like *praematurus* and *praeacutus*. *Praemature* at Pl. *Most.* 500 refers to the premature death of the pretended ghost but originally the word probably designated crops or fruit which had ripened 'before the expected time' (i.e., 'too early', cf. *praeliganeus*). When the harvest arrived, the fruit was thus 'overripe'. Compare the semantic development of *praecox* (Enn. +), *praefestinatim* (Sisenn. +), *praeproperus* (Pl. +), and, perhaps, *praeuiridans* (Laber. +, cf. n. 81). Temporal *prae-* with intensive connotations is also attested in *praefidens* (ap. Cic. *de Orat.* III. 41. 166, attributed to Accius by Ribbeck). The relative productivity of this group of adjectives in Republican Latin was doubtless related closely to the preverbal use of *prae-*, in words like *praefestino* (Pl. +) and *praegestio* (Cic., Cat.).[61] In fact the temporal connotation of each of these forms clearly distinguished this use of *prae-* from the highly productive *per-* and, during the development of intensive *prae-*, prevented any synonymic conflict between the two prefixes, at least until the Augustan period.

59. On the redactional confusion of preadjectival *prae-* and *per-*, note *praegraues* beside *pergraues* (Varro ap. Non. 440. 14), *praeferuidus* beside *perferuidus* (Columella, *RR* III. 1. 3).

60. K. von Garnier, *Die Präposition als sinnverstärkendes Präfix* (Dissertation, Leipzig 1906), p. 57. Meanwhile, intensive *per-* was highly productive: André lists forty-six pre-Ciceronian examples and over one hundred more from Cicero. Wölfflin's ingenious suggestion (*ALLG* (1884), 99) that *per-* implies a comparison with an inherent quality while *prae-* compares different objects possessing the same quality is, as André convincingly demonstrates (pp. 136–7), not borne out by the evidence.

61. *Cael.* XXVIII. 67: *praegestit animus iam uidere...* conceivably mimics the language of Clodia's set (cf. Cat. LXIV. 145: *animus praegestit apisci...* and *praetrepidans* at XLVI. 7). The Ciceronian context is unusually racy (cf. *quadrare*, ibid., XXIX. 69 and *quadrantaria*, ibid., XXVI. 62, with Austin's note (Cicero: *Pro Caelio*³ (Oxford 1960), pp. 124–5, 171), an epithet to which Catullus seems to allude in the *quadriuia* of LVIII. 4).

Two kinds of intensive *prae-*, comparative and superlative (cf. Engl. 'too' and 'very'), seem to be attested. The comparative use of preadjectival *prae-* is, however, not always clearly distinct from its superlative use. A distinction between Plancus' use of *prae-* in the phrase *praematura denuntiatio* (Cic. *ad Fam.* x. 8. 4) and Cicero's in *haec praepropera prensatio* (*ad Att.* I. I. I, cf. *ex tuis litteris cognoui praeproperam quandam festinationem tuam, ad Fam.* VII. 8. I, and Livy XXXVII. 23. 10) is hard to draw: the *denuntiatio* and *prensatio* occurred both 'too soon' and 'very hastily'. In several words, the distinction was probably blurred and depended on the meaning of the simplex. If the simplex had positive connotations (e.g., *maturus*), comparative and superlative uses of an intensive prefix could plausibly be distinguished (i.e., fruit which is 'very ripe' is not necessarily 'overripe'). On the other hand, given a semantically negative simplex (e.g., *properus*), intensive *prae-* would have been more ambiguous: 'very hasty' action is also likely to be 'too hasty'. These potential ambiguities doubtless affected the use of words attested at the beginning of the Augustan period when intensive *prae-* became productive: was the *homo praecanus* at Hor. *Ep.* I. 20. 24 very grey, too grey, or prematurely grey? The resonance of *praecanus* probably included all three senses (cf. *corpora praedura*, Verg. *G.* II. 531). Since the comparative use of intensive *prae-* as an adjectival prefix in pre-Augustan Latin appears to have been much more extensive than that of its superlative counterpart, the evidence of this relative productivity may therefore be justifiably cited as a significant factor in the interpretation of Augustan usage.

The contribution of forms like *praeacutus* to the history of intensive *prae-* can now be discussed. *Praeacutus* originally meant 'sharp in front' (i.e., 'with a sharp point'; cf. *praeferratus, praepilatus*, and *praefringo, praeseco, praetrunco, praeuro* etc.). This meaning is still implied by Caesar (e.g., *praeacutis cacuminibus, BG* VII. 73. 2, cf. id. II. 29. 3, Sall. *Cat.* LVI. 3). André ('Les adjectifs et adverbes', p. 140), however, argues that at *BG* IV. 17. 3 (*tigna...paulum ab imo praeacuta*), *praeacutus* is solely intensive. While André's interpretation implies a curious homonymy among Caesar's uses of *praeacutus* and is not absolutely required by the context, the passage may indeed provide a transitional example of the semantic development of locative to intensive *prae-* at a time when the productivity of locative *prae-* was generally losing ground. Thus, beside intensive *per-*[62] and obsolescent *prae se* 'ahead' (p. 7), Sallust provides the following unambiguous example of intensive *prae-*: *quorum proxuma terrae praealta sunt, cetera, uti fors tulit, alta*

62. Cf. *peridoneus* (ap. Non. 310. 14), *-ignarus* (ibid., 554. 19), *-incertus* (ap. Gell. XVIII. 4. 4). The use of *per-* as an adjectival prefix meaning 'thoroughly', hence 'very', is not only older than that of intensive *prae-* but has a somewhat different origin. Intensive *per-* derived in part from its use as a preverbal prefix and also under the influence of adverbial *per* (on which see Leumann, 'Lat. enklitisches *-per...*', cit. supr., and André, 'Les adjectifs et adverbes', passim). The transition from verbal to adjectival prefix most probably occurred by way of the past participle; for example, *percolo* 'honor greatly' (Pl. *Trin.* 280): *percultus* (id., *Poen.* 232), cf. *perterreo* 'thoroughly terrify': *perterritus*, hence, *peraresco*: *peraridus* (cf. Plautine *perbonus, -doctus, -dudum, -facile* etc., André, p. 146). The comparable use of locative *ex-*, for example, in *elixus* 'thoroughly boiled' (Pl. *Poen.* 279, as a pun) probably derived from the analogy of *eximius, excello* etc.; compare the corresponding influence of *praecipuus, praecello* etc. on the development of intensive *prae-*. Vergil uses *edurus* (beside *praedurus*) and *efferus* but the construction never gained much currency, at least in the literary language. Contrast the massive productivity of intensive *per-* in Republican Latin, especially in Cicero's letters (cf. André, 'Les adjectifs et adverbes', pp. 144–7); note also Lucretius: *perdelirus* (I. 692), *-dulcis* (IV. 635), *-paruus* (III. 216), *-subtilis* (III. 179), beside *praeproperanter* (III. 779), and Caesar: *-angustus* (*BG* VII. 15. 5), *-exiguus* (id. V. 14. 4 etc.), *-facilis* (id. I. 2. 2 etc.), *-gratus* (*BC* I. 86. 1), *-idoneus* (id. II. 24. 2), *-magnus* (*BG* VII. 31. 4), *-multi* (*BC* III. 43. 1), *-pauci* (*BG* I. 53. 2 etc.). Isidore (X. 233) attributes *praeuarus* to Cicero, but, in view of Cicero's overwhelming preference for *per-*, the authenticity of this form is dubious (leg. *peruarus?*). Cicero mostly uses *praepotens*, a word belonging to the traditional literary vocabulary (e.g., Pl., Acc.), in grandiloquent contexts (cf. *Rab. Post.* XVI. 44, also in reference to Jupiter, *Diu.* II. 18. 42) or when speaking of the past (e.g., Scipionic Carthage, *Balb.* XV. 34). Though the productive relation of *impotens*: *potens* could have doubtless suggested the analysis of *prae-* in *praepotens* as a separable (intensive) prefix, Cicero was apparently not influenced by this descriptive possibility. Thus the fact that he did not employ prefixational *prae-* as an intensive prefix meaning 'very' – in addition to underscoring his preference for *per-* – suggests that he viewed *praeclarus* as an indivisible word parallel to *praecipuus* rather than as a construct of intensive *prae-* + *clarus*. The same conclusion is also suggested by his use of *praeclarissimus*, since the superlative of intensive adjectives was commonly avoided during the Classical period (cf. André, 'Les adjectifs et adverbes', pp. 137–8, 141). *Praeclarus* (of *insignia caeli*) at *Arat.* XX. 2 Traglia therefore probably means 'brilliant' in the archaizing, locative sense of 'shining in front' rather than 'very bright' (Lewis and Short, *praeclarus* 1; cf. Lucr. II. 1032, of *lux*, V. 120, of *sol*). These observations make the anomalous presence of *praegestit* at *Cael.* XXVIII. 67 (n. 61) even more remarkable. André (pp. 138f.) has correctly noted that prevocalic hiatus in the case of intensive *prae-* strongly favored the use of *per-*. Words like *praeacutus* whose etymological construction was not intensive were obviously not affected by this restriction.

alia, alia in tempestate uadosa (*Iug.* LXXVIII. 2). At the end of the Republic, preadjectival *prae-* gradually became productive as an intensive prefix on the combined models of *praeclarus*: *clarus*, *praematurus*: *maturus*, and *praeacutus*: *acutus*, and, in Vergil, Livy, and Ovid, its use was fully exemplified.[63] In the *sermo cotidianus* of the first century A.D., intensive *prae-* was extended at the expense of *per-*.[64] The elder Pliny also favored intensive *prae-*,[65] which reached its highest productivity during his period. Nevertheless *per-* continued in use and, after the third century, began again to spread at the expense of *prae-*.[66] Despite this fact, and by contrast with the other functions of *prae*, its intensive use alone survived directly in Romance where it is attested as *prea* in Rumanian, 'wohl unter Einfluss von slav. *prě*'.[67]

63. Vergil coined *praecelsus, -diues* (cf. Ov., Livy, *per-* Cic.), *-dulcis* (*per-* Lucr.), *-durus, -pinguis* (cf. *praepes* n. 51), *-ualidus*: I. Dousa (followed by Warmington) read *praeualidus in funibus* in Lucil. ap. Non. 234. 37 (= fr. 389 Marx), but Marx prints [*quae*] *ualidis*...(cf. *Lucilius: Opera* II (Leipzig 1905), p. 148 ad loc.). Compare Ovid: *-nubilis, -frigidus* (*per-* Cic.), *-lustris, -signis*, Livy: *-ferox* (cf. *perferus* Varr., *efferus* Lucr., Verg.), *-gelidus, -grauis* (cf. *-dexter* Grat.).

64. Cf. André, 'Les adjectifs et adverbes', pp. 143–4. In particular, André notes the following evidence: four examples of *prae-* in Persius, none of *per-*, six of *prae-* and two of *per-* in Juvenal, twenty-six of *prae-* and nineteen of *per-* in Apuleius. Persius coined *praelargus* and *-trepidus* (cf. *-trepidans*, Cat. XLVI. 7).

65. While his older contemporary Celsus favored intensive *per-* (cf. André, 'Les adjectifs et adverbes', p. 147), the senior Pliny coined the following forms: *praeceler* (*per-* Cic.), *-crassus* (*per-* Cels.), *-densus* (*per-* Col.), *-diuinus, -fecundus* (*per-* Mela), *-lucidus* (*per-* Cic.), *-mollis* (*per-* Quint.), *-parcus, -tener, -tenuis* (*per-* Cic.), *-uelox*. Note the use of *praeposterus* in Pliny in reference to inverted births (*HN* VII. 8. 46, implying locative *prae-*) and, homonymously, of figs ripening out of season (i.e. 'too late', as an antonym of *praematurus*, id. XVI. 27. 117). Other first-century forms are found in Calpurnius: *praetorridus*, Statius: *-cultus* (*per-* Pl.), *-doctus* (*per-* Pl., Cic.), *-grauidus*, Tacitus: *-calidus* (*per-* Pliny), *-gracilis* (*per-* Pliny), [Quintilian]: *-rigidus*, Val. Probus: *-rancidus*, Frontinus: *-uiridis* (*per-* Cels.), Columella: *-sulsus*. Between the death of Cicero and the close of the first century A.D., new coinages with intensive *prae-* outnumbered those with *per-*.

66. Cf. André ('Les adjectifs et adverbes', pp. 148f., especially 153): 'aux ive–vie siècles, période de créations nouvelles pour les deux formations, œuvre d'une multiplicité d'auteurs: pour *per-*, 47 auteurs, 83 formes; pour *prae-*, 23 auteurs, 35 formes. L'ampleur du mouvement va s'atténuant régulièrement jusqu' au vie siècle'. Cf. E. Löfstedt, *Philologischer Kommentar zur Peregrinatio Aetheriae* (Uppsala 1911), p. 92.

67. W. Meyer-Lübke, *Romanisches etymologisches Wörterbuch*[3] (Heidelberg 1935), no. 6707.

The history of intensive *prae-* illustrates how a single, specialized function can be derived from relatively separate origins. This development corresponded to the increasing productivity of temporal and comparative uses of *prae-*, following a period in which its interpretation as an intensive prefix had been inhibited by the lingering use of locative *prae-* and the high frequency of intensive *per-*. The fact that intensive *prae-* was most productive during the century immediately following that in which *per-* had been predominant exemplifies a recurring aspect of linguistic change which Meillet described in these terms:

> La valeur expressive des mots s'atténue par l'emploi, la force en diminue; et ils tendent à se grouper ensemble. Pour maintenir l'expressivité dont on a besoin, on est donc conduit à renouveler les termes; c'est ainsi que les mots qui marquent le superlatif, comme *très*, *fort*, *extrêmement*, etc. tendent à sortir de l'usage au fur et à mesure que, grande au début, la force en décroît.[68]

PREADVERBIAL *PRAE-*

In addition to derivatives based on forms which have already been discussed, only *praefiscini*, *praemodum*,[69] *praesertim*, and *praesto* attest the use of *prae-* as an adverbial prefix. *Praesertim* (originally 'in the front rank') can be connected with *sero* 'link' (cf. Walde–Hofmann, II 522, Ernout–Meillet, pp. 618–19) and exemplifies the locative use of *prae-*. *Praefiscini*, an apotropaic term meaning 'touch wood' or 'no offence' is more complicated. From a descriptive standpoint, *praefiscini* and *praebia* imply a similar use of *prae-*, although the etymology of *praefiscini* remains obscure.[70]

68. *Introduction à l'étude comparative des langues indo-européennes*[8] (Paris 1937), p. 20.

69. *Praemodum* 'beyond measure' (Liv. Andr. *Od.* 39R[2]) represents an allegro form of *praetermodum*; compare Gell. VI. 7. 12: *Liuius in Odyssia 'praemodum' dicit quasi admodum...dictum...est quasi praetermodum* (also late Latin *peradmodum*, Hofmann–Szantyr, p. 164). On the confusion of *prae* and *praeter* in late Latin, see J. Svennung, *Wortstudien zu den spätlat. Oribasius-recensionen* (Uppsala 1932), p. 111 and J. Biletchi, 'Ist *prae-* in der Zusammensetzung mit Verben gleich *praeter*?', *Woch. f. kl. Phil.* (1916), 280f. Note, however, Livy's use of *praefluo* and *praelatus sum*, discussed on pp. 43f.

70. Cf. Walde–Hofmann (I 459) and Hofmann, *Lateinische Umgangssprache*, p. 131, for suggestions. It is hard to reconstruct the original context from

Praefiscine at Pl. *Rud.* 461 (beside *-ini* at *Asin.* 491), if genuine rather than redactional, implies its early reinterpretation as an adverb with the characteristic suffix *-e*.

Though the etymology of *praesto* 'at hand' has been contested, locative *prae-* is descriptively guaranteed.[71] *Praesto* can be plausibly derived from a phrase like *prae situ (: *situs*) *esse* 'be in place *prae*' with locative *prae* used adverbially (cf. *praefiscini*). Interpreted as an adverbial phrase + *esse* on the analogy of *prae manu*, *prae situ could have become *praestu* by syncope. A remodeling of *praestu* as *praesto* may be attributed to analogical pressure from the more frequently occurring adverbial type of *uero*, *multo* etc. Curtius Valerianus (ap. Cassiod. VI. 157. 22) actually cites a form *praestu*: *praesto nos per o scribimus, ueteres per u scripserunt. Sed sic praesto dicendum est, ut sedulo et optato et sortito* (cf. *CIL* VI. 2193). Although the antiquity of *praestu* has frequently been doubted,[72] it may indeed be genuine and thus support the etymology suggested above.

Praefiscini, *praesertim*, and *praesto* were all in use before 150 B.C. In each case *prae-* can be regarded as etymologically locative and,

which *praefiscini* developed. Moreover, *-fiscini* (:*fascinum*, with vowel assimilation, cf. *uiginti*) can imply either the evil eye or an apotropaic charm (cf. Porph. ad Hor. *Epod.* VIII. 18, Varr. *LL* VII. 97). If *-fiscini* refers to the evil eye, *praefiscini* might continue a phrase such as *prae fascini uereor* 'I fear the *fascinum* which is *prae*' (with the pre-Classical use of *uereor* + gen.).

71. Despite the apparent parallel with *prae manu*, Wackernagel's opinion (*46 Jhb. d. Schw. Gymnas.* (1919), 168f.) that *praesto* derives from a phrase *prai hesto 'bei der Hand' (cf. Sanskrit *hásta-*) 'se heurte au fait que le mot sanskrit n'a de correspondant nulle part' (Ernout–Meillet, p. 532). Solmsen (*Glotta* 3 (1911), 245f.) interpreted *praesto* as an archaic adverbial specialization of a first person singular present formation in its etymological meaning 'I stand in front'. According to Persson, *Beiträge zur indogermanischen Wortforschung* (Uppsala 1912), p. 240 (cf. Prellwitz, *BB* 19 (1895), 318), '*praestō* stellt wahrscheinlich einen erstarrten Kasus eines Stammes *prae-sto-* "dabei stehend, bei der Hand seiend" dar.' The evidence which Persson cites in defence of *prae-sto-*, namely, adjectival *praestus* (*CIL* VI 12013) is, however, more plausibly interpreted as a late back formation from *praesto* (so Walde–Hofmann II 356). Bréal (*MSL* 2, 44f.) suggested that *praesto* continued *praesito, but the meaning of such a form remains somewhat unclear and *praesino is not otherwise attested. As Ernout–Meillet remarked (loc. cit.), 'il a été proposé...des explications diverses dont aucune ne s'impose' (cf. Hofmann–Szantyr, p. 269: '*praesto* unerklärt').

72. Walde–Hofmann (loc. cit.: '*praestu*...ist wohl sek., nicht alt') follow Persson in questioning the antiquity of *praestu*. Persson's objection may, however, be overridden since its sole support appears to be his unnecessary reconstruction of a thematicized *prae-sto-* as the source of adverbial *praesto*.

from a descriptive standpoint, would surely continue to be understood in that sense.

PREVERBAL *PRAE-*

By far the most productive use of *prae-* was as a verb prefix. The locative use of preverbal *prae-* remained productive until the Augustan period during which temporal *prae-*, originally productive especially with verbs of speaking, became increasingly frequent. These changes are first clearly noticeable in the language of Ovid.[73] During the first century A.D., the productivity of locative *prae-* correspondingly decreased and after A.D. 100 became relatively uncommon.[74]

In discussing the specialized meanings of verbs prefixed with *prae-*, one may usefully distinguish between *homonymous* and *polysemous* usage. When a word is used in two or more different senses in identical syntactic and semantic contexts, it can be said to exhibit homonymy. On the other hand, if the semantic distinctions between uses of the same word can be predicted and there-

73. Ovid introduced the following examples of temporal *prae-* during this period of transition: *praecerpo* (n. 78), *-compono*, *-consumo*, *-contrecto*, *-corrumpo*, *-delasso*, *-fodio* (pp. 42f.), *-medico* (cf. n. 79), *-morior*, *-queror* (n. 80), *-sono*, *-tempto*, *-tepesco*, *-tingo*, *-uitio*. In addition to evidence discussed in nn. 80, 81, and 85, note the following examples of temporal *prae-* attested before A.D. 100 (post-Augustan usage is so indicated): *-cedo* (n. 74 and pp. 35f.), *-cogito* (Sen.), *-cipio*, *-cognosco*, *-colo*, *-damno*, *-destino*, *-disco*, *-dispono*, *-domo* (Sen.), *-finio* (pp. 39f.), *-floro* (n. 78), *-formo* (Quint.), *-germino* (Plin.), *-gusto*, *-innuo* (Varr. ap. Non. 91. 4, dub. l.), *-iudico* (cf. *praeiuratio*, Paul. ex Fest.), *-iuuo* (Tac.), *-lego* (Plin.), *-libo* (Stat.), *-ludo* (Plin.), *-mando*, *-meditor*, *-mercor*, *-migro*, *-modulor* (Quint.), *-molior*, *-mollio* (Quint.), *-monstro*, *-narro*, *-nosco* (cf. *praenotio*, p. 20), *-occido* (Plin.), *-occupo* (pp. 39f.), *-olo*, *-paro*, *-ripio*, *-rogo*, *-scio*, *-scisco*, *-scribo*, *-sidero*, *-significo*, *-signo*, *-spargo*, *-sterno*, *-stino* (cf. Paul. ex Fest. 249. 27: *praestinare apud Plautum praeemere est, id est emendo tenere*, on which see O. S. Powers, *Commercial vocabulary of early Latin* (Chicago 1944), pp. 22f.; the etymological significance of *prae-* in *praestinare* may have been locative, i.e., 'stand in front of [sc. to signify purchase]'), *-stituo*, *-struo*, *-sudo* (Stat.), *-uerno* (n. 81), *-uerto* (pp. 41f.).

74. Verbs of motion are listed as examples of locative *prae-*; their potential ambiguity is discussed on p. 38: *praebeo* (*praehibeo*, Pl., contrast *posthabeo*, Ter.), *-cedo* (n. 73 and pp. 35f.), *-celero* (Stat.), *-curro*, *-cutio*, *-dico* (n. 84), *-duco*, *-eo* (p. 38), *-fero* (n. 75 and p. 43f.), *-festino*, *-ficio*, *-fluo* (p. 44), *-fodio* (n. 73 and pp. 42f.), *-fulcio* (n. 79), *-fulgeo* (n. 81), *-fulguro* (Stat.), *-grado*, *-gredior*, *-grauo*, *-iaceo* (Plin.), *-icio* (Col.), *-labor*, *-lego* (Tac., Suet.), *-luceo*, *-mitto*, *-nato*, *-nauigo* (Plin.), *-pandeo*, *-pendo*, *-pondero*, *-pono*, *-porto*, *-rumpo*, *-seruio* (cf. *-ministro*, Gell.), *-sideo*, *-sto* (n. 88, cf. Powers (above, n. 73), pp. 25f.), *-sulto* (cf. *praesul*, p. 22), *-tego* (Plin.), *-tendo*, *-torqueo*, *-umbro* (Tac.), *-uado* (Sen.), *-uehor*, *-uolo*.

fore defined in terms of the syntactic or semantic context in which they occur, the relationship between them can be termed polysemous. Within the group of verbs under discussion, the distinction between polysemous and homonymous relationships can be illustrated by two examples, *praecedo* and verbs prefixed with *prae-* which refer to 'cutting, biting', etc.

Verbs like *praecedo*, prefixed with *prae-* and denoting superiority or preference, are already common in Roman comedy and were still slightly productive in post-Augustan Latin.[75] If a verb belonging to this subclass denoted both superiority and physical location, the distinction was in most cases syntactically predictable. For example, *praecedo* 'go in front' was constructed with a direct object in the accusative or used absolutely (e.g., Livy VII. 13. 2: *is praecedens agmen militum ad tribunal pergit*, abs., XXX. 13. 2; with an *ut*-clause, XXII. 51. 2). *Praecedo* 'excel', however, governed an indirect object in the dative in Roman comedy (e.g., Pl. *Asin.* 629: *ut uestrae fortunae meis praecedunt, Libane, longe*, cf. *Truc.* 372: *hoc tuis fortunis, Iuppiter, praestant meae*), but, in Classical Latin, a direct object in the accusative and also an ablative of respect (e.g., Caes. *BG* I. 1. 4: *Heluetii...reliquos Gallos uirtute praecedunt*). (Many other verbs denoting superiority continued to govern the dative, with or without an accompanying ablative of respect, e.g., *praestare*.) The relation between *praecedo* 'excel' and *praecedo* 'go in front' can therefore be regarded as a polysemous one, since their different meanings can be syntactically (and chronologically) predicted.[76] In terms of the principle of complementary distribution, a polysemous relationship involves semantic complementation while an homonymous relationship involves semantic contrast.[77]

75. Cf. *-cello* (cf. *ante-*), *-ditus*, *-emineo* (Tac.), *-fero*, *-gredior* (n. 74), *-luceo*, *-nito*, *-opto*, *-polleo*, *-pondero* (n. 74), *-possum* (cf. *praepotens*, p. 27f., and n. 62), *-radio*, *-sto* (n. 88), *-sum* (pp. 40f.), *-ualeo* (Stat.), *-uenio* (Col.), *-uerto* (n. 73 and pp. 41f.), *-uenio* (n. 79). The influence of such verbs on the development of comparative and intensive *prae-* has already been noted.

76. Contrast, for example, the homonymy of locative and intensive *prae-* in Pliny's use of *praeposterus* (n. 65, cf. *praecerpo*, p. 36).

77. Complementary distributions have most commonly been investigated with regard to phonological and morphological environments, but Weinreich has rightly emphasized that 'the distinction between contrastive [i.e., homonymous] and complementary [i.e., polysemous] senses is a prerequisite for descriptive semantics' ('Webster's *Third*: a critique of its semantics', *IJAL* 30 (1964), 406). In the argument concerning *praecedo*, syntactic context is used as an approximate guide to the classification of semantic relationships. Semantic

Prefixed to verbs which denote cutting, biting, breaking etc., preverbial *prae-* meant 'at the front (-end) of', hence 'from the end of'. *Praecido* (originally 'cut at the front') became comparable in meaning with *amputo* (cf. Lucil. 280–1 Marx: *'anu noceo' inquit | praecidit caulem testisque una amputat ambo*) and *ecfodio* (cf. Pl. *Aul.* 189: *quoi ego iam linguam praecidam atque oculos ecfodiam domi*). This specialization of preverbal *prae-* was semantically predictable in Republican Latin since it was associated only with *uerba secandi* and was thus in complementary distribution with *prae-* 'in front of'. During the Augustan period, however, the productivity of this construction lapsed, a fact which contributed to the possible reinterpretation of *prae-* in words like *praeacutus* as an intensive preadjectival prefix. As temporal *prae-* became increasingly frequent, the likelihood of homonymous uses of the same word obviously arose. *Praecerpo* is a good example of this development. Originally meaning 'pluck at the front of', hence 'diminish' (cf. Cic. *Verr.* ii. 4. 80), and used in its strictly locative sense by Statius (*Th.* ix. 193), *praecerpo* at Ovid, *Her.* xx. 143 had the temporal sense of 'pluck beforehand'. In the first century A.D., therefore, two homonymous uses of *praecerpo* were attested.[78]

Preverbal *prae-* with predominantly locative sense occurs in many compounds implying hindrance (e.g., *praecludo*, *praepedio*, *praesaepio*, etc.).[79] This use of *prae-* is comparable with the earlier

context will be invoked in our discussion of *praefero* (pp. 43f.) and of the development of locative and temporal uses of *prae* (pp. 54f.).

78. It is possible that *praefloro* (cf. Livy xxxvii. 58: *gloriam eius uictoriae praefloratam apud Thermopylas esse*, Plin. *Pan.* lviii: *decus praecerptum praefloratumque*) which functioned as the transitive of *defloresco* influenced the development of temporal *praecerpo*. (Ovid's authorship of *Her.* xx is notoriously disputed, but, even if non-Ovidian, the poem is unlikely to have been written more than fifty years after his death and thus at least supplies a valid example of first-century usage.) For other verbs of this type, compare *-acuo*, *-cido*, *-cingo*, *-ferratus* (n. 79), *-figo* (n. 79), *-fringo*, *-lambo*, *-mordeo*, *-pilatus*, *-rado*, *-rigesco* (Tac., n. 81), *-rodo*, *-scindo*, *-seco* (cf. *-segmen*, Pl. *Aul.* 313 and Non. ad loc.), *-suo*, *-tero*, *-texo*, *-trunco*, *-uro*, *-uello*, *-uerro*.

79. Cf. *-ferratus* (Pl. *Pers.* 24, beside Cato, *Agr.* xi, cf. n. 78), *-figo* (n. 78), *-foco*, *-ligo*, *-lumbo*, *-medico*, *-obturo*, *-uaricor*. *Praeuenio* 'prevent' variously implies locative or temporal *prae-*, depending on its context. In post-Augustan Latin, the temporal connotations predominate (cf. *praemunio*, p. 39f.). Just as causal *prae-* was not used exclusively in privative contexts in early Latin (cf. *prae laetitia lacrimae prosiliunt*, Pl. *Stich.* 466), so this use of prefixational *prae-* did not always imply hindrance in its early constructions (cf. *praefulcio* 'place in front as a prop', Pl. *Pers.* 12).

history of causal *prae* in construction with nouns denoting emotion
(see above, pp. 10f.). In compounds like *praecludo*, the locative
sense of the prefix is especially clear (but note *praeuenio*, n. 79).
On the other hand, the quasi-intensive function of verbs like
praegestio (Cat. LXIV. 145, Cic. *Cael*. XXVIII. 67, n. 61) clearly
derives from the temporal use of *prae*-. *Praetrepidans* at Cat.
XLVI. 7 – *iam mens praetrepidans auet uagari* – connotes both anticipation and intensity.[80] Along with the corresponding intensive
adjectives, the intensive use of preverbal *prae*- became relatively
productive in Silver Latin, especially in the elder Pliny,[81] and
its development included locative as well as temporal reference
(cf. *praelongo* beside *praecoquo*). In later Latin locative *prae*- continued to yield to the increasing productivity of temporal *prae*-.[82]

When *prae*(-) was constructed (as adverb or prefix) with verbs
of motion, its meaning was potentially ambiguous: *i prae* implies

80. Given the emotional connotations of the underlying verbal stem, one
cannot easily ascertain the stage at which temporal *prae*-, prefixed to words
like -*gestio* and -*trepido*, developed an intensive as well as an anticipatory function.
The context of *praetimet* at Pl. *Amph*. 29 suggests that a precautionary, temporal
sense predominates and this meaning is probably also appropriate to *praeme-
tuens* in Caesar, *BG* VII. 49. 1 (cf. Lucr. III. 1019). On the other hand, *prae*- at
Aen. II. 573 aptly intensifies Helen's dread, and, regardless of the authenticity
of the Helen-episode (on which, see G. P. Goold, *HSCP* 74 (1970), 101f.), this
interpretation is in keeping with other Vergilian experiments with intensive
prae- (n. 63). Intensive *prae*- continued to be associated with verbs of emotion,
for example, -*furo* (Stat. *Th*. II. 420), -*gaudeo* (Sil. XV. 307), -*queror* (Ov. *Met*. IV.
259), in later Latin, -*iactito*, -*patior*, -*stupesco*, and, with verbs denoting fear:
-*commoueo* (Sen.), -*formido* (Quint.), and, later, -*moueo*.

81. Comparative *prae*-: -*sanesco*, -*sano*, -*uernat*; superlative *prae*-: -*coquo* (: -*cox*),
-*duro* (: -*durus*), -*longo* (: -*longus*), cf. -*ualesco* (Col. : -*ualidus*), -*rigesco* (Tac.).
Praefestino, *praefulgeo*, and *praeuirido* are attested in Republican Latin. Again
it is uncertain how early *prae*- developed intensive connotations in these three
verbs. *Praefulgeo* (*ad Her*. III. 19. 32), however, seems to be used intensively and
the same is true of *praeuiridans* in Laber. *mim*. 158 Bonaria: *cur cum uigebam
membris praeuiridantibus*. These suggestions leave open the possibility that
praeclarus in the poetry of Cicero and Lucretius means 'very bright' (n. 62).

82. Locative *prae*-: -*ambulo*, -*cadens*, -*clareo*, -*clueo*, -*eligo*, -*fundo*, -*guberno*,
-*gypso*, -*lino*, -*loco*, -*mico*, -*nexus*, -*noto* (infr.), -*palpans*, -*strangulo*, -*tondeo*, -*uelo*,
-*uincio*. Temporal *prae*-: -*accipio*, -*aequo*, -*audio*, -*caeco*, -*catechizo*, -*coepi*, -*commodo*,
-*concinno*, -*condio*, -*condo*, -*crepo*, -*culco*, -*curo*, -*datus* (beside earlier -*ditus*), -*demonstro*,
-*designo*, -*determino*, -*esus*, -*fatigo*, -*figuro*, -*fomento*, -*fotus*, -*fugio*, *genero*, -*gero*,
-*infundo*, -*lasso*, -*lauo*, -*laxo*, -*lumino*, -*macero*, -*maledico*, -*mando* (cf. earlier -*mordeo*,
-*rodo*), -*metor*, -*minor*, -*misceo*, -*modero*, -*mundo*, -*noto*, -*nuncupatus*, -*oleo*, -*ordino*,
-*oro*, -*ostendo*, -*pignero*, -*plecto*, -*poto*, -*purgo*, -*roboro*, -*sago*, -*semino*, -*sepelio*, -*sero*,
-*seruo*, -*sicco*, -*sideo*, -*spero*, -*spicio*, -*surgo*, -*suspecto*, -*taedescit*, -*tango*, -*testor*, -*torreo*,
-*tumeo*, -*ulcero*, -*ungo*, -*uallo*, -*uaporo*, -*ueto*, -*uexo*.

both 'go ahead (place)' and 'go first (time)' (cf. also *prae se, praeposterus, praeproperus*). *Praeeo*, for example, means 'lead the way by action (or precept)' where both locative (cf. *praetor*) and temporal interpretations are descriptively possible. In its more frequent meaning of 'recite', locative and temporal uses have been separately specialized. Temporal *prae-* is thus implied by the meaning 'precede someone in reciting a formula etc.', locative *prae-* by 'recite in front of someone'. From an etymological standpoint, however, both these uses can be derived from locative *prae-*, specialized in either a religious or secular sense. A context such as Pl. *Cas.* 447–8: *protello mortem mihi; | certum est, hunc Accheruntem praemittam prius* also illustrates how a change from locative to temporal sense could have occurred (cf. n. 10).[83]

In construction with verbs of speaking, however, a temporal sense was generally specialized at an early date (e.g., *praedicere* Ter., *praefari* Cato, *praeloqui* Pl.).[84] If the verb was intransitive

83. (On *praeire*, see G. I. Luzzatto, 'Il verbo *praeire* delle più antiche magistrature romano-italiche', *Eos* 48 (1956), 439f.) Towards the end of the Republic and during the Augustan period, many intransitive verbs of motion (and position) prefixed with *prae-* came to be used transitively: *praecedo* (Caes.), *-curro* (Cic.), *-eo* 'recite', *-fluo, -gredior, -uenio* (Livy, n. 79), and later in Tacitus, *-cello, -emineo, -eo* 'precede' etc. (cf. *antecedo, -cello, -eo, -gredior, -uenio*). H. J. Roby (*A Grammar of the Latin language* II (London 1889), p. 49) has therefore supposed that these verbs 'have become transitive...by being compounded with the preposition'. This interpretation is mistaken to the extent that it implies a productive construction according to which the prefixation of *prae-* renders an intransitive verb transitive. These secondary, transitive uses developed by syntactic analogy, not as a result of, but only after the establishment of the prefixed verb. Verbs like *supero* and, in particular, semantically compatible verbs like *praeuerto(r)* which were used both transitively and intransitively (cf. pp. 41f.) contributed to this development in the following manner: after a sentence of the type *prae* (adv.) *alicui aliqua re cedit* was restructured as *alicui aliqua re praecedit, alicui* was replaced by *aliquem* on the syntactic analogy of a sentence like *aliquem aliqua re superat*. *Praecedo* thus came to be used transitively.

84. *Praedico* 'make public' is thus exceptional in that its early use suggests locative *prae-*: *ut faciam praeconis compendium | itaque auctionem praedicem ipse ut uenditem* (i.e., 'announce in public', rather than 'in advance', Pl. *Stich.* 194–5, cf. *praeco*, n. 45; Kranz, '*Pro*' et '*prae*', pp. 48f., unnecessarily insists on a temporal interpretation, 'vorher bekanntmachen'). Locative *prae-* is even more evident in (homonymous) *praedico* 'extol' (e.g., Ter. *Eun.* 565: *quid ego eius tibi nunc faciem praedicem aut laudem*) and is either analogical to verbs like *praefero, praepono*, or old. The anomalous use of *praedico* may be best explained by the fact that, unlike *praedico, praeloquor* etc., it can be derived as a denominative from **prai-dik-o-s* 'one who speaks in front' (cf. *praefica, praesul*). On the

it meant 'speak first, or beforehand' (e.g. *praeloqui* at Pl. *Rud.* 119), if transitive, to 'say something first' (ibid., 248), hence to 'foretell, predict the future before it occurs' (e.g., *futura praenuntio* Cic. *Diu.* I. 6. 12, *praenuntius* Lucr. v. 737, *-ia* Cic. *ND* II. 5. 14, cf. Gk. προαγγέλλω).[85] In this last use, verbs of speaking and perception prefixed with *prae-* were closely comparable with *prouideo* (cf. Caes. *BG* VII. 30. 2: *animo prouidere et praesentire*).

In the examples discussed so far, the attitude of the verb subject towards the future has been a solely descriptive one. Such an attitude was also likely to have a more normative, admonitory counterpart, subdivided into two categories of *instruction* and *warning*. Admonitory verbs constructed with prefixational *prae-* are indeed attested (e.g., *praecipere, praedicere, praedocere*, and *praescribere*, beside *praemonere*). *Obedience* and *precaution* may be regarded as the semantically middle counterparts of *instruction* and *warning*. Prefixational *prae-* occurred with verbs denoting precaution (e.g., *praecauere*,[86] *praefinire, praemunire, praeoccupare*) but not with verbs denoting obedience, e.g., **praepareo*. This development is highly significant since it parallels the privative specialization of causal *prae-* and, more particularly, the use of locative *prae-* with verbs of hindrance. For example, the meaning of *praecaueo*, like that of *praesentio*, is obviously close to the meaning of *prouideo* and Cicero seems to have regarded these verbs as synonymous (e.g., *quod a me ita praecautum atque ita prouisum est, ad Att.* II. 1. 6, cf. *Verr.* II. 4. 91, *Planc.* XXII. 53). The following passage, however, clearly shows that *praecaueo* implied not merely that a crisis was foreseen, but that effective steps were taken to prevent it: *id ne accideret, magno opere sibi praecauendum Caesar existimabat* (Caes. *BG* I. 38. 2).

It is therefore apparent that the specialization of locative *prae-*

use of *praedicare* in Christian Latin, see Chr. Mohrmann, '*Praedicare, tractare, sermo*. Essai sur la terminologie de la prédication paléochrétienne', *La Maison-Dieu* 39 (1954), 97f.).

85. Cf. *praecino, -cano* (Plin.), *-canto, -cento, -dico, -diuino, -for, -sagio, -sipio, -sentio, -uideo*.

86. At first sight the use of temporal *prae-* with a verb already meaning 'take heed (sc. for the future)' might seem pleonastic. On the other hand the formation of *praecaueo* (Pl. +) was probably influenced by verbs like *praetimeo* (Pl. +) and the characteristic occurrence of causal *prae* in privative contexts. (On *praecipio*, see P. Colaclidès, 'Note sur le sens de *praecipio*', *Glotta* 38 (1959–60), 309f.)

in verbs of hindrance was closely analogous to that of temporal *prae-* in certain verbs of admonition. Both uses suggest prevention and precaution, one spatial, the other temporal. The coincidence between the two uses is nicely illustrated by verbs like *praefinio* (Lucr. 1. 618), *praemunio*, and *praeoccupo*. *Praemunio* is a particularly informative example. Caesar uses *praemunio* in a context where both locative and temporal interpretations are plausible: *aditus duos...magnis operibus praemuniuit castellaque his locis posuit* (*BC* III. 58. 1). By Suetonius' time, however, temporal *prae-* was productive while locative *prae-* had become relatively obsolete. Suetonius' use of *praemunio* was thus unambiguously temporal: *metu uenenorum praemuniri medicamentis* (*Cal.* XXIX).

Many verbs which, at least from an etymological standpoint, contain locative *prae-* had undergone considerable semantic change by the beginning of the literary tradition, for example, *praesum/praesens*. *Praesum* 'am in command of' was common through Republican Latin but, during the Augustan period, its use declined. At this time, Ovid, notwithstanding his predilection for temporal *prae-* (n. 73), recomposed *prae-* + *esse* in the archaic sense of 'be in front' (i.e., 'defend': *stant quoque pro nobis et praesunt moenibus urbis | et sunt praesentes auxiliumque ferunt, Fast.* v. 135f.). Note the implied contrast of *pro*+personal complement (*nobis*) but *prae*+impersonal complement (*moenibus*). Although the indicative *praesum* gradually went out of use, its homonymous participial form, *praesens*, was frequent and productive (cf. *praesentia, praesentarius, repraesento* etc.) at all stages of the language. From a descriptive standpoint, *praesens* functioned as the participle to *adsum*; **adsens* is not attested. Wackernagel (cf. n. 40) thought that *praesens* was calqued on Greek παρών but, as Benveniste objects ('Le système sublogique', p. 179), 'outre que *prae* n'est pas symétrique de Gr. παρά, cela laisse sans réponse la question essentielle: alors que **adsens* était appelé par la proposition *absum:absens/adsum:x*, quelle raison a fait choisir *prae-*?' In answering this question, Benveniste emphasizes the immediacy which *prae-* connoted in such contexts as Pl. *Pseud.* 502f. (*quia illud malum aderat, istuc aberat longius; | illud erat praesens, huic erant dieculae*):

> La liaison de *adesse* et de *praesens* ressort clairement, mais aussi leur différence. Par *praesens*, on entend non pas proprement

'ce qui est là,' mais 'ce qui est à l'avant de moi,' donc 'imminent, urgent'...; ce qui est *praesens* ne souffre pas de délai (*dieculae*)...*Praesens* s'applique à ce qui est 'sous les yeux visible, immédiatement présent' [cf. the origin of causal *prae*, pp. 12–14] et peut sans pléonasme s'adjoindre à *adesse*, comme dans le texte cité de Plaute.[87]

Moreover, **adsens* and *absens* would have been virtual homophones and the specialization of *praesens* thus relieved the potential confusion between *adesse* and *abesse* at one point in their paradigm. The attempt to distinguish these two antonyms as clearly as possible, in addition to the factors which Benveniste has stressed, doubtless influenced the characteristic use of *praesens* (and *praesto*) in construction with *adsum*. The specialization of *praesens* paralleled that of *praesum* to the extent that both implied immediacy, one with reference to the actual here and now, the other to a more conventionally determined relationship of superiority or command.

Several instances of homonymous usage have already been discussed (e.g., *praecerpo*, *praedĭco*, *praeposterus*). Plautus' use of *praeuorto* provides a good example of both contrastive and complementary distribution (n. 77). Contrasting locative and temporal senses of the prefix give rise to homonymous uses of *praeuorto*, each of which includes further semantic distinctions whose interrelationship can be regarded as polysemous:

praeuorto 1 (loc. *prae-*): (a) 'prefer' (*aliquem prae aliquo | aliqua re*, *Amph.* 528 / Class. *alicui*, Cic. *Diu.* 1. 6. 10)

(b) 'be more important than' (*alicui* [*rei*], *Pseud.* 293), in complementary distribution with:

praeuortor (pass.) 'give priority to' (*alicui rei*, *Merc.* 376, *aliquid*, *Pseud.* 602, *in aliquid* id. 237).

praeuorto 2 (temp. *prae-*): (a) (act.) 'take beforehand' (hence, 'too soon', cf. *praecox*, *MG* 654), in complementary distribution with:

87. Cf. Pl. *Stich.* 577: *lupus praesens esuriens adest*; Cic. *de Off.* 1. 4. 11: [*belua*] *ad id solum quod adest quodque praesens est se accommodat* (cf. Löfstedt, *Syntactica* 1² (Lund 1942), p. 89 n. 3, and the meaning of English 'presence' and 'present', also G. Pascucci, '*Consens, praesens, absens*', *SIFC* 33 (1961), 1f.).

praeuortor (pass.)   'anticipate, outrun' (*Cas.* 509).[88]

Homonymous uses of prefixed verbs cannot always be explained solely in terms of a semantic distinction in the prefix. Such differences in meaning must often be attributed to contrasting senses of the underlying verb. For example, *praefodiunt* at Verg. *Aen.* XI. 473f.:

> *praefodiunt* alii portas aut saxa sudesque
> subuectant,

clearly means 'dig in front of' (cf. Serv. ad loc.: *id est ante portas fossas faciunt*). On the other hand, at Ovid, *Met.* XIII. 58f.:

> quem male conuicti nimium memor iste furoris
> prodere rem Danaam finxit fictumque probauit
> crimen et ostendit, quod iam *praefoderat*, aurum,

praefoderat means 'had buried beforehand'. The homonymy which exists between the Vergilian and Ovidian uses of *praefodio* (with locative and temporal *prae-*, respectively) cannot be explained simply by recalling Ovid's experimentation with temporal *prae-* (n. 73, cf. *praecerpo*) since the homonymous uses of *-fodio* 'dig' and 'bury' are not solely attributable to different uses of *prae-*.

Pliny (*HN* XVII. 16. 79) uses *praefodio* to mean 'dig beforehand', at a period during which the productivity of temporal *prae-* was increasing while that of locative *prae-* was declining. Locative *prae-* was still attested in new formations during Pliny's lifetime, so homonymous uses of *praefodio* – 'dig in front' and 'dig beforehand' – presumably coexisted at some point during the first century A.D., but it is at least possible that, by Pliny's time, the ambiguity had been resolved by favoring the temporal over the locative use. The history of *praefodio* therefore illustrates the

---

88. Similarly, in place of the elaborate schema implied by Lewis and Short, the Ciceronian usage of *praesto* can be classified as follows: *praesto* 1 (*a*) 'excel' (*alicui aliqua re*; cf. impers. *praestat* 'it is better'), (*b*) 'manifest' (*se, aliquod*), *praesto* 2 (*aliquod alicui* [originally *praes stat*? cf. n. 42]) (*a*) 'guarantee' (ps.), 'fulfill' (fut., pret.); cf. E. Wistrand, 'Absolutes *praestare*', *Eranos* 55 (1957), 188f.). Although the uses of *praesto* 1 (*a*) 'excel' and (*b*) 'manifest' are syntactically distinguishable, there may be semantic grounds for regarding them as homonyms. Note the function of tense in characteristically distinguishing the complementary uses of *praesto* 2.

importance of comparing usage within as well as across linguistic and literary periods.

The specific use of a compound is affected not only by the meanings of each member, but by its wider semantic context. Apparent differences in meaning between uses of the same word can often thus be attributed to its context. Frequent use of a word in a specific context can lead to semantic change as soon as that characteristic use is extended to other contexts in which its meaning is not so readily predictable. The Classical use of *praefero* can profitably be considered in these terms.

In Classical Latin *praefero* has at least two homonymous uses, 'carry in front' and 'prefer'. Lewis and Short's distinction between 'general' and 'particular' uses of *praefero* 'carry in front' is illusory. If there is any difference between carrying the *fasces* in front of the city praetor (Cic. *Verr.* II. 5. 22) and the *signa militaria* at the head of a procession (Livy III. 29. 4), that difference presumably refers to the connotations of the objects themselves and only indirectly to the meaning of *praefero*. Similarly, the use of *praefero* at Cic. *Sull.* XIV. 40; *clarissimum lumen praetulistis menti meae*, is closely comparable with that at *Verr.* II. 4. 74: *dextra ardentem facem praeferebat*. The difference is occasioned by the presence of *menti meae* (as opposed, for example, to *faciei meae*) in the first passage. Lewis and Short's gloss 'expose' (II B 3) can also be predicted from the semantic context which characteristically includes nouns like *amor*, *amicitia*, and *sensus*. No Classical author uses *praefero* (*pace* Lewis and Short II B 2) to mean 'anticipate' (in the sense of 'look forward to'); at Verg. *Aen.* v. 541, Eurytion graciously allows Acestes the 'preferred' honor (*nec...Eurytion praelato inuidit honori*) and, at Livy XXXIX 5. 11–12, Marcus Fulvius does not 'anticipate' the day of his triumph so much as 'advance' it. On the other hand, temporal *prae-* meaning 'beforehand' is probably attested in *praetulit* at Stat. *Th.* VI. 476: *nec praetulit* [PωS: *pertulit* A, Baehrens] *ullam | frater opem*. As Barth (ad loc.) notes, *praetulit...opem* means 'ante casum ei subvenit' (cf. *ante | obstitit* in v. 477f.). This reanalysis of *prae- +fero* is in keeping with the increasing productivity of temporal *prae-* in post-Augustan Latin.

Livy also uses *praeferor* in the sense of 'hurry past'. At VII. 24. 8: *praeter castra etiam sua fuga praelati*, the meaning of *praelati* may be

influenced by *praeter*. On the other hand, Livy provides other
examples of *prae-* and *praeter-* in closely parallel uses:[89] the main
distinction between *praefluo* in *infima ualle praefluit Tiberis* (I. 45. 6)
and *praeterfluo* in...*amnemque praeterfluentem moenia* (XLI. 11. 3) is
one of transitivity. Like *praefluit* in the first passage, *praelati* (*praeter
castra*) at VII. 24. 8 is intransitive. At V. 26. 7, however, *praelati*
functions transitively: *effusa fuga castra sua...praelati*. Livy's use
of *praelati* therefore illustrates two important developments. On
account of its characteristic juxtaposition with words like *fuga*,
praelatum esse became partially synonymous with verbs denoting
flight. As a result, although originally intransitive, *praelatum esse*
became transitive by syntactic analogy with the construction of
verbs like *fugio*, whose semantic function it partially shared
(cf. n. 83). At least from a syntactic standpoint, *praelatum esse*
'hurry past' can be reconciled with *praefero* 'carry in front', since
its transitive use is restricted to the passive voice. The semantic
diversification of *praefero* can therefore be summarized as follows:

praefero 1 (act. tr.) (a) 'carry in front' (*fasces*, *signa*; cf.
                         'present' *lumen menti*, *uitam* etc.; 'ad-
                         vance' *diem*, Livy), in complementary
                         distribution with:
                     (b) 'manifest' (*amorem* etc.) and:
praelatum esse   'hurry past' ([*praeter*] *castra* etc.)
(pass. intr. or tr.)
praefero 2   'prefer'
[*praefero* 3 (post-Augustan) 'offer, take beforehand']

The relationship between prefixational and prepositional usage
and the mutual influence of each in occasioning syntactic and
semantic change has been amply demonstrated by the preceding
discussion. The development of *prae*, however, cannot be fully
understood without reference to other prepositions and prefixes
of similar and sometimes opposite meaning (e.g., *pro*, *ante*, and

89. The idiosyncrasies of Livy's dialect deserve thorough reinvestigation.
P. G. Walsh (loc. cit.) has briefly noted some peculiarities of Livy's prepositional usage (cf. n. 18). In general, see O. Riemann, *Études sur la langue et la
grammaire de Tite-Live*[2] (Paris 1885), and Walsh's useful chapter, 'Livy's
latinity' (*Livy*, pp. 245–70). (For further examples of an apparent alternation
between *prae-* and *praeter*, see n. 69 and Biletchi, 'Ist *prae-*...?' (above,
n. 69).

post). The connections between intensive *per-* and *prae-*, and the semantic convergence of causal *prae* and *propter* in Petronius have already been noted. The development of *pro* must now be considered in a setting which will clearly articulate its relationship to *prae*.

PREPOSITIONAL *PRO*

The adverbial use of *pro* implies movement forwards (pp. 3–4). During its obsolescence, a context such as *pro* (adv.) / *moenibus ierunt* 'they came forward from the city walls' could be syntactically reinterpreted as *pro* (prep.) *moenibus* / *ierunt* 'they went in front of the city walls' (cf. the original syntax of causal *prae*). In his *epitome* of Festus (257), Paulus, however, reports that *pro significat in, ut pro rostris, pro aede, pro tribunali*. Just as *pro* as a preposition meaning 'in front of' derived from its adverbial use with verbs of motion, so prepositional *pro* '*in*' can be most plausibly explained as a development of adverbial *pro* with verbs of speaking (especially in public). Thus a sentence like *pro* (adv.) / *rostris loquitur* 'he speaks forth from the *rostra*' could be reinterpreted as *pro* (prep.) *rostris* / *loquitur* 'he speaks on the *rostra*'. The collocation of *pro* in Festus' gloss with nouns denoting public forums supports this account. The development of prepositional *pro* '*in*' and *pro* 'in front of' are therefore structurally parallel. The homonymy between these uses of *pro* was resolved by generalizing *pro* 'in front of' at the expense of *pro* '*in*' which was in any case rendered redundant by the established use of prepositional *in*.[90] With its development as a preposition meaning 'in front of', *pro* became approximately parallel in meaning to *ante* and *prae*. Except in later Latin, however, prepositional *pro* never referred to time. After the attested uses of *pro* have been discussed the development and resolution of this potential convergence between *pro*, *prae*, and *ante* will be reconstructed.

Locative *pro* is already found in early Latin, though not in

---

90. For a somewhat different view, see Tenney Frank, '"*Pro rostris, pro aede, pro tribunali*"', *Riv. d. Fil.* NS 3 (1925), 105f. Festus' gloss doubtless refers to a relatively early stage in the development of prepositional *pro*. The use of preverbal *pro*(-) to connote publicity will be discussed below (p. 52 and cf. n. 109). Nevertheless, the fact that *pro*(-) may connote publicity scarcely justifies DeWitt's view (*CJ* 37 (1941), 32f.) that its 'primary signification' is 'before one's eyes'.

comedy (e.g., Naev. 34 Morel [following K. O. Müller = Enn. *Ann.* 628V³]: *apud emporium in campo hostium pro moene*, Cato, *Orig.* IV. 14: *proelium factum depugnatumque pro castris*, cf. Kranz, '*Pro*' *et* '*prae*', pp. 2f.). Several specialized functions derived from this use. Compare the dedicatory inscription of Marcus Aemilius and Gaius Annius (*CIL* I² 20, iii cent. B.C.: [*M. Aim*]*ilio M. f.*, *C. An*[*io C. f.*||||[*prai*]*toris pro po*[*plod* | *uic. parti*] | *Dioue dede*[*re*]) with the opening of the *lex agraria* of 111 B.C. (ibid. 585. 1: *pro tribu Q. Fabius Q. f. primus sciuit*). Quintus Fabius, standing at the head of his tribe, casts the vote as their representative, 'on their behalf'. Similarly, Marcus Aemilius and Gaius Annius dedicate a small brass plate 'in front of the people' (i.e., 'on their behalf', cf. Cato, *Agr.* CXLIII. 1: *pro tota familia rem diuinam facere*).[91] As a result of this development, *pro* became an antonym of *contra* (cf. Cic. *de Orat.* III. 20. 75: *hoc...non modo non pro me, sed contra me est potius*, id. *Sull.* XVII. 49: *qui contra uos pro huius salute pugnabant*, cf. *propugnare*, Claud. Quadr. 12; *propugnacula*, Pl. *Bacch.* 710).

Other commonly listed uses of *pro* such as 'instead of' and 'in return for' are derived from, and in early Latin remained in complementary distribution with, *pro* 'on behalf of'. This phase of the history of *pro* can be sketched briefly since it is not directly relevant to *prae*. In the *Mostellaria* 1171f:

TR. promitte: ego ibo pro te, si tibi non lubet.
TH. uerbero, etiam inuides? TR. quian me *pro te* ire
    ad cenam autumo?

91. Cf. Pl.*Pseud.* 232: *ego pro me et pro te curabo* and *Stich.* 94: *bene procuras mihi.* This relationship of *pro aliquo curare*: *alicui procurare* is equivalent to that of *prae aliquo aliquem praeuortere*: *alicui aliquem praeuortere* and possibly influenced the development of comparative *prae* (cf. *Capt.* 437, Enn. *tr.* 136V³, also *promereo, -pugno, -sum*, and Kranz, '*Pro*' *et* '*prae*', p. 30). By substituting *res publica* (or *patria*) for *populus* or *tribus*, the class of potential complements of *pro* could be extended to include abstract nouns; cf. Cic. *de Fin.* I. 7. 24: *sed ut omittam pericula, labores, dolorem etiam, quem optimus quisque pro patria et pro suis suscepit*, id. *TD* IV. 19. 43: *conuenit dimicare pro legibus, pro libertate, pro patria.* Adelaide Hahn has convincingly argued that Vergil 'uses geographical and ethnological terms interchangeably' so that at *Aen.* VII. 670–1:
    tum gemini fratres Tiburtim moenia linquunt,
    fratris Tiburti dictam cognomine gentem
'the *city* and the *people* are... treated as interchangeable' ('A linguistic fallacy', in E. Pulgram (ed.), *Studies presented to Joshua Whatmough* ('s-Gravenhage 1957), pp. 62–3). This interchangeability was probably a traditional one and may thus have contributed to the specialization of *pro* 'on behalf of'.

Tranio recommends Theopropides to accept an invitation to dinner, otherwise, he, Tranio, will go on Theopropides' behalf, that is, 'instead of' him. Compare Lucilius fr. 671–2 (Marx):

> publicanus uero ut Asiae fiam, ut scripturarius,
> *pro Lucilio*, id ego nolo, et uno hoc non muto omnia.

The semantic distinction between *pro* 'on behalf of' and *pro* 'instead of', slight as it is, can be summarized as follows: the latter, unlike the former, necessarily implies the absence of the person in place of whom one is acting. Moreover, *pro* 'on behalf of' implies that one is working for the benefit of a person or a cause. The plausibility of this distinction is increased by the fact that *pro* 'instead of' can provide a transitional stage between *pro* 'on behalf of' and *pro* 'in return for'; compare the following contexts:

> *pro hisce aedibus*
> minas quadraginta accepisti a Callicle (Pl. *Trin.* 402f.)
> tris minas *pro istis duobus* praeter uecturam dedi (id. *Most.* 823)
> *pro eo agro* uectigal Langenses | Veituris in poplicum Genuam
>   dent in anos singulos uic. n. CCCC 'in return for the land'
>   (*Sententia Minuciorum inter Genuates et Viturios*, CIL I² 584,
>   24–5, 117 B.C.)
> par pari datum hostimentumst, opera *pro pecunia* (Pl. *Asin.* 172,
>   see Kranz, '*Pro*' et '*prae*', pp. 26–7, for further examples).

This use of *pro* became widespread in the later Republican and Augustan periods.[92]

The so-called 'proportional' and 'causal' uses represent specializations of *pro* 'in return for'. *Pro* expresses proportion in the following passages:

> quae probast mers, pretium ei statuit, *pro uirtute* ut ueneat
>   (Pl. *MG* 728, cf. tua te *ex uirtute*...accipiam, ibid. 738)
> *pro re* nitorem et gloriam pro copia qui habent (id. *Aul.* 541)
> *pro opibus nostris* sati' commodule...(id. *Stich.* 690)
> meus pater nunc *pro huius uerbis* recte et sapienter facit (id.
>   *Amph.* 289)

---

92. Cf. Cic. *ad Att.* 1. 3: *misimus qui pro uectura solueret*, Livy XXXVIII. 49: *pro eo quod...uos...fatigaui ueniam...petitam* and Ov. *Met.* II. 750: *proque ministerio ...aurum.*

This use of *pro* derives elliptically from the prepositional phrase *pro portione* as an expression of equivalence. *Pro portione* originated in turn from contexts like the following: *e[i]s quei posidebant uectigal Langensibus pro portione dent ita ut ceteri | Langenses, qui eorum in eo agro agrum posidebunt fruenturque* (*CIL* I² 584. 29–30). The burden of this passage is that, under prescribed stipulations, any Genoan or Viturian who possesses land *intra eos fines* (28) must pay tax *pro portione* 'for his plot', 'just as' (*ita ut*) the Langenses do (not necessarily, with Warmington, 'in the same proportion as the other Langenses'). The transfer of the meaning of the whole phrase *pro portione* to its prepositional member is typologically comparable to the development of intensive *prae-* (cf. Livy's transitive use of *praelatum esse*).⁹³

The causal use of *pro*, like that of *prae*, was at first highly restricted. The term 'causal' is in fact somewhat misleading. As an example of this usage Hofmann–Szantyr (p. 270) cite Pl. *Trin.* 26: *concastigabo pro commerita noxia* beside *ob meritam noxiam* (ibid. 23). The passage from the *Trinummus* actually illustrates the generalization of *pro* 'in return for' from the limited context of trade and taxation to include the payment of penalties for misdemeanors, as in Enn. *tr.* 226V³: *pro malefactis Helena redeat, uirgo pereat innocens*.⁹⁴ The relationship between *pro* and *ob*, implied by Hofmann–Szantyr, did not become productive until Late Latin,⁹⁵ when its causal use was in part due to the well-known convergence of *pro* and *prae*.

93. Note Livy's use of *quam pro* at XXI. 29. 2: *proelium atrocius quam pro numero pugnantium editur* (cf. Riemann (above, n. 89), p. 275). Compare the earlier development of *praequam* and *praeut*; for *pro quam* (Lucr. II. 1137) and *prout* (Titin., Cic. +), see n. 7.

94. The following examples illustrate the development in early Latin: *quin ut quisque est meritus praesens pretium pro factis ferat* (Naev. *tr.* 9R²), *cui nemo ciuis neque hostis | quibit pro factis reddere opis pretium* (Enn. *Epigr.* 19f.V³), *nam si pro peccatis centum ducat uxores, parum'st* (Pl. *Trin.* 1186), *sex talenta magna dotis demam pro ista inscitia* (id. *Truc.* 845), *ut pro huius peccatis ego supplicium sufferam* (Ter. *Andr.* 888), *ego pol te pro istis factis et dictis scelus | ulciscor* (id. *Eun.* 941f.). This use was maintained in Classical Latin, for example *atque etiam supplicatio dis immortalibus pro singulari eorum merito meo nomine decreta est* (Cic. *Cat.* III. 6. 15).

95. J. Svennung, *Orosiana* (Uppsala 1922) [= *Uppsala Universitets Årsskrift* (1922), 5], pp. 41f., also id., *Untersuchingen zu Palladius* (Uppsala 1936), pp. 377f., E. Löfstedt, *Late Latin* (Oslo 1959), pp. 54–5, Meyer-Lübke (above, n. 67), no. 6762, and, for further bibliography, Hofmann–Szantyr, p. 271 Zus. *b*.

The connotation of substitution (combining with that of *pro* of price) provided the starting point for the use of *pro* in the meaning 'as if' (i.e., 'equivalent to', cf. *pro portione*). Contrast *pro patre huic est* 'he is like a father to him' (Ter. *Ad.* 951) with *pro patre stat* 'he stands in front of his father' (or 'on his behalf'). The point of this example is to show the transition from acting 'on behalf of' and 'instead of' to acting 'as though'. The contrast is fully expressed in the following passage: *hoc quidem edepol hau pro insano uerbum respondit mihi* (Pl. *Men.* 927, 'he didn't reply like a madman, as though he were mad', not 'he didn't reply on behalf of the half-wit'; cf. ibid. 298: *pro sano loqueris* 'as though you were sane...'). Another influence in this development could have been provided by contexts such as *utrum pro ancilla me habes an pro filia* 'do you think I'm here "instead of" ("in the guise of" / "as though I were") the maid?' (Pl. *Pers.* 341; cf. *iam hercle ego uos pro matula habebo, nisi mihi matulam datis*, id. *Most.* 385, and *omne ego pro nihilo esse duco*, id. *Pers.* 637, a context which nicely illustrates the derivation of *pro* 'as if' from *pro* of price). The usage was still common in Augustan literature (cf. Livy II. 7. 3: *inde abiere, Romani ut uictores, Etrusci pro uictis*) and remained especially popular in the *sermo cotidianus* (cf. *mortuus pro mortuo*, Petr. XLV. 11).[96]

As a specialization of its proportional use, *pro* came to mean 'according to, by virtue of' (cf. Pl. *MG* 728, *Aul.* 541, *Amph.* 289 cited above, p. 47). In this sense *pro* is approximately synonymous with *ex*, a fact which recalls the earlier connection between the two prepositions. The following examples are typical of this use of *pro*: *tam etsi pro imperio, nobis quod dictum foret,* | *scibat facturos,* Pl. *Amph.* 21f., also *Poen.* 44; cf. Pacuv. *tr.* 41R²: *pro imperio agendum est,* Cic. *Verr.* II. 4. 49: *qui haec...palam de loco superiore ageret pro imperio et potestate.* An extension of this use can be seen in Lucil. fr. 1266 (Marx): *pro obtuso ore pugil pisciniensis reses* 'judging by his battered face...'. Common phrases like *pro sua parte* (e.g., *ubi poetae pro sua parte falsa conficta autumant* | *qui causam humilem dictis amplant,* Pacuv. *tr.* 337–9R²) and *pro uirili parte* derive from this usage.

All these uses of *pro* can thus be derived from a single locative origin. During their early development, they were presumably

96. V. Väänänen, *Ann. Acad. Sc. Fenn.*, B 73, 1 (1951), 14f.

in complementary distribution with each other, occurring only in readily definable contexts. As these contexts became generalized, however, a specific use of *pro* was not necessarily predictable from the semantic class of its complement (e.g., *pro insano, pro mortuo*), and homonymous usage arose. Gellius (XI. 3. 3) aptly describes this diversification as follows: *has omnes dictiones qui aut omnino similes et pares aut usquequaque diuersas existimaret, errare arbitrabar; nam uarietatem istam eiusdem quidem fontis et capitis, non eiusdem tamen esse finis putabam.*

PREFIXATIONAL *PRO*-[97]

Pro- occurred productively as a preverb and, unlike *prae*-, as a noun prefix. It is, however, virtually unattested as an adjectival prefix.[98]

PRENOMINAL *PRO*-

Pro- was productive as a prefix to kinship terms at all stages of the language. In the genealogy, *pater, auos, proauos, abauos, atauos, tritauos* (Pl. *Pers.* 57), *proauos* means 'great-grandfather'.[99] *Pronepos*, however, can refer to a 'great-grandson' and *pronurus* to his wife. It is mistaken to assume that *pro*- refers equally to future and to past time. A simpler rule governed the use of *pro*- in this context: *pro*- prefixed to a kinship term meant 'add one generation away from *ego*'. The underlying sense of 'forwards' in which all distinction between past and future time has been

97. On prefixational *pro*-, see Wackernagel, *Vorlesungen über Syntax* II², pp. 237f., id., 'Sprachliche Untersuchungen zu Homer', *Glotta* 7 (1916, also *separatim*, Göttingen), 238f., and Hofmann–Szantyr, pp. 270–1 Zus. *a*.

98. *Procliuis* and *profundus* are derived from *proclino and profundo*. *Profanus* either represents the remodeling of a prepositional phrase, *pro fano* (cf. *praegnas, proconsul*) or continues an adverbial use of *pro! fano* (ablative of separation, n. 9). *Probus* and -*procus*, as in *reciprocus* (n. 45, cf. *procul*) are inherited from Proto-Indo-European (cf. Walde–Hofmann II 366–7, 424).

99. Cf. *proamita* 'great-grandfather's sister' (*Dig.* XXXVIII. 10. 1) beside *amita* 'grandfather's sister', *propatruus* 'great-grandfather's brother' beside *patruus* 'father's brother', by analogy with *proauunculus* 'great-grandmother's brother' from *proauunculus magnus: auunculus maior*. (On *prognatus*, see E. Schwyzer, *ZVS* 56 (1929), 10f.)

neutralized is clearly illustrated by this use. The contrast between
the temporal use of *pro-* and *prae-* in this regard is striking (cf.
praegnas, praematurus/praeposterus, and *praefero/profero,* discussed
below).

The other productive use of *pro-* as a noun prefix in Classical
Latin is grammatically parallel to the use of *prae-* in *praecordia,
praenomen* etc. (p. 21), and means 'on behalf of, instead of'. From
contexts such as *neue magistratum | neue pro magistratud neque uirum
[neque mul]ierem quiquam fecise uelet (CIL* I² 581. 10, 186 B.C.) or
*auspicio [Ant]oni [M]arci pro consule classis | Isthmum traductast
missaque per pelagus (CIL* I² 2662. 3–4, c. 102 B.C.), the more
general use of *pro* exemplified by *istum appelles Tyndarum pro
Philocrate* (Pl. *Capt.* 546) became typically associated with terms
denoting public officials. The prepositional phrases *pro magistratu(d),
pro consule* etc. were then remodeled as the nouns *promagistratus*
and *proconsul.*[100] The earlier usage was still understood in the
late Republic, maintained as an archaism in legal discourse, and
thus give rise to Cicero's pun at *Phil.* XI. 8. 18: *nam Sertorianum
bellum a senatu priuato datum est, quia consules recusabant, cum L.
Philippus pro consulibus eum se mittere dixit, non pro consule.* This
construction was also productive with other classes of complements
(e.g., *pronomen* (cf. n. 100), *prouerbium*; compare the construction,
and contrast the meaning, of *praeuerbium*). In post-Augustan
usage, doubtless under Greek influence (cf. n. 100), *pro-* was
used in the temporal sense 'before' (e.g., *procupido* 'a previous
desire'). *Pro-* was never productive as a noun prefix meaning
'forwards'.[101]

100. Compare the derivation of *praegnas* from the prepositional phrase
*prai gnatid (p. 26f.) and note the possible influence of verbs like *procuro, -pugno*
etc. Greek terms like προήγορος (cf. προηγορέω, Xen. + and πρόαγορος, a
magistrate at Catana, Cic. *Verr.* II. 4. 50, note also *praes,* n. 42) may have
contributed to this remodeling since prefixal *prae-* in its productive correspondence to προ- (n. 39) refers only to position (or time) 'in front'. Contrast
the semantics (and derivational syntax) of *praefectus* and *proconsul.* (For *pronomen,* see H. Delehaye, *ALMA* (1927), 28f.) *Pro-* is also found in trans-
literations of Greek words (e.g., *proboscis, prodromus, prologus, prooemium,* and
propnigeum, cf. *praefurnium,* nn. 39, 42; on *prologus,* see S. Trenkner, 'L'éty-
mologie du mot latin *prologus', Charisteria Th. Sinko [Varsaviae Soc. Philol.
Polon.]* (1951), 365f.).

101. *Procella* was derived from *procello* and *promunturium* acquired the connotation of land 'jutting forward' by popular association with *promineo*; compare
Pacuv. *tr.* 94R²: *Id[ae] promunturium quoius lingua in altum proicit.*

PREVERBAL *PRO-*

Preverbal pro- retained the historically primary meaning of 'forth' in the majority of its uses (cf. *procedo, produco, proicio, prosequor* etc.). Whether the movement 'forwards' had the further implication of 'away from' or 'towards' was doubtless originally determined by the connotations of the simplex, just as *pro-* prefixed to *uerba pendendi* like *procumbo, proclino, propendo* implied 'down in a forward direction' (cf. *pronus, prorsus*). There is, however, reason to suppose that the implication of movement 'away from' was specialized early in the history of Latin (cf. Kranz, '*Pro*' et '*prae*', pp. 3f., and n. 97). The fact that prepositional *pro* governs the ablative rather than the accusative case (like *ante* and *ad*) partly supports this conclusion. Matching prepositional usage, preverbal *pro-* also means 'on behalf of' (e.g., *procuro, propugno, prodest*; cf. *prouideo, prospicio* at Pl. *Capt.* 643, *Most.* 526, and *Trin.* 688). Note, however, that at least in the late Republic, *propugno* means 'rush forth' (cf. Caes. *BG* v. 9. 5, II. 7. 2) and thus contrasts with *propugno* 'defend' (cf. id. *BC* III. 45. 3, Cic. *TD* v. 27. 79). *Pro-* 'forth' also developed the sense of 'openly, in public', particularly in construction with verbs of speaking (e.g., *profiteor, proloquor*; cf. *prostituo, prosto*; cf. the meaning of *pro rostris* etc. ap. Fest., discussed on p. 45) and this use was already frequent in early Latin (cf. Kranz, '*Pro*' et '*prae*', pp. 19–22 for examples). Towards the end of the Republic, this function of preverbal *pro-* was largely usurped by the adverbial phrase *prae se* (cf. pp. 6f.).

Relatively few verbs of the Classical period were prefixed with both *prae-* and *pro-*, a fact which in part reflects the semantic distinction between the two forms. Thus *prouideo* and *prospicio* already occur in Plautus but *praeuideo* dates from the late Republic and *praespicio* from the fifth century A.D. Conversely, *praescio* is attested in Terence but **proscio* never existed (cf. *praecaueo* Pl. +, not **procaueo*; *praesentio* Pl. +, but *prosentio* only at *MG* 1152, dub. l.). In Plautus *prouideo* and *prospicio* generally refer to place (cf. *Asin.* 450, *Amph.* 1059, *Curc.* 317; cf. *prospectus, MG* 609). At *Amph.* 1071, however, *prouidimus* means 'foresaw': *neque nostrum quisquam sensimus, quom peperit, neque prouidimus*, and, in Ennius and Terence, the temporal use became more general and *prudens* (from *prouidens*) similarly referred to foreknowledge. The earliest use of temporal *pro-* is at Liv. Andr. *Od.* 11R[2]: *quando dies adueniet quem profata Morta est.* Ennius, however (*Ann.* 563V[3]: *contra carinantes uerba aeque obscena profatus*; cf. Pacuv. *tr.* 145R[2]), uses *profor* in the locative sense of 'forth' (cf. *proloquor, prodico, pronuntio*).

The evidence suggests that the partial transition of preverbal *pro-* from locative to temporal reference was still in process at the end of the third century B.C., by which time the temporal meaning of *prae-* had already been specialized with verbs of speaking and perception (pp. 38f.). When *pro-* was prefixed to verbs of this type, it meant either 'forth (locative)' or 'in front (locative or temporal)'. The temporal meaning became synonymous with that of temporal *prae-*. These considerations help to explain the relative infrequency of temporal *pro-* and also, at least until the late Republic, that of verbs prefixed with both *prae-* and *pro-* (meaning 'in front, beforehand') unless the two forms were kept distinct by semantic specialization: compare *profor* 1 'speak forth' (Enn., Pacuv. +), 2 'foretell' (Liv. Andr. +), but *praefor* 1 'say a prayer' (Cato +) and, only later, *praefor* 2 'foretell' (Cat. LXIV. 383, beside *profor* 2, Lucr. I. 739, v. 112). In Augustan poetry and in Silver Latin, however, temporal *pro-* became slightly productive (cf. *prologuar*, Prop. III. 13. 59, *ad pugnam proludit*, Verg. *G.* III. 234) – probably under the combined influence of *prouideo* and Greek προ- (cf. *procupido*) – but never challenged the use of temporal *prae-*.

The semantic distinction between verbs prefixed with both *pro-* and *prae-* is usually very clear (e.g., *praedico/prodico, praeduco/produco*, and *praenuntio/pronuntio*). In some cases the meanings are exactly opposite: contrast *quod si laxius uolent proferre diem* (sc. *auctionis*) (Cic. *ad Att.* XIII. 13-14. 4) in which *proferre* means 'to adjourn, postpone (the day of the auction)' with *praetulit triumphi diem* (Livy XXXIX. 5. 12, cf. p. 43), where Marcus Fulvius 'advanced' the time of the triumph. In others (e.g., *praebeo/prohibeo*), potential synonymy was resolved by specializing the meaning of each word in different directions: *prohibeo* thus came to signify obstruction while *praebeo* meant 'offer'.[102] One must therefore recognize

---

102. Cf. *praebia* (p. 23) which, however, became descriptively associated with verbs of hindrance (cf. *praecludo* etc., also *praefiscini*).

three homonymous uses of preverbal *pro-* in Classical Latin: 'forth (locative)', 'beforehand (temporal)', and 'on behalf of'.[103]

CONCLUSIONS

It is now possible to reconstruct the semantic development of *prae* and *pro*, their relation to each other and to other prepositions, and the correspondence of their prepositional and prefixational usage. During the prehistory of Latin, *prae* first denoted position *in front*. A complementary distribution between its reference to place and time developed, according to which *prae* referred to time when it qualified a verb phrase or a verbally derived noun denoting an event; otherwise it referred to place. Thus *prae* referred to place in *praecordia*, derived from *prai corde, and in *praefica* (literally 'one who performs appropriate rites *at the head of* a funeral procession'). *Gnatis 'birth', however, denoted an event, and *praegnas* (from *prai gnatid, pp. 26–7) therefore contains the temporal use of *prae*. This complementary distribution of time–space reference was at first realized equally by prepositional and adverbial usage. With verbs of speaking, *prae* referred to either time or place depending on the syntax of the explicit or implied complement: if *ciuis Romanus* spoke *prae* a tribunal, *prae* denoted location; if he spoke *prae* an event, *prae* denoted time, that is, he 'foretold' that event. The complement of temporal *prae* was not necessarily specified: *praematurus* thus meant 'ripening ahead of the harvest' (i.e., the normal time for ripening). Verbs of perception (e.g., *praesentio*) and verbs expressing fear or precaution (e.g., *praecaueo*) contributed to this development. *Prae tet tremonti* in the *Carmen Saliare* illustrates the locative use of *prae*,

---

103. Garnier (*Die Präposition...*, p. 61) considered *pro-* in *propalam* at Pl. *Epid.* 12 (cf. *MG* 1348 corr. Camerarius, *Pers.* 446) to be an intensive usage. Indeed from a semantic standpoint, its construction is analogous to that of *praeclarus*. Unlike *praeclarus*, however, the potential comparison of *propalam: palam* never led to the productivity of *pro-* as an intensive prefix. Skutsch, *CQ* (1960), 190, 193f., rightly rejects Nonius' gloss of *prognariter – strenue fortiter et constanter* (150. 5) – at Ennius, *Ann.* 208–10V³:

> diui hoc audite parumper:
> ut pro Romano populo *prognariter* armis
> certando prudens animam de corpore mitto.

Prognariter qualifies *prudens* and certainly refers to time; note, however, the *paronomasia* in the sequence of *pro...prognariter...prudens* (*prouidens*).

while *prae morte tremunt* implies time. In verbs prefixed with *prae-* and denoting speech or perception, temporal reference was specialized early (but note denominative *praedicare*, nn. 45, 84). In verbs of motion, the reference of *prae-* was frequently ambiguous, at least before the first century A.D., when the productivity of temporal *prae-* became predominant. By early Latin the pre-positional use of locative and temporal *prae* was obsolete. The corresponding prefixational uses could generally be distinguished by reference to the underlying simplex and clearly homonymous usage was not widespread until the late Republican and Augustan periods.[104]

Like *prae*, *ante* also referred both to time and space. *Ante* originally denoted the act of *facing opposite* (cf. Greek ἀντίος) and therefore governed the accusative case. In its temporal reference, *ante* was distinguished from *prae* by being characteristically con-structed with nouns denoting time towards which the present implicitly faced (e.g., *diem*, *lucem*, *noctem*). Although temporal *prae* lacked this directional implication, both forms specifically denoted 'time before which' rather than 'in the future'.

Pro, on the other hand, implied movement *forwards* and was originally neutral in its reference to direction *away*, *towards*, or *down* (p. 52). Its relation to *ante* became more symmetrical after the specialization of *pro* in the sense of *forwards from*.[105] The correspondence of *ad* and *in* (+ accusative) to their antonyms *ab* and *ex* thus paralleled that of *ante* and *pro*, while *prae* and *in* (+ ablative) referred, without directional implications, to *place where*. The distinctive meanings of *ante*, *pro*, and *prae* were neutralized in their antonym *post*. At this stage of the development, an attacking army would stand *ante moenia*, the defending army, *pro moenibus*. To the objective observer, both armies would be *prae moenibus*.

104. Cf. *praecerpo* (p. 36). Cicero's use of *praeripio* 'forestall' (*ad Att.* x. 1. 2, cf. *de Off.* 1. 30. 108) provides a good example of the transition from polysemous to homonymous uses of *prae-*. Note, however, the early homonymy exemplified by *praeuorto* (p. 41f.).

105. Cf. Pl. *Rud.* 295: *ex urbe ad mare huc prodimus pabulatum* where movement *from* and movement *towards* are equally implied. (The historical resolution of the early convergence of *pro* and *ante* is discussed on pp. 57f.) The partial specialization of *pro-* in terms of movement *from* is also suggested by the development of prepositional *pro* 'in front of' (p. 45; cf. n. 97).

By contrast with *prae*, both *ante* and *pro* implied direction, but, unlike *in/ad* and *ex/ab*, they also signified *place*. The second contrast became productive as *ante* and *pro* began to usurp the function of *prae*.[106] The brief attestation of adverbial *prae* and the gradual transition from locative to comparative *prae* in the second century B.C. suggests that these changes were still in progress at the beginning of the literary tradition.

Such an inference is further supported by the distribution of the prepositional use of *pro* and locative *ante* in early Latin.[107] At least for a time, *ante* and not *pro* fulfilled the semantic function of obsolescent locative *prae*: the strictly locative use of *pro* does not occur in Roman comedy. The fact that *ante*, unlike *pro*, was closely comparable with *prae* in both locative and temporal uses, at first favored *ante* in this reorganization. Indeed the relation between prefixational *prae-* and both prepositional and adverbial *ante*, particularly in their temporal functions, remained productive throughout the history of Latin.[108]

The historical development of *praebeo* and *prohibeo* (p. 53) provided an example of the resolution of potential synonymy by specializing the uses of each word in different semantic directions. The case of *ante* and *pro* is somewhat similar. Despite the close relationship between these prepositions, and considerable evidence for the early replacement of obsolescent *prae* by *ante*, it was *pro* – perhaps already in Naevius – and not *ante*, which finally continued the locative function of prepositional *prae*. The potential synonymy of *pro* and locative *ante* was resolved by specializing the latter in its etymological sense of 'facing opposite' while *pro* became the general term for position 'in front', retaining its

106. The fact that this development was a Latin innovation is indicated by the retention of locative and temporal uses of Proto-Italic **prai* in Oscan and Umbrian (n. 14). Moreover, the early productivity of locative *prae* in all types of prefixation (e.g., *praecordium*, *praeceps*, *praecedo*, etc.) and its preservation in idioms like *prae manu* and *prae se* amply demonstrate that the innovation occurred at a relatively late date in the prehistory of Latin (cf. temporal *prae* in *praegnas* and in *praeloquor*, *praesentio*, etc.).

107. Cf. Pl. *Epid.* 568: *iube Telestidem huc prodire filiam ante aedis meam*, id. *Cas.* 295: *uxorem huc euoca ante aedis* etc. (and not *pro aedibus*, cf. Kranz, loc. cit., for further examples).

108. E.g., *nonne oportuit | praescisse me ante?* (Ter. *Andr.* 238f.), *praetorum est ante et praeire* (Lucil. ap. Varro, *LL* v. 80), *nisi aquam praecepimus ante* (Lucr. VI. 803, cf. p. 7).

earlier implication of 'forwards from'. This distinction was generally maintained until the post-Augustan period.[109]

Several factors favored prepositional *pro* over *ante* as the replacement of locative *prae*. Although the meanings of *prae* and *ante* were similar in many respects, one important semantic fact distinguished them: *prae* implied position, *ante* direction. This distinction had its syntactic counterpart. *Prae* governed the ablative case, *ante*, the accusative. Due to the prehistoric syncretism between inherited ablative and locative cases, the Latin ablative was governed by prepositions which denoted both position (*prae, in*) and separation (*ex, de*). *Pro* 'in front of' seems to have derived from reanalysis of the construction of adverbial *pro* 'forwards' with the ablative of separation as a prepositional phrase (p. 45). The fact that *pro* governed the ablative, while *ante* governed the accusative not only reflected their earlier semantic contrast ('forwards from' versus 'facing towards'), but provided strong syntactic pressure for keeping their meanings distinct. *Pro*, governing the ablative, could therefore inherit the locative function of prepositional *prae* while maintaining the implications of its own earlier collocation with the ablative of separation. (The phonological similarity between *pro* and *prae* may also have contributed to this development). Once the use of *pro* 'in front of' (+ ablative) was clearly established, the contrasting syntax of *ante* (+accusative) both reflected and continued to emphasize its semantic differentiation from *pro*. Under these circumstances, though *ante* no longer fulfilled the function of locative *prae*, its use as a preposition denoting time was extended to include noun complements which temporal *prae* had previously governed (cf. p. 27), for, in this use, *ante* and *pro* were not in competition.

It would be improper to account for the obsolescence of locative *prae* solely in terms of the generalization of other locative prepositions. Prepositional *prae* apparently became obsolete in its locative function at a time when its causal and comparative uses

109. Cf. Cic. *Phil.* II. 26. 64: *hasta posita pro aede Iouis Statoris bona Cn. Pompei...uoci acerbissimae subiecta praeconis* (where Caesar has ordered the *hasta* to be fixed *in front of* the temple to advertise the *public* (cf. n. 90) auction of Pompey's goods) and Livy I. 45. 6: *bouem Romam actam deducit ad fanum Dianae et ante aram statuit.*

were being established. Comparative (and perhaps also causal) *prae* can be considered as specializations of the etymologically locative function (pp. 10f. and n. 30). As these historically secondary uses became increasingly productive, potential homonymy between locative and comparative (or causal) *prae* was avoided or resolved by generalizing the use of other related prepositions, in particular, *ante* and *pro*. Meanwhile, prepositional *prae* developed comparative and causal functions which were shared by neither *ante* nor *pro*. The linguistic economy which these developments imply is remarkable.

This economy is also reflected in the prefixational use of *prae-*, *ante-*, and *pro-*. The balance between prepositional *ante* and prefixational *prae-* has already been noted. On the other hand, beside the considerable productivity of preverbal *prae-*, preverbal *ante-* was relatively rare. When preverbal *pro-* and *prae-* were constructed with the same verb, their meanings were usually quite distinct (pp. 52f.). In most cases, a commonly occurring verb prefixed with *prae-* was not also prefixed with *pro-*, and vice versa, at least in the same period, and the productivity of temporal *prae-* inhibited any extensive development of temporal *pro-*. Antonymous forms are, however, frequently prefixed to the same simplex, for example, *praefero*: *postfero*, *praepono*: *postpono*, *antehabeo*: *posthabeo* (+ *prae* in Terence, p. 18 and n. 32), and *prospicio*: *respicio*. Note also the formation of *praeposterus* and *reciprocus* which each include the parallel use of antonyms (cf. *reppulit propulit*, Pl. *Rud.* 672, *rursus*: *prorsus* etc.).

The interaction between adverbial, prepositional, and prefixational uses of the same form can be clearly observed. The original time–space references of adverbial and prepositional *prae* are reflected in its prefixational use, just as preverbal *pro-* occurs most commonly in the meaning 'forwards'. More interesting than these reflexes of the inherited implications of each form is the continuing relationship between secondary specializations of both prepositional and prefixational uses. Comparison was expressed both by prepositional *prae* and by prefixational *prae-*, in verbs denoting superiority. Implied hindrance provided a significant restriction on the use of causal *prae* in Classical Latin and was also reflected in verbal and nominal prefixation (e.g., *praecludo*, *praebia*). Likewise, the prepositional use of *pro* 'in front of' affected the meaning of prefixational *pro-* in words like *prostituo* (cf. *prouideo*). The derived meaning of prepositional *pro* 'on behalf of' was also implied by verbs like *procuro* and *propugno*.

In later Latin further changes occurred before *prae* and *pro* converged with *per*. Causal *pro* became productive, ultimately derived from phrases like *pro malefactis*. In the second century, temporal *pro* was used by Irenaeus (I. 13. 6) in *pro aeone* (for *ante saecula*) under the influence of Greek πρὸ αἰῶνος. Apart from its temporal and intensive functions, *prae* was gradually abandoned. Meanwhile, on an evening walk in Praeneste, Aulus Gellius had looked back at the *ueterum scripta* and pondered *qualis quantaque esset particularum quarundam in oratione latina uarietas* (XI. 3. 1). This *uarietas* indeed provides a rich example of the systematic reorganization of lexicon, syntax, and sense.

Greek poetry in Cicero's prose writing*

H. D. JOCELYN

I. THE DISTRIBUTION OF POETIC QUOTATIONS IN CICERO'S EXTANT WORKS

IT HAS often been remarked[1] that Cicero's quotations of and references to poetry are far more copious in his rhetorical and philosophical writing than in his private letters and public speeches. Latin poetry and its subject matter decorate in quantity only a few of the speeches, namely the defences of Sextus Roscius Amerinus (80 B.C.) Marcus Caelius (56), Publius Sestius (56) and Rabirius Postumus (54), the prosecution of Caius Verres (70) and the senatorial denunciation of Lucius Calpurnius Piso (55). A speech defending a man of Greek birth who wrote verses contains the only two mentions of Greek poetry.[2] In the letters to Pomponius (Atticus) literal quotations of the Greek poets abound, in those to Papirius Paetus and Trebatius Testa quotations of the Romans. Poetry in either language, however, is conspicuously rare in the letters addressed to other eminent senators and equestrians. What little survives of speeches[3] and letters[4] composed by other men during the period of the Republic suggests that there was nothing very unusual about Cicero's practice.

* I am grateful to D. B. Gain and D. O. Ross for the supply of certain information.

1. Cf. J. Kubik, 'De M. Tullii Ciceronis poetarum latinorum studiis', *Diss. Phil. Vindob.* 1 (1887), 242, M. Radin, 'Literary References in Cicero's Orations', *CJ* 6 (1911), 209ff., W. Zillinger, *Cicero und die altrömischen Dichter* (Dissertation, Erlangen, Würzburg 1911), pp. 5of. Quintilian's statements about the quotation of poetry by Cicero and others at *Inst.* 1. 8. 10–12 (cf. v. 11. 39–40 and XII. 4. 1–2) are characteristically inaccurate, being based more on the Greek rhetorical tradition than on accurate study of the Republican texts.

2. *Arch.* XIX, XXIV. Aulus Gellius (XIII. 1. 2) imagined a reference to Hom. *Il.* XX. 336 to be detectable at *Phil.* I. 10. See also the story related by Quintilian at *Inst.* VI. 3. 86.

3. For Titius and poetry see Macrob. *Sat.* III. 13. 13; for M. Crassus see Cic. *Cael.* XVIII; for Asinius Pollio see Tacit. *Dial.* XXI. 7, Quintil. *Inst.* I. 8. 11.

4. For quotations of poetry in letters by M. Terentius Varro see Nonius, pp. 263. 3, 423. 6; for quotations by Caelius see Cic. *ad Fam.* VIII. 2. 1; for quotations by Paetus see Cic. *ad Fam.* IX. 16. 4.

Less remarked has been the fact that the relatively few
quotations of Latin poetry which do appear in the speeches and
the letters are dominated by the dramatic scripts performed at
the public festivals, particularly the versions of Attic tragedy
made in the previous century, to the almost complete exclusion
of the epic poetry of Ennius[5] and the satires of Lucilius. Yet this
is a significant fact. During the first century many young men of
the senatorial and equestrian classes were made to study at school
Latin poems of both the dramatic and the non-dramatic genres.[6]
Just how many studied them and in what depth, of course, is
not plain.[7] Certainly the rhetorical and philosophical dialogues,
which Cicero addressed to the same classes which heard his
speeches and read his letters,[8] cite Ennius' *Annales* and Lucilius'
satires as freely as they do tragedy and comedy. It is unlikely that
the peasant and city working-classes had any advanced literary
education, but attendance at the public festivals[9] would have
acquainted them with the plots[10] and the songs[11] of the classic
plays. These indeed were thought to be somewhat vulgar objects
of knowledge and enjoyment.[12] Nevertheless, however offensive
the festivals might be to conservative antiquarians,[13] they gave
the poetry associated with them a certain traditional legitimacy
denied to epic and satire. Their management was an important
step in a statesman's career;[14] at them the mood of the people
concerning the issues and personalities of public life manifested

5. But cf. *Balb.* LI, *de Prou. Cons.* XXI, *Mur.* XXX.

6. See Rhet. anon. *ad Her.* IV. 7, Cic. *de Orat.* I. 154, I. 246, Hor. *Epist.*
II. 1. 50ff., Phaedr. III *epil.* 34, Sen. ap. Gell. XII. 2. 8, Suet. *Gramm.* passim.

7. See Cic. *de Orat.* II. 1 for evidence that in Cicero's youth some looked
with suspicion upon an excessive amount of literary education.

8. See Cic. *Fin.* I. 4–8 on the audience sought for the philosophical dialogues.

9. For a list of performances recorded from the first century see G. Kró-
kowski, 'De ueteribus Romanorum tragoediis primo post Chr. n. saeculo adhuc
lectitatis et de Thyeste Annaeana', *Tragica* I (*Prace Wrocławskiego Towarzystwa
Naukowego* Ser. A Nr. 41, Wrocław 1952), pp. 114–15.

10. In one of the few extant speeches whose audience extended outside the
equestrian and senatorial classes Cicero felt able to refer to the story of
Medea and Absyrtus as something well known (*Leg. Man.* XXII).

11. Cf. Suetonius, *Iul.* 84.

12. Cf. Cic. *ad Fam.* VII. 1, *Fin.* V. 63, *TD* I. 36–7, I. 106–7.

13. Cf. Varr. *RR* II *praef.* 3, *Ant. rer. diu. fr.* I. 55 Agahd (= Aug. *Ciu.* IV. 31),
Liv. VII. 2. 13.

14. Cf. Cicero's description of life at Rome in 49: *ad Att.* IX. 12. 3 *praetores
ius dicunt, aediles ludos parant, uiri boni usuras perscribunt.*

itself in regular if informal ways;[15] they could be regarded as having a tenuous connection with the business of government. Accordingly it would be considerations about the dignity of the occasion that made Cicero tend to avoid some kinds of poetry altogether and to be sparing with other kinds when he spoke to the people or the Senate or a jury[16] or wrote to a magistrate or a senator. The literary culture of first-century Romans, or lack of it,[17] had little to do with Cicero's practice.

It is also of some significance that poets are mentioned by name in Cicero's speeches and formal letters less often even than their works are quoted or referred to. Some Roman aristocrats might encourage antiquarians and poets to link their families with the ancient kings or even with the heroes of Greek saga[18] but the poet as such bore no authority among them; heads of families were the sole source of moral and political wisdom.[19] The kind of argument employed by Aeschines in fourth-century Athens against Timarchus[20] would have been inconceivable in republican Rome. A Roman orator could quote from the repertory of the public festivals to please and divert or to mock but not to prove a point or to persuade.[21] He had always to be careful lest he be thought frivolous or vulgar or both. The unusual number of poetic quotations in the speeches delivered by Cicero in the years 56 and 55 should be attributed not to carelessness, over-confidence or growing 'Asianism'[22] or to reading done in preparation for writing the dialogue *de oratore*,[23] but rather to the special circumstances of each case.[24]

15. Cf. Cic. *ad Att.* II. 19. 3, x. 12a. 3.

16. Cf. the apologetic tone of *Arch.* II, *Verr.* IV. 109, *S. Rosc.* XLVI, *Sest.* CXIX, *Pis.* LXX–LXXI.

17. So C. Knapp, *AJPh* 32 (1911), 19f.

18. On this see E. Norden, *NJbb* 7 (1901), 256ff. (= *Kleine Schriften* 367ff.), and F. Münzer, *Römische Adelsparteien und Adelsfamilien* (Stuttgart 1920), p. 65.

19. For the inferiority of poetry to politics see Cic. *de Orat.* I. 212, *Brut.* III, *Parad.* XXVI, *Fin.* I. 24, V. 7, *Sen.* L; for the parallel inferiority of philosophy see *Ac.* II. 5–6, *Fin.* I. 1, *de off.* II. 2.   20. Cf. 141ff.

21. For the theory of quoting poetry in public orations see Aristotle, *Rhet.* I. 15. 13–14 (1375b–1376a), II. 21 (1394a–1395b), Hermogenes, *Meth.* XXX, Rhet. anon. *ad Her.* I. 10, Cic. *de Orat.* II. 257, *Top.* LXXVIII, Quintil. *Inst.* VI. 3. 96. Roman practice should be sharply distinguished.

22. So Radin, 'Cicero's orations', p. 216.

23. So Zillinger, *Cicero und die altrömischen Dichter*, pp. 67f.

24. So R. G. M. Nisbet in T. A. Dorey (ed.), *Cicero* (London 1964), p. 69.

II. THE NUMBER OF QUOTATIONS OF GREEK POETRY IN CICERO'S LETTERS TO ATTICUS

It is only in Cicero's private letters that literal quotations of Greek poems are found. The letters to T. Pomponius (Atticus) contain most of these. Cicero won notoriety in his youth for Greek learning[25] and Atticus, seven years his elder, lived in Athens itself between the years 88 and 65, taking an active part in Athenian life.[26] Both men must have possessed considerable skill in using Greek and some knowledge of the classics of Greek poetry. The seventy or so quotations in Cicero's letters need not, however, imply the deep knowledge of the original poems which enthusiasts often claim for him.[27] Some are clearly requoted from Atticus' own letters[28] while most are of a gnomic character, as likely to come from the cultural ambience as from the poems themselves.

Deductions about the general level of Greek knowledge among upper-class Romans on the basis of Cicero's correspondence with Atticus are even more dubious.[29] The tone of the prefaces to the philosophical dialogues suggests that, at the time these were written, Greek was a special accomplishment and that more men claimed than really possessed an effective knowledge of the language and its literature.[30] The many anecdotes related in extant literature about the knowledge of individuals[31] have a tone indicating that such knowledge was not thought to be commonplace. Cicero's use of Greek and allusions to Greek literature as a kind of code in some letters to Atticus,[32] points to the same conclusion. The relative absence of Greek from the letters to

25. See Plut. *Cic.* v.
26. See Nep. *Att.* ii–iv.
27. E.g. E. Lange, *Quid cum de ingenio et litteris tum de poetis Graecorum Cicero senserit* (Dissertation, Halle 1880), p. 33, J. Tolkiehn, 'De Homeri auctoritate in cotidiana Romanorum uita', *NJbb* Suppl. 23 (1896), 223ff., P. T. Pütz, *De M. Tulli Ciceronis bibliotheca* (Dissertation, Münster 1925), pp. 25ff., E. Malcovati, *Cicerone e la poesia* (Pavia 1943), pp. 48ff. For a more sober view see R. B. Steele, 'The Greek in Cicero's Epistles', *AJPh* 21 (1900), 410.
28. Cf. vii. 3. 5.
29. E.g. those of H. I. Marrou, *Histoire de l'éducation dans l'antiquité*[4] (Paris 1958), pp. 330, 351.
30. See *Fin.* i. 10. Cf. *TD* v. 116.
31. See W. Kroll, *Die Kultur der ciceronischen Zeit* ii (Leipzig 1933), pp. 118ff.
32. vi. 4, vi. 5.

other friends and acquaintances does not, on the other hand, itself prove anything. Feelings about the dignity of a correspondent or the solemnity of an occasion might suffice to keep his Latin free of foreign interpolation.[33]

III. THE DISTRIBUTION OF POETIC QUOTATIONS IN CICERO'S RHETORICAL AND PHILOSOPHICAL WRITINGS

All the personages of the dialogues which Cicero wrote concerning rhetoric and philosophy are Roman senators. No equestrian, nobody professionally concerned with poetry, grammar, rhetoric or philosophy appears in them. The occasions of meeting are private ones and thus permit the senators to say things that they never could be imagined saying in the curia, before a jury, before an assembly, or even in formal correspondence.[34] Nevertheless, they are given an oratorical mode of speaking appropriate to their public dignity[35] rather than the colloquial manner that must have been employed at such private meetings in real life. This oratorical mode manifests itself most obviously in the conscious avoidance, wherever possible, of Greek words and phrases and of literal quotations of Greek authors.[36] The dialogues present us with a strange conflation of two literary traditions,[37] Roman oratory and Greek technical exposition. Those who have observed the large amount of poetical quotation in them[38] attribute this simply to the freedom which the dialogue

33. Compare his pretended uncertainty about the source of a Latin tragic verse in a letter to Cato (*ad Fam.* xv. 6. 1) with *S. Rosc.* xlvi, *Sest.* cxviii, *Phil.* ii. 65, xiii. 49.

34. Cf. *ND* i. 61. I leave aside the problem that troubled Cicero himself (*de Orat.* ii. 1–9, *Ac.* ii. 7, *ad Att.* iv. 16. 3) of the verisimilitude of Roman aristocrats possessing technical knowledge of esoteric matters.

35. Cf. *Fin.* ii. 17, *TD* i. 7, ii. 26, *Diu.* ii. 7, *Fat.* iii, *de Off.* i. 2–3, *Parad.* v. The *sermo uulgaris* of the Epicurean writers, Amafinius and Rabirius, is sharply attacked (*Ac.* i. 5, *TD* i. 6, ii. 7, iv. 6). Cicero was not alone in his opinion of these writers; cf. Cassius ap. Cic. *ad Fam.* xv. 19. 2.

36. Cf. *de Orat.* i. 144, *Or.* cxxxii, *Ac.* i. 25, *Fin.* ii. 13, iii. 15, *TD* i. 15, *de Off.* i. 111.

37. For their tenuous link with the literary traditions of the Academy and the Lyceum see below, p. 68. The only known previous Latin dialogues, those of M. Iunius Brutus on the civil law, represented Brutus speaking with his son (see Cic. *Clu.* cxli, *de Orat.* ii. 224.

38. See above, p. 61.

form gave Cicero to indulge his natural love of poetry and to display his vast knowledge of the classic Greek and Roman works.[39] I should contend, however, that while some of the quotations are decorative in the very manner of those in the public orations (if they are more frequent, it is because of the more relaxed character of the philosophical orator's themes), the majority are probative and reflect the character of certain Greek technical expositions used by Cicero as sources of information. There is more method in the distribution of the quotations than has hitherto been observed.

A marked difference can be seen in the number of quotations of, and references to, Greek poetry between the rhetorical and the philosophical writings. Those in the former are comparatively few[40] and none consist of literal translations by Cicero himself into Latin verse. One reason would be that Cicero put more care into the composition of the rhetorical works[41] and was much less dependent on particular Greek sources.[42] Oratorical practice, however, if not oratorical theory, had a long and honoured history at Rome and a Latin theoretician was bound to keep the tone of his discourse as Roman as possible. The philosophical dialogues which bear most on matters of traditional concern, that *de republica* and that *de legibus*, likewise make few references to Greek poetry.

The view of rhetoric put by M. Antonius and L. Licinius Crassus in the *de Oratore* and by Cicero himself in the *Orator* is closely akin to the one developed by Aristotle and Theophrastus.[43] These thinkers regarded the study of the poets' ways of expression as useful to the budding orator[44] and, while keeping rigidly distinct the poetic and the oratorical manner,[45] thought it appropriate to illustrate both types of argument and types of verbal

39. E. Bertrand, *Cicéron au théâtre* (Grenoble 1897), p. 91, declares that the quotations in the philosophical dialogues were put there 'pour séduire les esprits rebelles et les gagner à la philosophie nationale'.

40. Cf. *de Orat.* I. 69, I. 196, I. 217, III. 57, III. 70, III. 138, III. 141.

41. Cf. *ad Att.* XIII. 19. 4.

42. Cf. *ad Att.* XII. 52. 3.

43. See *de Orat.* I. 43, II. 160, III. 67–8, *ad Fam.* I. 9. 23, *Or.* CLXXII.

44. See Quintil. *Inst.* X. 1. 27 on Theophrastus and cf. Cic. *de Orat.* I. 158, III. 39, III. 48.

45. See Arist. *Rhet.* III. 2, III. 3. Cf. Isocr. *Euag.* IX. ff., Strab. I. 2. 6, Cic. *de Orat.* I. 70, III. 27, *Or.* LXVI–LXVIII, *TD* III. 20, *Pis.* LXXIII.

expression from the poems which were read at school and still heard
at the public festivals. They also found it useful to consider the orator
and the theatrical actor together where gesture and delivery were
concerned.[46] There were more practical and less literary approaches
to the training of the orator such as that of the anonymous
treatise addressed to Herennius, in which contemporary examples
of debate are preferred to mythical ones and poetry is cited
merely to illustrate faults of argument.[47] Cicero perhaps diverged
a little from his Peripatetic masters in making Antonius keep
away from poetry in his discourse on the orator's subject matter
but followed them closely in strewing Crassus' exposition of style
and delivery with quotations.[48]

The views of the four major Athenian schools, Plato's Academy,
Aristotle's Lyceum, Epicurus' Garden and Zeno's Porch, are
expounded in Cicero's philosophical dialogues. The manner of
Latin exposition reflects on the whole quite accurately the
differing attitudes to poetry in the four schools.

Theorists had found fault as early as the sixth century with the
way the epic poets represented reality.[49] Plato represented
Socrates as hostile not only to Homer and Hesiod and Orpheus
but also to the Attic tragedians, regarding them as purveyors
of lies and immorality and as of no service to men seeking after
the truth of things.[50] On the other hand the Socrates whom
Plato depicted was not unmindful of the persuasive power of the
poets and the beauty of their verses.[51] He did not pretend
ignorance of the poems which the schools and public life of
Athens made familiar.[52] Later Academic philosophers remained
more or less loyal to Plato's view of poetry but did not disdain

46. See Arist. *Rhet.* III. 1, III. 2, III. 12. Cf. Cic. *de Orat.* I. 18, I. 128, I. 251, II. 194, III. 214ff.

47. See IV. 1–7.

48. See particularly *de Orat.* III. 152–70 and III. 217–19.

49. See Xenophanes ap. Sext. Emp. IX. 193, Heraclitus ap. Diog. Laert. IX. 1. 1.

50. See *Apol.* 22b, *Men.* 99b, *Phaedrus* 229b, *Protag.* 347c–348a, *Rep.* 376e, 378a, 387b, 392d, 398a, 595c, 597e, *Tim.* 19d. Nothing is certainly known about the real Socrates. Xenophon represents him as appealing to the poets in justification of argument (*Mem.* I. 2. 56–9, I. 3. 3, I. 3. 7, II. 1. 20, III. 2. 1) and many anecdotes are told about his predilection for the philosophical Euripides.

51. See *Phileb.* 47e–48b, *Rep.* 607a; cf. *Leg.* 653d, *Ion* passim.

52. Cf. *Gorg.* 525e–526d, *Phileb.* 47e. The great sophists, of course, are represented as quoting the poets very freely.

the help of poetic quotation in making their lectures and published writings more attractive to men of education.[53] Aristotle's view of poetry was in detail more complex than Plato's but over all differed little: philosophical enlightenment could not in his view be found in the works of the poets[54] but since these often expressed true observations about the world and human life in an eloquent and attractive way, they might be quoted with advantage by a serious philosopher in support of, although not as authority for, a particular statement. It is not clear how much Aristotle or some later member of his school was responsible for the notions that late fourth-century Athenian comedy reflected real life truly[55] and that its practitioners were not poets at all.[56]

Cicero claimed in his maturity formal allegiance to the Academy and particularly to the doctrines and method of inquiry taught in the school by Arcesilas and Carneades.[57] Nevertheless, he saw no great intellectual differences between the Academy and the Lyceum[58] and found the views of Aristotle and his successors on literary style particularly sympathetic.[59] He sent his own son to Cratippus, the contemporary head of the Lyceum. The dialogue form of his writings on rhetoric and philosophy was meant to remind his readers of the classic publications of the early Academy. His view of the nature of the poet's inspiration was one traditionally associated with Plato as well as with Democritus.[60] Not surprisingly, therefore, where he speaks in his own person[61] in the dialogues or uses another person to state Academic[62] or Peri-

53. For Crantor and poetry see Diog. Laert. IV. 26; for Philo see Cic. *TD* II. 26; in general see Plut. *Mor.* 16. The *Consolatio ad Apollonium* differs radically from the Academic Plutarch's genuine philosophical works in its large number of quotations of poetry.

54. Aristotle's basic contempt for poetry comes out clearly at *Rhet.* III. 1. 8–10, III. 5. 4.

55. Cf. Cic. *S. Rosc.* XLVII and ap. Donat. *exc. de com.* p. 22. 19.

56. Cf. Cic. *Or.* LXVII, Hor. *Sat.* I. 4. 45–8.

57. See *Mur.* LXIII, *de Cons. suo*, fr. 2. 71–6 (*Diu.* I. 22), *Ac.* I. 43, II. 61, II. 65, *ND* I. 11–12, *Diu.* I. 6–7, II. 1, II. 150, *TD* III. 12, V. 33, *de Off.* I. 2, II. 8, *Fin.* II. 7. Cf. Plut. *Cic.* III–IV.

58. See *de Orat.* III. 67, *de Cons. suo*, fr. 2. 71–6 (*Diu.* I. 22), *Ac.* II. 15, *TD* II. 9, *Fin.* I. 7, I. 14, *de Off.* I. 2, II. 8.

59. See *Fin.* V. 7, *TD* III. 22; cf. *Or.* CLXXII, *Ac.* II. 132, II. 143, *TD* IV. 6.

60. See *Arch.* XVIII, *TD* I. 64; cf. *de Orat.* II. 194, *Diu.* I. 80.

61. Cf. *Leg.* I. 3–4, I. 40, II. 41, *Fin.* IV. 10, *Diu.* II. 113 (cf. the apologies put into Quintus' mouth at I. 68), *TD* I. 36, I. 65, II. 27, III. 3, IV. 69–70.

62. Cf. *Leg.* I. 5, *ND* III. 77, III. 91, *Lael.* XXIV.

patetic⁶³ views the ancient suspicion of poetry as a source of
truth and sound moral instruction frequently finds expression.
Wherever the line of argument is openly Academic verses appear
only seldom and then either as decoration or *ad hominem*.⁶⁴

Epicurus and his followers maintained the old hostilities more
strongly than Plato and much more strongly than the atomist
Democritus. They not only regarded the poets as liars⁶⁵ but
affected to scorn their ways of expression as artificial and worth-
less.⁶⁶ Thus the Epicurean arguments of Torquatus in the first
book *de finibus bonorum et malorum*⁶⁷ and of Velleius in the first
book *de natura deorum* are left by Cicero practically bare of
quotations and both speakers are made to assert the traditional
Epicurean contempt for poetry.⁶⁸

Perhaps in the sixth century, certainly in the fifth, there were
theorists who found virtue and wisdom in poetry.⁶⁹ They became
common enough to be a butt of the comedians' humour.⁷⁰ Zeno,
the principals of the Athenian Porch who followed him, and
Posidonius of Rhodes all regarded the ancient pre-philosophical
traditions of the Greeks as containing a large element of truth
and the poems of Homer and the Attic tragedians as giving a
valid and authoritative expression of this truth.⁷¹ Accordingly
they quoted frequently and extensively from those poems which
seemed to them to foreshadow and support their own doctrines.⁷²
Chrysippus in particular was notorious for the length of his
quotations⁷³ and still in the late first century B.C. the Stoic

63. Cf. *Fin.* v. 49, v. 52, v. 64.
64. Cf. the quotations in *ND* III. 65–93; Cicero's source here clearly attacked
an argument slightly different from that represented at *ND* II. 153–67, which
contains remarkably little poetry for a Stoic argument (for the source of this
see below, p. 88).
65. See Plut. *Mor.* 15d, 1087a, Athen. 5. 187c, Heracl. *Alleg.* IV, Sext. Emp.
Adu. Math. I. 272.
66. See Cic. *Pis.* LXIX–LXX, Diog. Laert. x. 121.
67. There is one slighting reference to *fabulae* at I. 65.
68. Cf. *Fin.* I. 65, I. 72, *ND* I. 42.
69. See K. Müller, 'Allegorische Dichtererklärung', *RE* Suppl. 4 (1924), 16ff.
70. Cf. Aristoph. *Batr.* 1471ff.
71. See Dio Chrys. LIII. 4 (on Zeno), Plut. *Mor.* 34b (on Chrysippus).
72. See Cic. *TD* II. 26, *ND* I. 41, Sen. *Epist.* VIII. 8, CVIII. 9ff., CXV. 12ff.,
Gell. VI. 16. 6, Galen, *Plac. Hipp. et Plat.* III. 2–3 (on Chrysippus), IV. 5 (on
Posidonius), Diog. Laert. VII. 180. At *Inst.* V. 11. 39 Quintilian is probably
referring to Stoic philosophers.
73. See Diog. Laert. VII. 180.

Dionysius could offend Academic stylistic tastes by his undisciplined and careless manner of quoting verse.[74] There are three outright statements of Stoic doctrine in Cicero's works, the one given to Marcus Cato in the third book *de finibus bonorum et malorum*, that to Lucilius Balbus in the second book *de natura deorum* and that to Quintus Cicero in the second book *de diuinatione*. The two latter are stuffed with poetic justifications of the arguments presented. The absence of poetry from Cato's discourse in the third book *de finibus* is puzzling but so too are the brevity and hesitant composition of both this and the opposing Academic discourse in the fourth book; we may have in the former only the sketch, not a full elaboration of Stoic doctrine on τὸ τοῦ βίου τέλος.[75]

The homily addressed by Cicero to his son *de officiis* was confessedly based on Stoic sources.[76] These sources, however, were heavily infected by Academic influences[77] and Cicero used them with considerable freedom. The number of quotations of poetry is smaller than in the Stoic parts of the dialogues *de finibus bonorum et malorum*, *de natura deorum* and *de diuinatione* but larger than in the Academic parts of the same dialogues. It is significant that as Cicero moves further and further away from his sources in the second and third books *de officiis* so the proportion of poetry to prose argument decreases.

The origin of the doctrines that Cicero puts into his own mouth in the second book *de finibus bonorum et malorum* and in the five books of the *Tusculanae disputationes* has long been a matter of contention.[78] Cicero's formal pose in both works is an Academic one[79] but Carneadean scepticism is rejected and divergence from

74. See Cic. *TD* II. 26.
75. M. Giusta, 'I dossografi di etica', I (Turin 1964 = *Università di Torino, Pubbl. della fac. d. lett. e filos.* 15. 3), pp. 23ff., argues that Cicero did not draw on one Stoic teacher's argument but a doxographical account which treated the ethical theories of several teachers topic by topic.
76. See I. 6, II. 60, III. 7, III. 20. Cf. Cic. *ad Att.* XVI. 11. 4, Plin. *HN praef.* 22, Gell. XIII. 28. 1. (For convenience of exposition I include this work with the dialogues.)
77. For Panaetius and Plato see Anon. *Ind. Stoic.* LXI, Cic. *TD* I. 79; for Posidonius and Plato cf. Galen, *Plac. Hipp. et Plat.* IV. 7.
78. See below, pp. 83ff.
79. See *Fin.* I. 5, I. 7, II. 1–3, II. 17, II. 68, II. 76, II. 119 (cf. v. 7); *Tusc.* I. 17, II. 9, III. 12, III. 59, III. 71, IV. 7, V. 11.

conventional Academic method and doctrine admitted a number of times.[80] The number of verses quoted in the second book *de finibus* loses its peculiarity once it is realized that most come from comedy or satire.[81] The verses pullulating in the *Tusculanae disputationes* cannot but be odd for an Academic setting.[82] Nevertheless, the quotation of poetry was common in epitaphic and consolatory speaking[83] and the *Tusculanae disputationes* were perhaps designed to remind readers of this as much as of ordinary philosophical disquisition.

IV. CICERO'S POETIC QUOTATIONS AND THOSE OF HIS RHETORICAL AND PHILOSOPHICAL SOURCES

The quotations of Latin poetry in Cicero's letters and speeches can for the most part be assigned to first-hand acquaintance with the actual poems. Of his love of the contemporary theatre and enthusiastic interest in the art of performing the old poetic scripts both he[84] and others[85] give good evidence. He seems to have genuinely admired the poems he read at school[86] and his youthful version of the Φαινόμενα of Aratus shows a better acquaintance with the verbal and metrical manner of Ennius' *Annales* than with the technicalities of astronomical observation.[87] The principal subject matter of the rhetorical and philosophical works, however, came ultimately not from the experience of first-century Romans but from Greek books. I have already shown that the general distribution of poetic quotations in these works was determined by certain Greek traditions. We must now con-

80. See *Fin.* II. 43, *TD* III. 13, v. 13, v. 33, v. 76, v. 82.
81. See above, p. 68.
82. Some of the poems quoted, however, are said to have philosophical sources (see III. 29, III. 31).
83. Cf. Menander's parody at *Aspis* 399–432 (411 ~ Cic. *TD* v. 25; 424–5 ~ Cic. *TD* IV. 63).
84. Cf. *Quinct.* LXXVII, *Q. Rosc.* XVII, XX, XXX–XXXI, *Sest.* CXX, *ad Att.* IV. 15. 6, *ad Fam.* XII. 18. 2, *Diu.* I. 79–80.
85. Cf. Plut. *Cic.* V, Macrob. *Sat.* III. 14. 11–12.
86. To be distinguished from stock judgements (e.g. *Opt. gen.* II, *Brut.* LX, LXXII, *Fin.* I. 4) are those which have a personal stamp: *Arch.* XVIII, *Sest.* CXX, *de Orat.* I. 198, *Diu.* I. 66, *TD* I. 107, III. 45 (a Greek comparison between Homer and Euphorion may, however, lie behind this; cf. *Diu.* II. 133).
87. See below, pp. 93–4.

sider the question of the relationship between Cicero's particular quotations and the sources of his knowledge of rhetoric and philosophy.

There had been Latin grammar and rhetoric since at least the turn of the century and Cicero's youthful treatise *de inuentione* almost certainly purloined its quotations of comedy and tragedy from earlier Latin books.[88] The discussion of humour at *de Oratore* II. 216–89 and that of vocabulary at III. 152–70 may get their quotations from some place other than Cicero's memory. The lengthy quotations of famous dramatic speeches in the discussion of *actio* at III. 213–27 on the other hand bear the stamp of originality. The polemical account of euphony in individual words at *Orator* 149–64 seems to be directed at analogist grammarians and strays from Cicero's main rhetorical argument; it has accordingly been thought to come from Varro's *de utilitate sermonis libri*.[89] In any case the error at section 157[90] gives away at least some of the quotations made in the course of the account as quite certainly stolen. As to the other references and quotations scattered sparingly through the *de oratore libri* and the *Orator*, those to Latin poems are as likely to be original as the ones in the letters and speeches while those to Greek poems generally occur in Greek contexts[91] and probably were first made by the Greek writer from whom the matter in question ultimately derived.

When Cicero began publishing philosophical dialogues there existed in Latin prose hardly any philosophizing except of an Epicurean bent, and this must have eschewed on principle[92] the quotation of poetry. P. Nigidius Figulus,[93] M. Terentius Varro[94] and M. Iunius Brutus[95] were composing and publishing works on philosophical themes at more or less the same time, perhaps always Academic or 'Pythagorean' in formal outlook but often drawing on Stoic sources. Some of the many quotations of poetry

88. On the relationship of the anonymous treatise addressed to Herennius and the *de inuentione libri* see D. Matthes, *Lustrum* 3 (1958), 81ff. (92f. on the poetic quotations shared by the two works).

89. See W. Kroll, *M. Tullii Ciceronis Orator* (Berlin 1913), 'Einleitung', pp. 12–13.

90. Two tragic senarii (Trag. inc. 194–5) are quoted as coming from the *Phormio* of Terence.

91. See above, n. 40.   92. See above, p. 69.
93. See Cic. *Tim.* 1–11.   94. See Cic. *Ac.* 1. 9.
95. See Cic. *Ac.* 1. 12, *TD* v. 1, *Fin.* 1. 8.

in Cicero's dialogues may be purloined from these men, but most must in some sense be Cicero's own.

Cicero's quotations fall into three groups, verses by Latin poets of the previous two centuries, verses published by Cicero himself in his youth[96] or middle age[97] or by contemporaries,[98] and Latin verses attributed to various classical Greek poets. There are no actual Greek verses as in the private correspondence; the oratorical style of the dialogues demanded Latinity as complete as possible.[99] Whereas indirect references to Greek poetry occur freely in the speeches of most of the philosophizing orators,[100] Latinized Greek verses tend to be restricted to Cicero's own speeches.[101] One batch of these verses is stated[102] to be unknown to an assembly of Cicero's friends imagined as taking place in June of 45 and several more are openly claimed[103] by Cicero as his own work. The modest tone in which Cicero describes his method of translation[104] contrasts strikingly with the brimming pride which shows through the remarks Lucilius Balbus is made to pass about the published *Aratus* and *Prognostica* in the second book *de natura deorum*.[105] Unlike some actual Greek verses quoted

96. E.g. the *Marius* quoted at *Diu.* I. 106 and the *Aratus* quoted at *ND* II. 104–15 (see Capitolinus, *Gordian.* III. 2, Jerome, *Chron. praef.* [+Cic. *de Off.* II. 87]). The phrase *utar...carminibus Arateis* at *ND* II. 104 (∼ *Leg.* II. 7) suggests that the *Prognostica* (quoted at *Diu.* I. 13–15) belongs to the same period. A second edition of the *Prognostica* need not be referred to at *ad Att.* II. 1. 11.

97. E.g. the *de consulatu suo libri* quoted at *Diu.* I. 17–22.

98. E.g. Q. Scaevola's epigram at *Leg.* I. 2.

99. See above, p. 65.

100. Care was taken about chronological accuracy; at *Rep.* I. 56 (set in 129 B.C.) the younger Scipio is made to refer indirectly to Aratus while at *Leg.* II. 7 (set sometime after Cicero's admission to the augural college [53 B.C.]; see II. 32) Cicero quotes his own version of the proemium of the Φαινόμενα.

101. The exceptions are at *Fin.* v. 49 (M. Piso quotes nine Latinized verses of Homer), *ND* II. 65 (Q. Lucilius Balbus quotes three Latinized verses of Euripides), *Diu.* I. 52 (Quintus Cicero quotes an anecdote containing an adapted verse of Homer), I. 81 (Quintus Cicero quotes an anecdote containing an iambic Pythian oracle).

102. *TD* II. 26. There is a similar implication in M. Piso's words at *Fin.* v. 49 (the scene is set in the year 79).

103. *Fin.* II. 105, *TD* I. 15, III. 29, *Diu.* II. 63, *de Off.* III. 82.

104. See *Fin.* II. 105 *concludam, si potero, Latine*, *de Off.* III. 82 *dicam, ut potero, incondite fortasse.*

105. II. 104. Cf. also what brother Quintus is made to say about the *de consulatu suo libri* (*Diu.* I. 17) and the *Marius* (*Leg.* I. 1).

in letters[106] and some Roman verses quoted in speeches, letters
and dialogues,[107] the verses in question never appear in abbreviated form.

One may reasonably assume that all Latin verses attributed to
a Greek poet were fashioned by Cicero on the basis of the Greek
originals,[108] while those verses quoted without any attribution
at all come from one of the Latin works of the previous two
centuries[109] or, perhaps, from one of Cicero's previously published
poems.[110] The aristocrats taking part in a dialogue were imagined
to possess an acquaintance with the classics of Greek and Roman
poetry; decorum prevented any speaker citing actual Greek verses,
verisimilitude any but Cicero himself[111] spontaneously putting
Greek verses into Latin equivalents. Such a method of reference
would have been systematic and easily comprehensible. It seems to
have been imitated by Seneca in his philosophical writing.[112]

106. Cf. *ad Att.* v. 10. 3 (~ *TD* i. 41), v. 11. 5, vi. 1. 16, vi. 5. 2.

107. Cf. *Planc.* lix, *Cael.* xviii, *Sest.* cxxi, cxxxvi, *ad Fam.* vii. 28. 2, ix. 22.
1, *ad Att.* vii. 26. 1, viii. 11. 3, xiv. 12. 2, *Orat.* clxiv, *TD* i. 34, i. 106,
iv. 77, *ND* iii. 72, *Fin.* ii. 71, *Ac.* ii. 88. The beginning or beginning and end
of a passage is quoted and the audience or reader is left to supply the rest.
To be distinguished are *Diu.* ii. 112, *TD* iii. 53, iii. 58, where the passages
abbreviated have been quoted in their entirety earlier in the dialogue.

108. It is not completely clear what assumptions the readers of late antiquity
made. Gellius (xv. 6. 4) and Augustine (*Ciu.* v. 8) may depend on statements
made by Cicero himself. Priscian (*Gramm.* iii. 426. 7) obviously uses his own
intelligence with regard to *TD* iv. 63. The general tendency of the grammarians
is to quote as by Cicero all verse to be found in a dialogue; cf. Non. p. 16. 6
(Enn. *tr.* 21), p. 122. 17 (Inc. trag. 135), p. 181. 1 (Enn. *tr.* 88), p. 272.
39 (Inc. trag. 75), Charis. p. 277. 3 (Pacuv. *tr.* 256), Serv. A. Virg. *Aen.* i. 726
(Enn. *tr.* 84). Thus no conclusions of any sort can be drawn from such
quotations as those of *TD* ii. 22–5 by Diomedes (*Gramm.* i. 366. 27), Priscian
(*Gramm.* ii. 542. 24) and Arusianus (*Gramm.* vii. 457. 7).

109. The assumption is confirmed for *ND* ii. 89 by Non. p. 90. 8, for
Fin. ii. 94 and *TD* ii. 19 by Non. p. 324. 26.

110. On *ND* ii. 159 see below, p. 89. I should interpret *Ac.* ii. 66 as
a reference not so much to the historical Aratus as to the speaker of the
verses in a poem which Cicero regarded as in some sense his own; this poem
was known not by a title translating the Greek Φαινόμενα but as the *Aratus*,
just as the dialogue de amicitia was named *Laelius* after its chief participant.

111. The exceptions listed above, n. 101, may be due to oversight in hasty
composition.

112. Contrast *Epist.* cvii. 10 (P. Burman, *Anthologia ueterum Latinorum epi-
grammatum et poematum* (Amsterdam 1759), i 605, and J. Tolkiehn, *Woch. f. kl.
Ph.* 22 (1905), 555–8, wrongly make Cicero responsible for translating
Cleanthes' verses; see August. *Ciu.* v. 8) and cxv. 14–15 with xcv. 53 and
cii. 16.

Directly beneath Cicero's philosophical dialogues lay various Greek professional treatises.[113] The haste with which Cicero wrote sometimes allowed the manner of the professional treatise to show through.[114] The classic Latin tragedies and comedies had been even more closely based on Greek works, these being works of the very same genre.[115] Many of Cicero's quotations of the Latin plays, like that of Ennius' *Medea* in the discussion of causation at *Fat.* XXXIV, merely replaced quotations in his sources of the originals of these plays.[116] In some cases, however, this is almost demonstrably not so. One of the stock examples employed in Greek discussion of the problem of perception was vv. 255ff. of Euripides' Ὀρέστης;[117] at *Ac.* II. 52 and II. 89 Cicero uses a parallel scene from Ennius' *Alcmeo*.[118] Greek discussions of death were often illustrated with the Homeric Priam's prophecy of his own end;[119] at *TD* I. 85 Cicero uses the Ennian Andromache's account of Priam's end.[120] The quotations of various tragedies by Ennius and Accius at *ND* II. 65, *TD* III. 28, III. 44–5[121] and III. 62 are plainly additions to the arguments of Cicero's sources. While quotations of the *Aratus* and the *Prognostica* may have replaced Greek philosophers' quotations of the Φαινόμενα,[122]

113. See *ad Att.* XII. 52. 3 and cf. Plut. *Cic.* XL. Larger claims are made at *Ac.* I. 10, *Fin.* I. 4–8, *de Off.* I. 6.

114. Cf. *Rep.* II. 9, *TD* II. 53, III. 52, v. 67, *ND* II. 65, II. 166, III. 59, *Diu.* I. 72, *Lael.* xv, XLVIII.

115. See Cic. *Opt. gen.* XVIII, *Ac.* I. 10, *Fin.* I. 4–6.

116. Clem. Alex. *Strom.* VIII. 930 shows that the Euripidean prologue was a stock example in such discussions. The argument of *TD* II. 48–50 reveals plainly that the Sophoclean Νίπτρα was quoted in the source.

117. See Chrysippus ap. Aet. *Plac.* IV. 12 (= *SVF* II.54), Sext. Emp. VII. 170, VII. 249.

118. This is no reason to assume that no Latin poet had translated the Ὀρέστης. The grammarians seem to know an *Orestes* (see Donat. *Gramm.* IV. 375. 25). Malcovati (*Cicerone*, p. 117) and others are wrong to suppose that Cicero was necessarily acquainted with all the Latin plays known to professional scholars. Even if he had been, he might still have avoided quoting in the dialogues those plays not well known to Romans of average education.

119. Hom. *Il.* XXII. 56ff. (Plut. *Mor.* 113f).   120. *Tr.* 86–8.

121. Returning to the argument of his source at III. 46 Cicero forgets he has quoted the speech of a female personage.

122. A Stoic argument that knowledge of the divine comes from contemplation of the cosmos is reported along with a quotation of Arat. *Phaen.* 545–9 by Aetius, *Plac.* I. 6. The same argument is illustrated at *ND* II. 104–15 by very extensive quotations from an earlier section of Cicero's published translation of the Φαινόμενα. R. Hirzel, who makes Posidonius Cicero's source

quotations of Ennius' *Annales*, Lucilius' satires, Afranius' *fabulae togatae* and Cicero's own *Marius* and *de consulatu suo libri* must be independent. Some indirect references to, and direct quotations of, Greek poems pretty certainly stem from Cicero's own independent knowledge[123] but most should be regarded as taken from the philosophical source Cicero happened to be following at the time.

Where anecdotes about Greeks or Romans speaking Greek are concerned there can be no reasonable doubt that Cicero's knowledge of the original poetic texts is not involved.[124] The only question is whether an anecdote comes from Cicero's memory or from a written source. Where, however, Cicero or one of his personages speaks as if from independent knowledge of a Greek poem it is theoretically possible that appearances do not deceive. Nevertheless, despite the fact that most of the late second- and early first-century philosophers with whom Cicero seems to have been best acquainted had little influence on the Greek philosophical texts which survive to the present day, sufficient analogues can be found in these of Ciceronian arguments together with their poetical illustrations to raise powerful suspicions. Ps.-Plutarch's *Consolatio ad Apollonium*, Galen's *De placitis Hippocratis et Platonis* and the writings of Sextus Empiricus offer parallels for most of the quotations and references in the *Tusculanae disputationes*.[125] One may suppose that writers like the

(*Untersuchungen zu Cicero's philosophischen Schriften* i (Leipzig 1877), p. 193), and L. Reinhardt, who makes the source Panaetius (*Die Quellen von Cicero's Schrift de deorum natura* (Breslau 1888), p. 35), regard the quotations simply as Cicero's own decoration of the original Greek argument. The copious modern literature on the source of the second book *de natura deorum* does not seem to touch on the problem.

123. Cf. *Fin.* v. 3 and the reference to the opening speech of Sophocles' ὁ ἐπὶ Κολωνῷ Οἰδίπους. It is possible that some Roman treatise on augury provided the quotation of Hom. *Il.* ix. 236–7 at *Diu.* ii. 82.

124. I refer to *TD* i. 115, ii. 60, iii. 18 (Hom. *Il.* ix. 646–7), iii. 59 (Eurip. fr. 757), iv. 63 (Eurip. *Or.* 1–3), v. 49, v. 101, *Diu.* i. 52, i. 81, ii. 115, *de Off.* iii. 82 (Eurip. *Phoen.* 524–5). A slightly different method of dealing with such anecdotes is found at *Deiot.* xxv: *de Domitio dixit uersum Graecum eadem sententia qua etiam nos habemus Latinum: pereant amici dum inimici una intercidant.*

125. Where other dialogues are concerned compare *Ac.* ii. 89 with Sext. Emp. vii. 249, viii. 67; *Fin.* ii. 105 with Plut. *Mor.* 630e; *Fin.* v. 49 with Sext. Emp. i. 42; *ND* ii. 65 with Clem. Alex. *Strom.* v. 717, Heracl. *Alleg.* xxiii; *Diu.* ii. 12 with Plut. *Mor.* 399a, 432c (see further below, p. 82 n. 164); Aug. *Ciu.* v. 8 with Sext. Emp. vii. 128.

Academic Crantor (340–275)[126] and the Stoic Chrysippus (280–
207)[127] interwove the discussion of certain themes with the
subject matter of epic and tragic poetry quite inextricably, de-
termining one of the stylistic features of all future discussion.[128]

The many errors made by Cicero about the speakers of Homeric
verses[129] enforce suspicion. In general it is less likely that he
should have misattributed verses he thought of himself to illustrate
a point[130] than that he misattributed verses he found already
quoted in a philosophical source but lacking a full or accurate
description of their original context. Read alone the verses
'ἀνδρὸς μὲν τόδε σῆμα πάλαι κατατεθνηῶτος, | ὅν ποτ' ἀριστεύ-
οντα κατέκτανε φαίδιμος Ἕκτωρ.' | ὥς ποτέ τις ἐρέει· τὸ δ' ἐμὸν
κλέος οὔ ποτ' ὀλεῖται'[131] might well be carelessly taken, as they
were by Cicero,[132] as an utterance by Ajax. The error about the
nature of the agricultural activity ascribed to Laertes by Homer[133]
and the muddling of Pelius and Aeson in the *de senectute liber*[134]
may come entirely from Cicero's own wandering mind, but the
nature of the misdescription at *TD* IV. 49 of Hector's state of
mind when about to meet Ajax in battle suggests strongly that
Cicero was drawing upon a source in which a quotation of the
Iliad stopped abruptly at VII. 217.

A decisive indication that Cicero at least very often took
quotations of and references to Greek poems from his philosophical
sources is provided by his tendency to translate Greek verses
with more attention to the argument they were supposed to
support than to their original context or actual wording.[135]

126. See Diog. Laert. IV. 26 for Crantor's admiration of Homer and
Euripides.
127. See Diog. Laert. VII. 180 for Chrysippus' notoriously lengthy quotations
of poetry.
128. See Cic. *Ac.* II. 87 on Academic use of Stoic quotations.
129. *Diu.* II. 63 (*Il.* II. 299ff.), II. 82 (*Il.* IX. 236f.), ap. Gell. XV. 6. 3 (*Il.*
VII. 89–91). Cf. the error about Eurip. fr. 324 at Sen. *Epist.* CXV. 15.
130. These errors are to be sharply distinguished from the sort committed
at *ad Att.* IV. 7. 2, VII. 3. 5, VII. 6. 2, XIV. 13. 2, *ad Q.fr.* III. 5. 4, which can
only be simple lapses of memory.
131. Hom. *Il.* VII. 89–91.   132. See Gell. XV. 6. 3.
133. *Od.* XXIV. 227.
134. LIV, LXXXIII (perhaps a true memory of Plaut. *Pseud.* 868–71 rather
than a false memory of the Greek myth).
135. This is different from the merging of a literal quotation into the
argument (cf. *ad Att.* IV. 7. 3, VII. 1. 2, VII. 6. 2, XVI. 6. 1, XVI. 13a. 3).

The version of ἀλλά μοι οἰδάνεται κραδίη χόλῳ, ὁππότε κείνων |
μνήσομαι ὥς μ' ἀσύφηλον ἐν 'Αργείοισιν ἔρεξεν | 'Ατρείδης,
ὡς εἴ τιν' ἀτίμητον μετανάστην[136] offered at *TD* III. 18, *corque
meum penitus turgescit tristibus iris | cum decore atque omni me orbatum
laude recordor*, ignores the particular circumstances of Achilles'
anger inasmuch as these are irrelevant to the point being argued,
namely the similarity of certain mental states to physical ones.

Chrysippus' advice to those grieving to accept necessity is
incorporated into the version of ἔφυ μὲν οὐδεὶς ὅστις οὐ πονεῖ
βροτῶν | θάπτει τε τέκνα χἄτερα κτᾶται νέα | αὐτός τε θνήσκει
καὶ τάδ' ἄχθονται βροτοί | εἰς γῆν φέροντες γῆν· ἀναγκαίως
δ' ἔχει | βίον θερίζειν ὥστε κάρπιμον στάχυν[137] offered at *TD*
III. 59, *mortalis nemo est quam non attingit dolor | morbusque. multis
sunt humandi liberi, | rursumque creandi, morsque est †finita† omnibus. |
quae generi humano angorem nequiquam adferunt. | reddenda terrae est
terra, tum uita omnibus | metenda ut fruges. sic iubet Necessitas.* Euripides'
Amphiaraus had merely described to the grieving Hypsipyle the
cycle of human life, glancing at its inevitability; Cicero's series
of gerundival phrases, the adverb *nequiquam* and the strong
personification of Necessitas make the Latin verses hortatory and
general.

The words *nemo possit maerore uacare* look to the context of
TD III. 65 and its general discussion of grief rather than to
Homer's πότε κέν τις ἀναπνεύσειε πόνοιο;[138]

The Aeschylean Prometheus' reply to Oceanus at *P.V.* 379–80,
ἐάν τις ἐν καιρῷ γε μαλθάσσῃ κέαρ | καὶ μὴ σφριγῶντα θυμὸν
ἰσχναίνῃ βίᾳ, sarcastically rejected the idea of medical attention
for the wrath of Zeus, arguing that the only way of assuaging the
god's wrath likely to succeed was soft flattery at an appropriate
moment. The version offered by Cicero at *TD* III. 76, *siquidem
qui tempestiuam medicinam admouens | non adgrauescens uolnus inlidat
manu*, universalizes the situation entirely and, besides shifting the
medical metaphor from the reduction of tumours to the treatment
of flesh wounds, makes Prometheus' reply coincide exactly with
the doctrine being promoted: *sumendum tempus est non minus in
animorum morbis quam in corporum.*

136. Hom. *Il.* IX. 646–8.
137. Eurip. *Hyps.* fr. 60. 90–4, p. 43 Bond.
138. *Il.* XIX. 227.

The verses οὐκ ἔστιν οὐδὲν δεινὸν ὧδ' εἰπεῖν ἔπος | οὐδὲ πάθος οὐδὲ ξυμφορὰ θεήλατος[139] were open to two interpretations[140] but the context of *TD* IV. 63 must have helped to push Cicero into translating them as *neque tam terribilis ulla fando oratio est | nec sors nec ira caelitum inuectum malum.*

The wording of *aethera | qui terram tenero circumiectu amplectitur* is less inconsistent with the Stoic theory being illustrated at *ND* II. 65 than that of the original αἰθέρα | καὶ γῆν πέριξ ἔχονθ' ὑγραῖς ἐν ἀγκάλαις.[141]

The words *uariis auido satiatus pectore musis* reflect the somewhat less than fully approving account of man's inborn thirst for knowledge at *Fin.* v. 49 rather than the simple τερψάμενος used in the speech of the Homeric Sirens.[142]

Tales sunt hominum mentes quali pater ipse | Iuppiter auctiferas lustrauit lumine terras mistranslates τοῖος γὰρ νόος ἐστὶν ἐπιχθονίων ἀνθρώπων | οἷον ἐπ' ἦμαρ ἄγῃσι πατὴρ ἀνδρῶν τε θεῶν τε[143] in such a way as to make these verses fit better the Stoic theory they were argued[144] to anticipate. In this and each of the other seven cases Cicero pretty certainly adapted from a single Greek source both his argument and the illustrative verse.

V. CICERO'S EXTENDED QUOTATIONS OF HOMER AND THE ATTIC TRAGEDIANS

Some scholars carelessly take all the references to Greek poems in the philosophical dialogues as evidence of Cicero's direct acquaintance with these poems.[145] Others see that those references which turn up in connection with similar arguments in extant Greek philosophical works must have been adapted by Cicero

139. Eurip. *Or.* 1–2.
140. See schol. ad loc. (p. 94 Schwarz).
141. Eurip. fr. 941. Lucret. I. 179, I. 207, II. 146 suggest that Cicero may also have had an Ennian phrase in mind.
142. *Od.* XII. 188.
143. *Od.* XVIII. 136–7.
144. See the fragment of the *de fato liber* quoted by August. *Ciu.* v. 8.
145. Cf. E. Lange, *Quid cum de ingenio et litteris tum de poetis Graecorum Cicero senserit* (Dissertation, Halle 1880), pp. 33, 49ff., E. Howind, *De ratione citandi in Ciceronis Plutarchi Senecae Noui Testamenti scriptis obuia* (Dissertation, Marburg 1921), p. 10, P. T. Pütz, *De M. Tulli Ciceronis bibliotheca* (Dissertation, Münster 1925), pp. 28, 33ff., E. Malcovati, *Cicerone*, pp. 49f. (but see pp. 63ff.).

at the same time as he adapted arguments from the sources of these works[146] but are reluctant to believe in such a mechanical procedure where the extant Greek works fail us, especially in the case of the very large pieces of translated verse at *Diu.* II. 63–4[147] and *TD* II. 20–5.[148] There is a widespread notion[149] that these and some of the smaller pieces were made by Cicero in his youth along with the translation of the Φαινόμενα.[150] A recent writer[151] seems, on the other hand, to want to associate them with Plutarch's story[152] of Cicero's production of 500 verses per night during Caesar's dictatorship.

It is quite possible that Cicero translated into verse other Greek poems besides the Φαινόμενα in his youth. The statement at *De oratore* I. 154 is not, however, evidence[153] that this was anyone's practice in the early first century; παράφρασις of poems into oratorical prose[154] is what Crassus describes. Cicero often represents shorter batches of verse as having been translated at the moment of speaking.[155] Dramatic propriety prevented the

146. There is reluctance, nevertheless, to accept the full logic of the situation. A. Lörcher, for example, argues, *Das Fremde und das Eigene in Ciceros Büchern de finibus bonorum et malorum und den Academica* (Halle 1911), p. 114 n. 3, that Antiochus, Cicero's alleged source at *Fin.* V. 49, merely referred in an indirect manner to the Sirens' address to Odysseus and that it was Cicero's decision to quote Homer's actual verses.

147. Cf. D. Heeringa, *Quaestiones ad Ciceronis de diuinatione libros duos pertinentes* (Dissertation, Groningen 1906), p. 35.

148. Cf. O. Heine, 'De fontibus Tusculanarum disputationum' (Progr., Weimar 1863), 4, 11, G. Zietzschmann, *De Tusculanarum disputationum fontibus* (Dissertation, Halle 1868), pp. 13f., M. Pohlenz, 'Das zweite Buch der Tusculanen', *Hermes* 44 (1909), 24.

149. Cf. C. F. A. Nobbe's 1827 Leipzig programme quoted by Orelli, vol. IV. ii, p. 514, Heine, 'De font. Tusc.', p. 11, Zietzschmann, *De Tusc. font.* p. 13, M. Grollmus, *De M. Tullio Cicerone poeta* (Dissertation, Königsberg 1887), pp. 51f., F. D. Allen, *AJPh* 13 (1892), 56, J. Tolkiehn, *NJbb* Suppl. 23 (1896), 223, A. S. Pease on Cic. *Diu.* II. 63 (*Illinois Stud. Lang. Lit.* 8 (1923), 268). A. Traglia, *La lingua di Cicerone poeta* (Bari 1950), p. 47, thinks that the verses in question were translated 'in diversi tempi e per diverse occasioni'.

150. See above, n. 73.

151. G. B. Townend in T. Dorey (ed.), *Cicero*, p. 117 and n. 13 on p. 133.

152. *Cic.* XL. 3.

153. As M. Schanz, C. Hosius, *Geschichte der römischen Literatur* I⁴, (Munich 1927), p. 537, J. W. Spaeth, *CJ* 26 (1930–1), 503, seem to think.

154. Cf. Plut. *Dem.* VIII. 2, Dio Chrys. *Or.* XVIII. 19, Theon, *Progymn.* IV, Hermogenes, *Meth.* XXIV.

155. See *Fin.* II. 105, *TD* I. 15, III. 29, *de Off.* III. 82. Cf. *TD* I. 115 (*huiusmodi uersiculos*), III. 18, *Diu.* I. 52, II. 82.

longer batches being similarly represented. The remark at *Fin.* v.
49, *nam uerti, ut quaedam Homeri, sic istum ipsum locum*, comes from
the mouth of M. Pupius Piso and should be regarded as part of
the imaginative paraphernalia of the dialogue rather than as hard
evidence for the biography of Cicero; if, however, it is a lapse
by Cicero into his own situation[156] it permits no deductions as
to chronology. The words introducing the verses translated from
Homer at *Diu.* II. 63, *ut nos otiosi conuertimus*, must have been
intended to suggest that they were made during the period of
political idleness forced on Cicero by Caesar's victory in the
civil war.[157] The words which discuss the verses translated from
tragedy at *TD* II. 20–5, *uidesne abundare me otio?...itaque postquam
adamaui hanc quasi senilem declamationem, studiose equidem utor nostris
poetis; sed sicubi illi defecerunt, uerti enim multa de Graecis, ne quo
ornamento in hoc genere disputationis careret Latina oratio*, are unfortunately of uncertain interpretation at a crucial point[158] but
they plainly were meant to imply that these and similar verses
had been made since Caesar's victory and for the very purpose
of equipping the philosophical dialogues. One could suppose
either that Cicero made the verses, as he seems to claim, within
the dramatic situations of the two dialogues, from the actual
texts of Homer and the tragedians without thinking of the specific
uses to which they were to be put or, as I think more likely, that
he made them straight from the texts of the professional treatises
upon which he based his dialogues. The notion that they come
from the period of his youth is quite untenable.

It is unlikely that Clitomachus, or whoever it was who provided
Cicero with the Academic argument of the second book *de
diuinatione*,[159] quoted the verses of Homer translated at II. 63.
Heeringa[160] is so far right to make Cicero here an independent
agent. The Stoic author of the source of the first book,[161] however,

156. See above, pp. 73–4.
157. Cf. *Ac.* I. 11, II. 6, *Fin.* I. 10, *TD* I. 1, v. 4–5, *ND* I. 7–9, *Diu.* II. 1–7, *de Off.* II. 2–7, III. 1–4.
158. Some editors mark a lacuna after *defecerunt*. Pohlenz interprets *enim* as representing a wave of the hand.
159. R. Hoyer, *Rh. Mus.* 53 (1898), 37ff., argued that Antiochus was Cicero's source. Cicero himself says that the argument against astrology in II. 87–97 comes from the Stoic Panaetius.   160. See above, n. 147.
161. T. Schiche's view (*De fontibus librorum Ciceronis qui sunt de diuinatione* (Dissertation, Jena 1875), p. 25) that Posidonius was the source seems generally

threw poetry about quite liberally and very likely quoted the
Homeric verses in question in what lies underneath 1. 72–9.[162]
Cicero may have translated them as he adapted this argument
but then decided that, while it was appropriate for his brother
Quintus to quote such of his poems as were already in the public
domain and might be memorized by admirers, namely the
Prognostica (quoted at 1. 13–15), the *de consulatu suo libri* (quoted
at 1. 17–22) and the *Marius* (quoted at 1. 106), Quintus could not
plausibly extemporize at such length[163] or draw on products of
earlier poetic activity. The translated verses, accordingly, would
have been kept for his own imagined reply to Quintus, to the
satisfaction of literary if not of philosophical[164] realism. The
mistaken attribution of the verses to a speech by Agememnon[165]
and the way in which Homer's emphasis on the prophecy of
victory is replaced in translation with one on that of nine years'
campaigning[166] suggest positively that an isolated passage in a
philosophical account of divination rather than a whole text of
the *Iliad* was Cicero's immediate source. The τέρας is treated in
verse after verse as a Roman *augurium oblatiuum* portending evil[167]
while Calchas θεοπροπέων is made to obscure the identification
of the devouring serpent with the conquering Achaean army[168]

accepted. K. Reinhardt, *Poseidonios* (Munich 1921), p. 422, has some reser-
vations.

162. Cf. 1. 72 *alia autem subito ex tempore coniectura explicantur ut apud Homerum
Calchas qui ex passerum numero belli Troiani annos auguratus est.*

163. He is made to translate single verses at 1. 52 and 1. 81.

164. The quantity of verses quoted in the second book drops to the
predictable level when one excludes these verses and those requoted from the
first book (45 ~ 19; 104 ~ 132; 112 ~ 66–7). The sceptical sentiments quoted
from the poets are meant not so much to enforce the Academic argument
itself as to form an ironic reply to Quintus' frequent appeals to poetic authority.
A Euripidean verse is introduced at II. 12 as *quidam Graecus uulgaris...uersus*;
the original verse is referred to as a παροιμία when quoted in support of
a similar sceptical argument at Plut. *Mor.* 399a but attributed to Euripides
in the course of the dogmatic argument at *Mor.* 432c.

165. See above, p. 77.

166. Cf. the wording of the philosophical argument: 1. 72 *ex passerum
numero belli Troiani annos auguratus est*, II. 63 *apud Homerum Calchantem dixisti ex
passerum numero belli Troiani annos auguratum*, II. 65 *quae tandem ista auguratio est
ex passeribus annorum potius quam aut mensium aut dierum?*

167. See below, pp. 105f.

168. *Nam quot auis taetro mactatas dente uidetis | tot nos ad Troiam belli
exanclabimus annos | quae decumo cadet et poena satiabit Achiuos* could hardly have
been written with much attention to *Il.* II. 326–9 ὡς οὗτος κατὰ τέκνα

and to make prominent both the horror of the serpent's attack[169] and the sufferings the campaign will bring.[170]

The thesis criticized by Cicero in the second book of the *disputationes Tusculanae*, namely *dolorem existumo maximum malorum omnium*, was one repulsive to both the Academics and the Stoics. Although Cicero maintains his customary formal Academic pose, he drew many of his arguments, most scholars would agree,[171] from a Stoic source. His several attempts to argue the antithesis with reference to the behaviour of the heroes of tragic poetry ill consort with the conventional Academic diatribe in II. 27 against the deleterious effects had upon morality by the stories of the poets.[172]

Sandwiched between a summary account of the various general philosophical doctrines on pain (II. 15–16) and the main discourse (II. 28ff.) is an assault on the supposed Epicurean doctrine that the wise man will get pleasure out of being tortured.[173] Cicero argues that not only such relative poltroons as the Accian Philoctetes but even the Hercules of Sophocles and the Prometheus of Pythagoras' pupil Aeschylus express anguish and despair as a result of physical torture. The Accian Philoctetes appears twice elsewhere in argument representing rather more fairly Epicurus' view of pain, at *TD* II. 31–3 and *Fin.* II. 92–5, both passages

φάγε στρουθοῖο καὶ αὐτήν, | ὀκτώ, ἀτὰρ μήτηρ ἐνάτη ἦν, ἣ τέκε τέκνα, | ὡς ἡμεῖς τοσσαῦτ' ἔτεα πτολεμίξομεν αὖθι, τῷ δεκάτῳ δὲ πόλιν αἱρήσομεν εὐρυάγυιαν.

169. For *taeter* (~ nothing in Greek) of unfavourable portents cf. Livy XXII. 9. 8.

170. For *exanclari* (~ πτολεμίξομεν) of enduring time with difficulty cf. Enn. *tr.* 90.

171. Cf. O. Heine, G. Zietzschmann, and M. Pohlenz, as cited above, n. 148, H. Uri, *Cicero und die epikureische Philosophie* (Dissertation, Munich 1914), pp. 74f., R. Philippson, *Rh. Mus.* 78 (1929), 353f., R. Kassel, *Untersuchungen zur griechischen und römischen Konsolationsliteratur* (Munich 1958), p. 25. Those who posit Academic sources (e.g. K. Hartfelder, *De Cicerone Epicureae doctrinae interprete* (Dissertation, Heidelberg 1875), pp. 43ff., R. Hirzel, *Untersuchungen zu Cicero's philosophischen Schriften* III (Leipzig 1883), pp. 406ff.) imagine these sources heavily infected with Stoicism.

172. Cf. Plat. *Rep.* 398a.

173. What Epicurus actually said was κἂν στρεβλωθῇ ὁ σοφός, εἶναι αὐτὸν εὐδαίμονα (fr. 601; cf. Aristot. *Eth. Nic.* VII. 14 οἱ δὲ τὸν τροχιζόμενον ... εὐδαίμονα φάσκοντες εἶναι ... ἢ ἑκόντες ἢ ἄκοντες οὐδὲν λέγουσι and the parallel Stoic doctrine, μηδὲν κωλύειν φασὶ πρὸς εὐδαιμονίαν τὰ ἔξωθεν ἀλλ' εἶναι τὸν σπουδαῖον μακάριον, κἂν ὁ Φαλάριδος ταῦρος ἔχῃ καιόμενον [*SVF* III. 586]). Fr. 598 (ὅτε μέντοι στρεβλοῦται, ἔνθα καὶ μύζει καὶ οἰμώζει) makes the erroneousness of Cicero's discourse quite clear.

formally Academic in tone but very probably drawn from Stoic sources;[174] in them Philoctetes is offered as an example of the pusillanimous person whose troubles could not be helped by the kind of advice given by Epicurus. Heine and Zietschmann[175] derived the argument of *TD* II. 16–25 from a Stoic source which quoted only a play about Philoctetes[176] and the long verse translations of speeches in Sophocles' Τραχίνιαι and Aeschylus' Προμηθεὺς λυόμενος from work done in Cicero's youth. Pohlenz[177] argued that Cicero himself botched *TD* II. 16–25 together from what he had already written at *Fin.* II. 92–5 with the principal aim of showing off his abilities as a translator of verse.

Against Pohlenz I should argue that Cicero was not alone in so misinterpreting Epicurus' doctrine on pain,[178] that he did not have the same pride in his versions of Homer and the tragedians as he had in his published translation of the Φαινόμενα,[179] that the tone of admiration for the poets[180] and their creations[181] perceptible in the very argument of *TD* II. 19–25 is quite inconsistent with the general polemic of II. 27 and must come from Cicero's non-Academic source rather than the literary superstructure; finally that both the Sophoclean and the Aeschylean passages seem to have been translated with as much attention to the context in which they appear as to their actual wording. Hercules' intensely dramatic baring of his body to all present on stage and in the theatre[182] is omitted as being either irrelevant to the argument or offensive to the audience of the dialogue.[183]

174. On *TD* II. 31–3 see above, n. 171. *Fin.* II. 86–108 was thought by Madvig (ed.³ p. 287) to come from Chrysippus; by Zietzschmann (*De Tusc. font.* p. 8) to come from Panaetius; by Hartfelder (*De Cic. int.* pp. 21ff.), Hirzel (*Untersuchungen* II (Leipzig 1882), pp. 654ff.), Lörcher (*Das Fremde*, pp. 64ff.), Uri (*Cicero*, pp. 54ff.) and R. Philippson (*RE* 7Ai (1939), 1137ff.) to come from a heavily Stoicizing Antiochus.

175. See above, n. 148.

176. It was probably through oversight that Zietzschmann thought Cicero's source to have quoted Accius.   177. *Hermes* 44 (1909), 24.

178. Cf. Sen. *Epist.* LXVI. 18, LXVII. 15, Lactant. *Inst. diu.* III. 17. 5, III. 17. 42, III. 27. 5.

179. See above, p. 73.

180. Cf. II. 23 *ueniat Aeschylus, non poeta solum sed etiam Pythagoreus*.

181. Allowances are made even for Philoctetes' moaning; see II. 19.

182. Vv. 1078–80.

183. For the Roman attitude to nudity see Cic. *Rep.* IV. 4, *TD* IV. 70; even fathers and sons did not bathe together (see Cic. *de Off.* I. 129, Val. Max. II. 1. 7).

His threat to mutilate Deianira[184] and his very vocal expressions of pain[185] are likewise omitted in order to make him a more sympathetic personage.[186] His plea to Hades to receive him[187] is sacrificed to the well-known story of his admission to heaven.[188] Like a true Stoic he is made to claim spiritual as well as physical powers of endurance.[189] The fully divine Titan Prometheus is made to crave death in just the same way as the mortal Philoctetes and the demigod Hercules do and as a Roman statesman[190] or Stoic wise man[191] would do in similar circumstances and a god could not.[192]

The Aeschylean Philoctetes,[193] the Aeschylean Prometheus[194] and the Sophoclean Hercules[195] all appeared in Greek philosophical discussions of pain. I should suppose that at *Fin.* II. 92–5 and *TD* II. 31–3 Cicero adapted an argument against Epicurus in which Aeschylus' crying Philoctetes figured and substituted the Accian hero;[196] behind *TD* II. 16–25 lay another argument against Epicurus invoking a trio of tragic personages,[197] one of which had a well-known Roman version while the other two

184. Vv. 1068–9.   185. Vv. 1078–84.
186. See Cic. *TD* II. 48 on the impropriety of excessive moaning.
187. V. 1085.
188. Cf. II. 20 *cum inmortalitatem ipsa morte quaerebat.* Sophocles' Τραχίνιαι ignores this story. From the third century onwards Hercules regularly appeared in lists of men who had obtained divinity because of their deeds on earth; cf. Aet. *Plac.* I. 6. 15 (*Dox. Gr.* p. 297; depending ultimately on Chrysippus' Περὶ θεῶν), Cic. *TD* I. 28, *ND* II. 62, III. 39, *Leg* II. 19 et al.
189. Cf. *corpore exanclata atque animo pertuli* ~ v. 1047 καὶ χερσὶ καὶ νώτοισι μοχθήσας ἐγώ.
190. See Cic. *Scaur.* III, *Sest.* XLVIII.
191. See Chrysippus ap. Plut. *Mor.* 1042d, Diog. Laert. VII. 130. The Academics (cf. Plat. *Phaed.* 62b; also, however, *Leg.* IX. 873c) and the Peripatetics (cf. Aristot. *Eth. Nic.* v. 15) were generally hostile to suicide. For the attitudes attributed to the various schools in Cicero's own day see Plut. *Brut.* XL, *Cat. min.* LXVII.
192. See below, p. 110.   193. Cf. Plut. *Mor.* 1087f.
194. Cf. Plut. *Mor.* 102b.
195. Cf. Diog. Laert. x. 137 (quoting Epicurus).
196. This does not mean that Cicero knew anything of Aeschylus' play or believed that Accius had translated it. For modern controversy about Accius' original see T. Zieliński, *Eos* 17 (1911), 129ff., W.-H. Friedrich, *Hermes* 76 (1941), 121ff.
197. For three mythological examples see *Rep.* I. 30, *Fin.* I. 65 (~ Plut. *Mor.* 93e), *Ac.* II. 88, *TD* IV. 52, IV. 49–50, v. 8, *de Off.* III. 94–5. There is perhaps also design in the sequence mortal (Philoctetes), demigod (Hercules), god (Prometheus).

did not and therefore required translating work from Cicero.
The former argument could have been either Stoic or Academic;
the latter, with its warm approval of Hercules and tolerance
for Philoctetes and Prometheus, could have only been Stoic.

VI. THE EDITING OF THE TRANSLATIONS OF GREEK VERSES FOUND IN CICERO'S PHILOSOPHICAL WORKS: SOME DIFFICULTIES

It has been established that any verse quoted directly in
Cicero's philosophical dialogues and not accompanied by a
specific attribution comes from the stock of Latin poems known
to the well-educated in the middle of the first century B.C.; those
verses, on the other hand, which are attributed to a Greek poet
or which occur in an anecdote about persons speaking Greek
were in all likelihood translated by Cicero at the time when he
was adapting the dialogues from Greek treatises which quoted
the original verses. The first editor of all Cicero's works to concern
himself with the fragments of those lost, Lambinus,[198] printed
verses only from poems known to have been separately published,
namely the *Aratus*, the *Prognostica*, the *Marius* and the *de consulatu
suo libri*, and did not separate the other verses which appear in
the philosophical dialogues from the edited texts of these dialogues.
C. F. A. Nobbe[199] and those who followed him[200] ought not to
have departed from this very sound procedure. Collectors of the
fragments of lost Roman poems, like E. Baehrens,[201] or of
Cicero's verses, like W. W. Ewbank[202] and A. Traglia,[203] could

198. *M. Tullii Ciceronis opera omnia quae extant*, IV (Paris 1566).

199. *M. Tullii Ciceronis...opera ex recensione I. A. Ernestii* (Leipzig 1827).

200. J. C. Orelli, *M. Tullii Ciceronis opera quae supersunt omnia ac deperditorum
fragmenta*, IV ii (Zürich 1828), pp. 514ff., printed only those Homeric verses
which occur at *Diu.* II. 63, *TD* III. 63, *TD* III. 18, *Fin.* v. 49, August. *Ciu.* v.
8. J. G. Baiter (see C. L. Kayser and J. G. Baiter, *M. Tullii Ciceronis opera
quae supersunt omnia*, XI (Leipzig 1869), pp. 89ff.) and C. F. W. Mueller
(*M. Tulli Ciceronis scripta quae manserunt omnia*, IV iii (Leipzig 1879), pp. 350ff.)
added other Homeric verses, the tragic verses and various oracles, proverbs
etc.

201. *Fragmenta poetarum Romanorum* (Leipzig 1886), pp. 306–15.

202. *The Poems of Cicero* (London 1933).

203. *Ciceronis poetica fragmenta* (Rome 1950), vol. I, pp. 29–41.

justify ignoring the distinction with the excuse of their readers' convenience.[204] The behaviour of W. Morel,[205] however, as of Nobbe and Orelli, in printing the Homeric but not the tragic verses alongside those of the published poems is to be condemned from every point of view.

A number of passages have caused or could cause difficulty.

An anecdote is told at *TD* II. 60 in which the Stoic philosopher Cleanthes quotes a verse 'ex Epigonis'. Some collectors of the verses translated by Cicero from the Greek, like H. Stephanus[206] and V. Clavel,[207] and some collectors of all Cicero's verses[208] have excluded this verse, *audisne haec Amphiarae sub terram abdite?* from their collections while some editors of early tragedy[209] have laid claim to it, F. H. Bothe[210] actually assigning it to the Latin *Epigoni* mentioned by Cicero at *Opt. gen.* XVIII and *de Off.* I. 114 and frequently quoted by the grammarians as by Accius.[211] If the primary quoter were a Roman a doubt might be permissible,[212] but since Cicero represents himself as quoting Cleanthes the verse should be regarded as one fashioned by Cicero on the basis of a verse from one of the Greek Ἐπίγονοι plays quoted in the source of the anecdote. Where Cicero substitutes an already known Roman verse for a Greek one quoted in an anecdote he draws attention to the fact.[213]

Exactly parallel is the reference to Theophrastus' quotation of Chaeremon's τύχη τὰ θνητῶν πράγματ', οὐκ εὐβουλία[214] at *TD* v. 25. Fortunate accident rather than intelligent design probably excluded the senarius *uitam regit fortuna non sapientia* from

---

204. As perhaps also G. Pascoli, *Epos* I[5] (Livorno 1938), who prints the Homeric pieces after the *de consulatu suo libri* and the *Marius* (pp. 69–71; see p. lviii for a hazy account of the status of the Homeric verses).

205. *Fragmenta poetarum Latinorum* (Leipzig 1927), pp. 73–9.

206. *Ciceronianum Lexicon Graecolatinum* (Geneva 1557).

207. *De M. T. Cicerone Graecorum interprete* (Paris 1868), pp. 54–65.

208. Baiter, C. F. W. Mueller, Baehrens, Traglia.

209. M. A. Delrius, *Syntagma tragoediae Latinae* (Antwerp 1593), p. 156, P. Scriverius, *Collectanea ueterum tragicorum...fragmenta* (Leiden 1620), p. 168.

210. *Poetae scenici Latinorum V: fragmenta* (Halberstadt 1823), p. 200.

211. Charis. p. 376. 11, Non. p. 16. 4 et al.

212. Cf. *de Off.* III. 82, where, however, Cicero makes it clear that he himself translates Caesar's quotation of Eurip. *Phoen.* 524–5.

213. Cf. *Deiot.* xxv and above, p. 76.

214. Cf. Plut. *Mor.* 97c and A. Nauck, *TGF*[2], p. 782. See now Menan. *Aspis* 411.

the early collections of tragic fragments. H. Stephanus[215] regarded
it as a Ciceronian verse but recent collectors[216] for no apparent
good reason ignore it.

At *Diu.* II. 133 Cicero quotes in his own voice the riddling
hexameter *terrigenam herbigradam domiportam sanguine cassum*. Baiter
printed this as a verse of Cicero's own making and later editors
all follow him.[217] Its manner of quotation, however, is no different
from that of many verses of Ennius and Lucilius in other parts
of the dialogue.[218] The γρῖφος quoted by Athenaeus (II. 63b),
ὑλογενής, ἀνάκανθος, ἀναίματος, ὑγροκέλευθος, may have stood
in Cicero's source; if Cicero had been compelled to translate this
himself he would have been a little more faithful to the Greek
wording. Ennius or Lucilius or some other early poet should be
regarded as the author of the Latin hexameter.[219]

At *ND* II. 154–67 it is argued that all things in nature were
designed for the benefit of mankind. Most scholars would agree[220]
that Cicero got the details of the argument from Posidonius.
After the suitability of the ox's neck for bearing the yoke and of
its shoulders and flanks for drawing the plough is remarked at
II. 159, a kind of parenthesis appears about the fabulous golden
generation of mankind and the fact that this generation refrained
from killing the useful ox. Since Posidonius is known to have
allegorized the golden generation of the poets as that stage of
civilization when philosophers ruled[221] it is likely that Cicero
drew this parenthesis from his Stoic source. In the middle of it
there comes without attribution a not-quite-accurate version of
vv. 129–32 of Aratus' Φαινόμενα:

215. *Lexicon*, p. 150. Cf. Clavel, *De M. T. Cicerone*, p. 67.
216. Baiter, Mueller, Baehrens, Morel, Ewbank, Traglia.
217. Cf. also Marx on Lucil. *dub.* 1377.
218. Cf. I. 29, I. 42, I. 65, I. 66–7, I. 80, I. 114, II. 30, II. 115.
219. G. J. Vossius, *De uitiis sermonis et glossematis Latino-Barbaris libri IV*
(Amsterdam 1645), I, ch. 28, and E. F. Corpet in his 1845 edition of Lucilius
gave it to the latter; so too E. Baehrens, *Frag. poet. Rom.* p. 258 (but see
p. 314).
220. Cf., among older students, Hirzel, *Untersuchungen* I, p. 224,
P. Schwenke, *NJbb* 119 (1879), 129ff. and Reinhardt, *Die Quellen*, pp. 54–5.
Among more recent students, however, J. Heinemann, *Poseidonios' meta-
physische Schriften* II (Breslau 1928), p. 219, argues strongly against Posidonian
authorship.
221. See Sen. *Epist.* xc. 5.

> ferrea[222] tum uero proles exorta repente est
> ausaque funestum prima est fabricarier ensem
> et gustare manu iunctum domitumque iuuencum.

Editors since Lambinus[223] have given these three verses to Cicero's published translation of the Φαινόμενα; perhaps rightly, since this translation is quoted at length earlier in Balbus' discourse[224] and since in some degree it probably possessed the status of a well-known classic.[225] Nevertheless there are at least two other possibilities worth considering.

Roman poets of the classical period localized the golden generation of Greek mythology in Latium[226] and often spoke as if there had existed only two generations, one of gold and a second of iron.[227] It is not impossible that they depend on Ennius' account of early Italy[228] and that the three verses in question come from this account.[229]

The second possibility is that the verses have been interpolated into our text of the *De natura deorum libri* from some younger poem like the *Epimenis* of Varro Atacinus.[230] Like many other sets of verses which appear in the dialogues[231] they could be excluded without damaging the surrounding discourse, in this case *quibus cum terrae subigerentur fissione glebarum ab illo aureo genere, ut poetae loquuntur, uis nulla umquam adferebatur. tanta putabatur utilitas percipi e bubus ut eorum uisceribus uesci scelus haberetur.*[232] This in itself is

222. *Ferrea proles* corresponds ill with Aratus' χαλκείη γενεή.
223. Vol. 4, p. 448, following G. Morelius, *Arati Solensis Phaenomena et Prognostica* (Paris 1559), p. 3.
224. II. 104ff.
225. See above, p. 73.
226. Cf. Virg. *Aen.* VI. 791–3, VIII. 313–29. For Saturn taking refuge from Jupiter in Italy cf. Ovid, *Fast.* I. 235–40.
227. Cf. Virg. *Aen.* VIII. 313–29, Ov. *Met.* XV. 96–142, 260.
228. Cf. *Ann.* 25, 26. In the *Euhemerus* Ennius brought Saturn to Italy in his flight from Jupiter (95ff.).
229. The Pythagorean slant of Ennius' poem is well known (cf. Porph. Hor. *Epist.* II. 1. 51). Aratus' account of the succession of the generations seems to have been popular with Pythagorean proponents of vegetarianism (cf. Plut. *Mor.* 998a).
230. See the verses quoted by Servius on Virg. *Georg.* I. 375 and Arat. 942ff.
231. Cf. *Rep.* I. 30 (Enn. *tr.* 199–201), *TD* II. 23 (Acc. *tr.* 533–6), *TD* III. 67 (Eurip. fr. 821), *Diu.* II. 30 (Enn. *tr.* 201).
232. Howind, *De ratione citandi*, p. 16 is wrong to parallel *TD* II. 44, where Pacuv. *tr.* 202 *iteradum eadem ista mihi* replaces an ordinary request for clarification.

not significant, but whereas other parenthetic verses elucidate
further the point being made, these merely make an awkward
repetition. Furthermore the phrase *ut poetae loquuntur* suggests
that Cicero intended to make no reference to any particular
poet's handling of the myth.[233] An interpolator could, of course,
as easily have inserted verses from Ennius' *Annales* or even from
Cicero's own *Aratus*. Against the latter hypothesis is the fact that
the verses make the warring, meat-eating generation one of iron;
a poet describing quickly the history of a particular place seems
a more likely author than one translating Aratus' account of
the successive mortal generations of gold, silver and bronze.

H. Columna[234] gave the verses introduced at *TD* I. 115 with
qua est sententia in Cresphonte usus Euripides to Ennius' *Cresphontes*,
Delrius[235] to an unknown tragedy. R. Stephanus[236] gave those
introduced at *TD* II. 20 with *quas hic uoces apud Sophoclem in
Tracchiniis edit...ait ille* to an unknown tragedy, Scaliger[237] to
an alleged *Trachiniae* of Accius, thus imposing upon Delrius,[238]
Scriverius[239] and Bothe.[240] Scriverius[241] and Bothe[242] gave those
introduced at *TD* III. 76 with *ut Prometheus ille Aeschyli cui
cum dictum esset...respondit* to the *Prometheus* of Accius, a play
from which two small fragments are quoted in our sources. One
of these, containing five uninformative words, *tum profusus flamine
hiberno gelus*,[243] seems to have been used by Flavius Caper in his

233. Cf. *Harusp. resp.* xx, lix, *S. Rosc.* lxvi, *ND* I. 112, *TD* II. 34, IV. 71,
v. 115, *de Off.* III. 97. The septenarius *ob scelera animique impotentiam et super-
biloquentiam* stands to the context of *TD* IV. 35, *pendet animi. quam uim mali
significantes poetae inpendere apud inferos saxum Tantalo faciunt*, in a similar way
and may itself be an interpolation. Ennius' phrase *pater diuomque hominumque*
(*Ann.* 581) was based on the Homeric πατὴρ ἀνδρῶν τε θεῶν τε, a fact which
explains the variation at *ND* II. 4 and II. 64.

234. *Q. Ennii poetae...fragmenta* (Naples 1590), p. 398.

235. *Syntagma* p. 159. Scriverius (*Collectanea*, pp. 14, 174) and Bothe (*Poetae
Scenici Latinorum*, pp. 40, 283) dithered.

236. *Fragmenta poetarum ueterum Latinorum* (Geneva 1564), p. 378.

237. *Coniectanea in M. Terentium Varronem de lingua Latina* (Paris 1565),
pp. 178–9.

238. *Syntagma*, p. 148.   239. *Collectanea*, p. 147.

240. *Poetae scenici Latinorum*, p. 245.   241. *Collectanea*, p. 143.

242. *Poetae scenici Latinorum*, p. 239. Cf. also *Aeschyli dramata quae supersunt*
(Leipzig 1805), p. 584.

243. The fragment may refer to Prometheus' place of punishment; cf.
Aesch. *P.V.* 993–4 λευκοπτέρῳ δὲ νιφάδι καὶ βροντήμασι | χθονίοις κυκάτω
πάντα καὶ ταρασσέτω.

de sermone dubio libri to exemplify masculine *gelus* and to have
passed from here to Nonius' article on *gelu* at p. 207. 32ff.[244] and
perhaps to Priscian's discussion of neuter nouns in *-u* at *Gramm.*
II. 210. 19ff.[245] The other, †tu mei† *uolans pinnata cauda nostram
adulat sanguinem*, of which at least the last five words appear in
the same order in the tragic senarii introduced at *TD* II. 23 with
ueniat Aeschylus...fert apud eum Prometheus...dicit haec, occurs in
Nonius' article on *adulatio* at p. 17. 2ff.[246] There has been, as
a result, continuing controversy to the present day about the
origin of the verses at *TD* II. 23–5. All collectors of Cicero's
verses follow V. Clavel[247] in claiming them for the orator–poet,
as do most who write about his verses[248] and most editors and
students of Aeschylus' fragmentary tragedies.[249] Nevertheless

244. On the structure of this and the contiguous articles see W. M. Lindsay,
Nonius Marcellus' Dictionary of Republican Latin (Oxford 1901), p. 61, *Philologus*
64 (1905), 438. L. Strzelecki, *Eos* 34 (1932–3), 113, *De Flauio Capro Nonii
auctore* (Kraków 1936), p. 30, shows fairly conclusively that Caper is the
source.

245. The entry in Priscian illustrates a word, *gelus*, omitted from the
introductory list and interrupts most illogically a series of consecutive entries
from Cicero's *Aratus* (149, 261f., 279f., 293, 332f.). It could originally have
been written as a marginal scholium against v. 292 of a copy of the *Aratus*
(*quam gelidum ualido de pectore frigus anhelans*). The *Lucretius* and *Accius in Troadibus*
entries disturb the logic of Priscian's arrangement almost as much and cannot
be similarly explained away. I should therefore prefer to attribute all three
entries to a hasty consultation of a second source, perhaps Caper. For Caper
as the source of Priscian's knowledge of old Latin poetry see L. Jeep, *Philologus*
67 (1908), 12ff., 68 (1909), 1ff.

246. For full discussion of this article see below, pp. 93ff.

247. *De M. T. Cicerone*, pp. 45ff.

248. M. Gündel, *De Ciceronis poetae arte capita tria* (Dissertation, Leipzig
1907), p. 37, C. Atzert, *De Cicerone interprete Graecorum* (Dissertation, Göttingen
1908), pp. 30ff., Putz, *De Ciceronis bibliotheca*, p. 33, E. Fraenkel, *Iktus und Akzent
im lateinischen Sprechvers* (Berlin 1928), pp. 316ff., Malcovati, *Cicerone*, pp. 64,
272, 276. Since my paper was written there has appeared J. Soubiran's
important 'Accius ou Cicéron? (à propos de *Tusc.* II, 10, 23–25)', *RPh* ser. iii, 44
(1970), 257–73.

249. Cf. C. G. Schütz, *Aeschyli fragmenta* (London 1782), p. 91, G. Hermann,
De Aeschyli Prometheo soluto dissertatio (Leipzig 1828), p. 19 (= *Opusc.* IV 271),
G. Dindorf, *Aeschyli tragoediae superstites et deperditarum fragmenta* (Oxford 1832),
p. 284, F. G. Welcker, *Die griechischen Tragödien* (Bonn 1839–41), p. 1387,
A. Nauck, *Tragicorum Graecorum Fragmenta²* (Leipzig 1888), p. 64, N. Wecklein,
Äschylos. Prometheus nebst den Bruchstücken des Προμηθεὺς λυόμενος *für den
Schulgebrauch erklärt³* (Leipzig 1893), pp. 125ff., H. Weir Smyth, *Aeschylus*,
vol. II (London 1926), p. 448, G. Thomson, *Aeschylus. The Prometheus Bound*
(Cambridge 1932), pp. 178f., H. J. Mette, *Die Fragmente der Tragödien des*

many editors of the remains of Roman stage tragedy[250] follow R. Stephanus[251] in assigning them to Accius' *Prometheus*; likewise a number of serious students of Aeschylus,[252] Accius[253] and Cicero.[254] Controversy about the verses at *TD* I. 115, II. 20, III. 76, on the other hand, has ceased.

The positive case for Ciceronian authorship of the verses in question is overwhelmingly strong. The conversation which follows their quotation implies, if it does not directly state, that they were unknown to the readership which Cicero expected for the *Tusculanae disputationes*,[255] i.e. that they were not from the pen of one of the famous Latin tragedians of the second century.[256] Their manner of being introduced (*apud eum* [*Aeschylum*] *Prometheus*) distinguishes them absolutely[257] from such as are introduced with, e.g., *ille apud Accium pastor* (*ND* II. 89) or *illa apud Ennium nutrix* (*TD* III. 63) or *apud Ennium Vestalis illa* (*Diu.* I. 40). The words of the following discourse, *uerti enim*[258] *multa de Graecis ne quo ornamento*

Aischylos (Berlin 1959), p. 118, A. D. Fitton-Brown, 'Prometheia', *JHS* 79 (1959), 57, C. J. Herington, 'Aeschylus, Prometheus Unbound, Fr. 193', *TAPhA* 92 (1961), 239ff.

250. Cf. Delrius, *Syntagma*, p. 146, Scriverius, *Collectanea*, p. 142, Bothe, *Poetae scenici Latinorum*, p. 239, A. Klotz, *Scaenicorum Romanorum Fragmenta* I (Munich), pp. 254f. (see also *PhW* 50 (1930), 1140–1).

251. *Fragmenta poetarum* (above, n. 236), pp. 36, 429.

252. Cf. U. von Wilamowitz-Moellendorff, *Aeschyli Tragoediae* (Berlin 1914), p. 73, *Aischylos. Interpretationen* (Berlin 1914), p. 127, F. Stoessl, *Die Trilogie des Aischylos* (Vienna 1937), p. 131.

253. Cf. Scaliger, *Coniectanea*, pp. 178–9, G. Przychocki, *Eos* 32 (1929), 215, L. Strzelecki, *Eos* 49 fasc. i (1957–8), 187.

254. Cf. M. Grollmus, *De M. Tullio Cicerone poeta* (Dissertation, Königsberg 1887), p. 51 (doubtfully).

255. The dramatic date of the dialogue is 16–20 June 45 and Cicero's interlocutor a young man of good education.

256. See above, p. 74.

257. G. Przychocki, *Eos* 32 (1929), 215, *PhW* 52 (1932), 159, argues that if we did not have Varro's testimony (*Ling.* VII. 11) we should attribute to Cicero the four anapaestic dimeters which follow *quo modo fert apud eum Prometheus dolorem quem excipit ob furtum Lemnium* (Scaliger persuaded Delrius and Scriverius of the link with Varro; Bothe, however, gave some of the words quoted to Accius' *Prometheus*). Not so. They are an incidental decoration of the main discourse of a type common in the philosophical dialogues. The awkwardness of their syntactical connection and their lack of fresh information suggest that they might even be an interpolation of the type discussed above, p. 89. Whoever put them in the text, whether an interpolator or Cicero himself, had his mind full of the *Philoctetes* (cf. the earlier quotation at II. 19).

258. On the textual difficulty here see above, n. 158.

in hoc genere disputationis careret Latina oratio, certainly do not refer directly or exclusively to the verses[259] but would have little point if Ciceronian poetry had not appeared in the immediate neighbourhood.

Those who deny the verses in question to Cicero do not seem to realize that their view entails the possibility of the verses at *TD* I. 115, II. 20–2, II. 60, III. 59, III. 67, III. 71, III, 76, IV. 63, *ND* II. 65, *de Off.* III. 108 not being by Cicero either but rather by some old dramatic poet and makes inescapably circular any attempt to argue about the verbal and metrical style of the verses. In any case, even if the dispute could be restricted to these verses alone, the presence therein of Accian features would have no probative value. As a rule the hexameters of Cicero's *Aratus*, *Prognostica*, *Marius* and *de consulatu suo libri* and of the versions of Homer in the philosophical works ape the style of the old epic[260] and one would expect to find a parallel state of affairs in tragic senarii composed by him.[261]

The entry in Nonius' article on *adulatio* can carry weight in favour of Accian authorship of the verses of *TD* II. 23–5 only while the rationale of Cicero's methods of citing poetry is not appreciated. Nevertheless the entry does present a problem. Many scholars have tried to solve it but none of their solutions seems fully satisfactory. I shall examine these solutions before proposing a new one of my own.

Turnebus[262] suggested that Cicero deliberately incorporated into a version of the Aeschylean Prometheus' account of his incarceration and punishment the words from Accius' *Prometheus* which Nonius quotes. A number of scholars have either accepted this suggestion fully[263] or treated it as a plausible

259. Przychocki, *PhW* 52 (1932), 159–60, is so far right to argue against the point made by Fraenkel at *Gnomon* 6 (1930), 663.

260. See M. Gündel, *De Ciceronis poetae arte*, pp. 42ff., R. Wreschniok, *De Cicerone Lucretioque Ennii imitatoribus* (Dissertation, Breslau 1907), pp. 3ff.

261. On the style of the two large batches of senarii at *TD* II. 20–5 see E. Lindholm, *Stilistische Studien* (Lund 1931), p. 99, Fraenkel, *Iktus und Akzent*, pp. 316–20, below, pp. 101ff. J. Soubiran, *RPh* ser. iii, 44 (1970), 263ff., detects a number of differences between the style of the second batch and that of Accius' tragic fragments.

262. *Aduersariorum libri XII* (Paris 1564), II 9.

263. Cf. J. Mercerus in his second edition of Nonius (Paris 1614), p. 647, V. Clavel, *De M. T. Cicerone*, p. 47, O. Ribbeck, 'corollaria', *Tragicorum*

one.[264] It is true that many Latin poets of Cicero's generation and the next repeated hemistichs and even whole verses from famous poems of the past in their own works[265] and very likely that Cicero's own *Aratus* contained Ennian hemistichs.[266] Sometimes there was a desire to ridicule the older poem, more often a spirit of emulation; the poet wished, by referring to the older poem, to make his readers aware of his ambition to surpass this poem in quality of thought, in elegance of language, versification and argumentative structure. Where, however, the versions of epic and tragedy in the philosophical works were concerned Cicero displayed what was for him an unusual degree of modesty.[267] Occasionally his memory of a phrase of one of the old poets replaced attention to the Greek text before him,[268] but he had no conscious desire to challenge comparison with them. Furthermore there is no great likelihood that Cicero knew the particular Accian tragedy quoted by the grammarians. If †tu mei† *uolans pinnata cauda nostrum adulat sanguinem* is a fragment of this tragedy, then it must have contained a description by Prometheus of what he was suffering at the talons and beak of the eagle, and if Cicero knew the tragedy then his failure to quote it *in extenso* at *TD* II. 23–5

*Romanorum Fragmenta*² (Leipzig 1871), p. lvii, *Die römische Tragödie im Zeitalter der Republik* (Leipzig 1875), p. 543.

264. Cf. M. Pohlenz, *Ciceronis Tusculanarum disputationum libri I et II erklärt von M. P.* (Leipzig 1912), p. 149, fasc. 44 of the Teubner Cicero (Leipzig 1918), p. 291.

265. Cf. Lucr. III. 1025 *lumina sis oculis etiam bonus Ancus reliquit* (~ Enn. *Ann.* 149 *postquam lumina sis oculis bonus Ancus reliquit*), III. 1035 *ossa dedit terrae proinde ac famul infimus esset* (~ Enn. *Ann.* 312–13), IV. 408–9 *uix absunt... uix etiam cursus quingentos saepe ueruti* (~ Enn. *Ann.* 353), VI. 357 *stellis fulgentibus apta* (~ Enn. *Ann.* 29, 159), VI. 856 *cum superum lumen* (~ Enn. *Ann.* 102), Varro Atacinus, *Argonaut.* fr. ap. Serv. Verg. *Aen.* X. 396 *semianimesque micant oculi lucemque requirunt* (~ Enn. *Ann.* 473), Hor. *Sat.* I. 2. 37–8 *audire est operae pretium, procedere recte | qui moechis non uoltis* (~ Enn. *Ann.* 465–6), II. 5. 41 *Furius hibernas cana niue conspuit Alpes* ('hic uersus Furi Bibaculi est' – Porphyrio). On Virgil's use of his predecessors see Macrob. *Sat.* VI. 1–5 and Servius, passim.

266. Cf. fr. 3. 2 *noctesque diesque* (= Enn. *Ann.* 334 ~ *Arat.* 20 πάντ' ἥματα), 101, 184 *spiritus austri* (= Enn. *Ann.* 443 ~ *Arat.* 321, 403), 104 *nocte serena* (= Enn. *Ann.* 396 ~ *Arat.* 323 καθαρῇ ἐνὶ νυκτί). Behind Cic. *Arat.* fr. 9. 5 *obstipum caput a tereti ceruice reflexum* (~ *Arat.* 58 λοξὸν δ' ἐστὶ κάρη), Lucr. I. 35 *tereti ceruice reposta* and Virg. *Aen.* VIII. 633 *tereti ceruice reflexa* there doubtless lies something Ennian (cf. *Ann.* 472 *caput a ceruice reuulsum*).

267. See above, p. 73.

268. See below, p. 103.

would contradict the statement of policy issued a little later: *studiose equidem utor nostris poetis sed sicubi illi defecerunt...* The great orator was surely not blind to truth and plausibility quite to that extent.

Jacobus Nicolaus of Loo[269] suggested that when Nonius made the entry *Accius Prometheo* †tu mei† *uolans pinnata cauda nostrum adulat sanguinem* at p. 17. 8, he had before him the text of the *Tusculanae disputationes* and that memory of the quotation of Accius' *Philoctetes* at II. 23 misled him as he was perusing the next set of verses quoted. Jacobus' suggestion was accepted by Davies,[270] Hermann,[271] and Ribbeck (at least for a time)[272] and although study of the arrangement of Nonius' dictionary cut the foundation from beneath this and similar suggestions as early as 1867,[273] it has been repeated by L. Mueller,[274] M. Pohlenz[275] and W. Kraus.[276]

The article on *adulatio* interrupts a sequence of articles whose leading quotations are drawn from the plays of Pomponius, no. 6 of the 41 sources postulated by W. M. Lindsay[277] for the dictionary. It is possible that the original leading quotation has been lost and replaced by the first extra quotation. This comes from no. 16 (Cic. *ND* II)[278] of the 41 sources; the next quotation comes from no. 20 (Cic. *de Off.* I); the following two, of Lucretius[279] and Accius, would come most probably from no. 27, an alpha-

269. *Epiphillidum libri*, VIII 6 (in J. Gruterus, *Lampas* v suppl. (Frankfurt 1606), pp. 586–7).

270. *M. Tullii Ciceronis Tusculanarum disputationum libri V* (Cambridge 1708).

271. *De Aeschyli Prometheo soluto dissertatio* (Leipzig 1828), p. 19 (= *Opusc.* IV 271).

272. *Tragicorum Latinorum Fragmenta* (Leipzig 1852), p. 300.

273. See A. Schottmüller, 'Ueber die Bestandteile des ersten Capitels des Nonius Marcellus', *Symbolae philologorum Bonnensium* (Leipzig 1864–7), pp. 807–32. Cf. P. Schmidt, *De Nonii Marcelli auctoribus grammaticis* (Leipzig 1868), pp. 65ff., 80ff.

274. On Nonius, p. 17. 8 (Leipzig 1888).

275. *Ciceronis Tusculanarum disputationum libri I et II erklärt*, p. 149.

276. *RE* 23 i (1957), 677.

277. *Nonius Marcellus' Dictionary*, pp. 7ff., 82ff.

278. There is a difficulty here in that source no. 16 is not used in the first book of the dictionary for leading quotations or elsewhere for extra quotations.

279. At p. 450. 8 the Lucretian verse is quoted with its book number, supposedly from source no. 35b (Gloss. iv). No pattern is apparent in the quotations of Lucretius without book number (pp. 103. 22, 158. 19, 197. 2, 229. 1, 245. 7, 310. 32, 408. 23, 453. 6, 458. 13).

betical list of verbs. There is only a remote possibility that the
Accius quotation comes from list 39 (Cic. *TD*), this list being
only twice used in the first book of the dictionary for 'extra'
quotations. Even if it did there would be no reason to make
Nonius himself responsible for the kind of error suggested by
Jacobus. Nonius never, so far as we can see, stopped in his hasty
process of excerption to mark the origin of an unattributed poetic
quotation in a work by Cicero. The dictionary as we have it
contains many pieces of old Republican poetry taken from works
by Cicero and simply labelled as Ciceronian.[280] The only way
to salvage Jacobus' theory would be to suppose that the author
of the glossary used by Nonius had a text of the *Tusculanae
disputationes* with a marginal scholium at II. 23 referring to an
account by Accius of the punishment of Prometheus and was
led into error by this scholium.[281] The Bodmer papyrus of
Menander's Σαμία (third century A.D.) has an obviously erroneous
reference to Euripides' Οἰδίπους in its margin at vv. 325–6, where
the speaker in fact quotes a tragedy set in Athens.

No solution to the problem is suggested by the many mechanical
errors arising from confusions and omissions in Nonius' listing
process.[282] To suppose that a piece of Cicero's *Tusculanae disputationes* consisting of a version of a piece of Aeschylus' Προμηθεὺς
λυόμενος got affixed through coincidence to the words introducing
a piece of Accius' *Prometheus* would stretch the bounds of coincidence beyond credibility.

Close examination of the transmitted text of the verses in
which Prometheus describes the eagle's mode of visitation reveals
a difficulty which might be solved along with that set by the
entry in Nonius' dictionary. The verses run

>   iam tertio me quoque funesto die   10
>   tristi aduolatu aduncis lacerans unguibus
>   Iouis satelles pastu dilaniat fero.
>   tum iecore opimo farta et satiata adfatim
>   clangorem fundit uastum et sublime aduolans
>   pinnata cauda nostrum adulat sanguinem.   15

280. See above, n. 108.
281. Cf. C. J. Herington, *TAPhA* 92 (1961), 245.
282. Lacunae are often postulated at pp. 75. 8, 90. 10, 116. 8, 170. 12,
176. 12, 209. 25, 223. 2, 479. 13, 515. 12 et alibi.

cum uero adesum inflatu renouatumst iecur
tum rursum taetros auida se ad pastus refert.

The words *tristi aduolatu aduncis lacerans unguibus* complicate unnecessarily the picture being presented and fit awkwardly into
the grammar of their sentence. Still it would be rash to delete
them, however much their deletion might improve the whole
passage. The words *et sublime aduolans pinnata cauda nostrum adulat
sanguinem* are, on the other hand, quite intolerable as they stand.
Turnebus[283] replaced *aduolans* with *auolans* and interpreted
pinnata cauda nostrum adulat sanguinem as 'tractu caudae sanguino-
lenta Promethei uulnera perstringit cruorisque aliquid deterget. . .
tactu caudae attingit et tamquam palpat sanguinem.' Turnebus'
text and interpretation have been taken over by most scholars
since the sixteenth century.[284] There is nevertheless no parallel
whatsoever for this use of *adulare/adulari* in recorded Latin. An
interpretation proposed and summarily discarded by Turnebus
himself, 'sanguinem expetit eique caudae motu blanditur', coheres
much better with the normal usage of the verb. The eagle would
be imagined as a dog wagging its tail before the bound Prometheus
in pleasurable anticipation of the bloody feast ahead.[285] For the
use of the normally intransitive *adulare* as a verb of desiring one
might compare that of *demori* at Plaut. *MG* 970, 1040, of *deperire*
at Plaut. *Amph.* 517, *Asin.* 527 etc., of *inhiare* at Caecil. *Com.* 147,
of *latrare* at Lucr. II. 17, of *sitire* at Cic. *Rep.* I. 66, *Phil.* II. 20. The
participle *aduolans* could now be interpreted as a neat variant
of *adueniens*, commonly used in stage drama with a past significance.[286] The surrounding context has hitherto prevented such

283. *Aduers.* II 14.
284. Cf. F. A. Wolf (Leipzig 1792): 'cauda quasi demulcet'; R. Kühner
(Jena 1829): 'terget, stringit, "streichelt"'; R. Klotz (Leipzig 1835):
'streichelt, wischt das Blut ab, als wolle er, dass die Leber bald wieder heile';
G. H. Moser (Hannover 1836): 'sanguinem deterget (sc. ut uulnus exsiccetur
et rursum consanescat)'; O. Heine (Leipzig 1864): 'er wischt mit dem
Schwanze meine blutige Wunde aus'; T. W. Dougan (Cambridge 1905):
'wipes off'; F. Gnesotto (Turin 1923): 'terge'; J. E. King (London 1927):
'wipes away'; J. Humbert (Paris 1931): 'les plumes de sa queue balayent les
flaques de mon sang'; W. W. Ewbank (London 1933): 'cleanses away the
gore'; K. Büchner (Zürich 1952): 'und streift mit seines Schwanzes Federn
unser Blut'.
285. Cf. Aesch. *P.V.* 1021–2 Διὸς. . .πτηνὸς κύων, δαφοινὸς αἰετός.
286. Cf. Plaut. *Amph.* 161, 613, 713 etc.

an interpretation being widely accepted.[287] I suggest that before the time of Arusianus,[288] perhaps through the inspiration of some scholar's commentary on the *Tusculanae disputationes*,[289] a reader inserted in the margin of his copy some words from Accius' account of Prometheus and the eagle and that these got accidently incorporated in the next copy made of Cicero's text,[290] forcing alteration to the words which followed *clangorem fundit uastum*. This would not be the only case of early interpolation of the verse quotations in the *Tusculanae disputationes*.[291]

VII. THE ACCURACY OF CICERO'S TRANSLATION OF SOME VERSES OF AESCHYLUS' (= fr. 193N²)

Practically all the Greek verses which Cicero translated when adapting his philosophical sources survive except those from Aeschylus' Προμηθεὺς λυόμενος translated at *TD* II. 23–5.[292] Those

287. In order to accommodate it J. Bouhier had to rearrange and rewrite the verses as:...*pastu dilaniat fero pennata cruda et nostrum adulat sanguinem. tum iecore opimo farta et satiata adfatim clangorem fundit uastum et sublime auolat. cum uero*...(I draw my information from J. H. Moser's edition, not having seen Bouhier's (Amsterdam 1737–9)). Without worrying about the context N. Wecklein, *Äschylos. Prometheus nebst den Bruchstücken des* Προμηθεὺς λυόμενος (3rd ed., Leipzig 1893), p. 126, writes 'προσσαίνει, "wedelt an". Vgl. *Eum.* 254 ὀσμὴ βροτείων αἱμάτων με προσγελᾷ'; H. Weir Smyth, *Aeschylus*, vol. II, p. 450, 'fawns upon'.

288. At *Gramm.* VII. 457. 6 Arusianus quotes *nostrum adulat sanguinem* as from *Cic....Tusc. II.*

289. For scholarly concern with the verse quotations in the *de republica libri* see Sen. *Epist.* CVIII. 32–3. On the early history of the text of the *Tusculanae disputationes* see Pohlenz's edition of 1918, *Praef.* pp. iv–v. On the alleged medieval glossemata see S. Lundström, *Vermeintliche Glosseme in den Tusculanen* (Uppsala 1964).

290. The text-book case is that of Soph. *Ant.* 277 written in the margin of M and P and in the text of other manuscripts of Aesch. *Pers.* 253.

291. O. Skutsch, *Rh. Mus.* 96 (1953), 197 (= *Stud. Enn.* p. 161), writes the text of *TD* III. 5 as *animusque aeger, ut ait Ennius, semper errat [neque pati neque perpeti potest] cupere numquam desinit* but makes Cicero himself responsible for the insertion. For suspicion about *TD* II. 23 see above, n. 257.

292. Missing also are the originals at *TD* II. 60 and *Diu.* II. 25. It is just possible that Pap. Heidelberg. 185 contains some of the original of *TD* XXIII–XXV; see E. Siegmann, *Literarische griechische Texte der Heidelberger Papyrussammlung* (Heidelberg 1956), pp. 21ff., K. Reinhardt, *Hermes* 85 (1957), 12ff., 125f. (= *Tradition und Geist* (Göttingen 1960), 182ff.), H. J. Mette, *Der verlorene Aischylos* (Berlin 1963), pp. 22ff., N. Terzaghi, *Athenaeum* 39 (1961), 3ff.

who in the past have accepted Ciceronian authorship of these senarii have usually believed that they follow the Greek words of Aeschylus more or less exactly.[293] But while there are grounds for thinking that Cicero paid more attention to what he was adapting in the case of the verses of the philosophical dialogues than in that of the *Aratus* and the *Prognostica*,[294] a restorer of the Προμηθεὺς λυόμενος might err badly by taking the verses of *TD* II. 23–5 at their face value. I shall argue a case for treating these verses sceptically, using those verses for which we possess the Greek originals and two assumptions, namely that the extant Προμηθεὺς δεσμώτης was actually written by Aeschylus[295] and that the now fragmentary Προμηθεὺς λυόμενος belonged with it to a trilogy.[296]

The Ciceronian senarii are represented as spoken from the Caucasus mountain by Prometheus to his Titan uncles; they describe (2–4) his imprisoned state, (5–9) the way in which Jupiter with the assistance of Vulcan fixed him to the mountain, (10–21) the periodic feasts of the eagle upon his liver, (22–4) Jupiter's refusal to let him die, and (25–8) the daily melting of the blood coagulated round the wedge driven through his chest. The philosopher Posidonius thought that the scene of the Προμηθεὺς λυόμενος was set on the Caucasus,[297] but the action of the previous member of the trilogy quite certainly took place a long way to the west of Armenia.[298] Many scholars have accepted the evidence of Posidonius and Cicero at its face value and postulated a change of scene within the trilogy. This is not in itself an impossible idea – the scene of the Ὀρέστεια changes

293. M. Valgimigli, *Eschilo: la trilogia di Prometeo* (Bologna 1904), pp. 240–2, and C. J. Herington, *TAPhA* 92 (1961), 239ff., attempt to extract Aeschylean words and phrases. G. Murray, *Aeschyli Tragoediae*[2] (Oxford 1955), p. 147, writes: 'haec si ab Accio scripta sunt Aeschylum fontem habent, si a Cicerone Aeschyli ipsa uerba reddunt.'

294. See above, p. 94.

295. Cicero's philosophical sources believed so; see *TD* III. 76 and Plut. *Mor.* 102b. For the controversy regarding authenticity see, most recently, C. J. Herington, *The Author of Prometheus Bound* (Austin 1970).

296. See Schol. Med. *P.V.* 511 ἐν γὰρ τῷ ἑξῆς δράματι λύεται. For an argument that Aeschylus wrote only a 'dilogy' see F. Focke, *Hermes* 65 (1930), 265.

297. Ap. Strab. IV. 183. Cf. also Hygin. *Astrol.* II. 15.

298. See vv. 707ff. and J. D. P. Bolton, *Aristeas of Proconnesus* (Oxford 1962), pp. 46ff.

from Argos to Delphi and then to Athens – but one would expect
to be able to see some motive for the change. In any case vv. 1015–
21 of the Προμηθεὺς δεσμώτης strongly suggests that the scene
of the Προμηθεὺς λυόμενος was intended to be the same.[299]
I should prefer to hold Posidonius and Cicero in error. The
regular post-fifth-century version of the myth set the episode
of the eagle on the Armenian Caucasus[300] and some careless
readers of the Προμηθεὺς δεσμώτης imagined this play as set
there.[301] Cicero refers to the Caucasus both in the remark
introducing the verses, *has igitur poenas pendens adfixus ad Caucasum
dicit haec*,[302] and in the concluding verse, *guttae quae saxa adsidue
instillant Caucasi.* Behind the former may lie an error of his
philosophical source, an error extended from there into his
version of Aeschylus' verses, which need not have specified the
name of the mountain.[303]

Cicero (or his source) was pretty certainly mistaken to make
the theft of fire the sole cause of the punishment exacted in the
Προμηθεὺς λυόμενος. Jupiter sent the eagle to torture Prometheus
because of the latter's refusal to reveal the oracle concerning
Jupiter's next marriage.[304] The verses of the philosophical
dialogues, like those of the *Aratus*,[305] show a marked tendency to
specify what was general or vague in the original. At *Fin.* v. 49
Homer's ὅσσα γένηται ἐπὶ χθονὶ πουλυβοτείρη[306] becomes
omnia…e latis regum uestigia terris; at *TD* II. 20 Sophocles'
θήρειος βία[307] becomes (erroneously)[308] *biformato impetu Centaurus*
and his ὅσην ἐγὼ | γαῖαν καθαίρων ἱκόμην[309] *saeua terris gens*

299. Cf. also vv. 26–7, 93–105.

300. Cf. Apollon. *Arg.* II. 1247ff., Eratosthenes ap. Arrian. *Peripl. Eux.* II. 5,
Virg. *Ecl.* VI. 42, Propert. II. 1. 69 et al.

301. See the hypothesis and the scholium on v. 347.

302. Cf. *TD* v. 8 *Prometheus adfixus Caucaso.*

303. Cf. F. D. Allen, *AJPh* 13 (1892), 51ff.

304. See Aesch. *P.V.* 944ff.

305. Cicero felt at liberty to specify τις ἀνδρῶν (*Phaen.* 373) as *ille astrorum
custos* (162) and to tell why Eridanus was thought to be πολύκλαυτος (*Phaen.*
360 ~ 147–8 *quem lacrimis maestae Phaethontis saepe sorores | sparserunt, letum
maerenti uoce canentes*).

306. *Od.* XII. 191.

307. *Trach.* 1059.

308. See vv. 1095–6 ~ *bicorporem…manum.* Cicero perhaps had Nessus in
mind.

309. *Trach.* 1060–1.

relegata ultimis, | *quas peragrans undique omnem ecferitatem expuli.*[310]
One must, therefore, be hesitant about accepting as Aeschylean
any specific statement in the verses at *TD* II. 23–5.

There can be no certainty that everything uttered by the
Aeschylean god was translated by Cicero or that his attitude
to the other persons of the drama was fairly reproduced. In
turning the speech of the Sophoclean Hercules to his son Hyllus
Cicero omitted the demigod's wish to mutilate the body of
Hyllus' mother, his baring of his own body, his cries of anguish
and his plea to Hades to receive him in the underworld forthwith.
I have explained these omissions as due in the main to the
context of Cicero's dialogue.[311] No necessary significance is
therefore to be seen in the fact that the Prometheus of the
Ciceronian senarii shows no hostility to the Titan uncles whom
he had helped Jupiter to defeat in battle[312] and makes none of
the sort of disparaging remarks about Jupiter that are made to
visitors in the Προμηθεὺς δεσμώτης.[313] Whatever stood in the
text of the Προμηθεὺς λυόμενος, the context of Cicero's argument
at *TD* II. 17–25 demanded that Prometheus be a reasonably
sympathetic character.[314]

The Ciceronian senarii contain one εἰκών, *religatum asperis* |
uinctumque saxis, nauem ut horrisono freto | *noctem pauentes timidi
adnectunt nauitae,* and a number of striking and powerful μεταφοραί;
the Titans are like a mass of suckers sprung up from the base of
a shrub (*Titanum suboles*); the ties of Prometheus and the Titans
are like those of the participants in a commercial or military
enterprise (*socia nostri sanguinis*); the eagle pours out its cry like
liquid (*clangorem fundit*); Prometheus is deprived of his physical

310. I should suggest that Cicero had in mind some rationalistic interpretation
of the stories of Geryon, Busiris and the Amazons. For Hercules as the
destroyer of tyrants and lawless savages cf. Dionys. Hal. *Ant.* I. 41. 1. Cicero
may also be thinking of the way in which the Romans had shifted troublesome
populations to distant places, e.g., the Picentes in 268 (Strab. v. 251) and
the Ligures Apuani in 180 (Liv. XL. 38). On Roman *relegatio* see below,
p. 107.

311. See above, p. 85.

312. See vv. 199–221.

313. See vv. 186–92, 221–5 etc.

314. Sympathetic, that is, to Roman aristocrats. Prometheus would of
course have been guilty in their eyes of *contumacia* towards legitimate authority
and *furtum*, perhaps even of *impietas* and *sacrilegium*. His punishment, nevertheless, was extreme.

powers as a man is of his sexual partner (*me ipse uiduus*); the blood congealed around the wedge driven through his chest is like woollen thread balled around a distaff[315] and the time of his punishment[316] like generations of ill-kempt spinning women (*saeclis glomerata horridis...clades*); his blood as it melts drips upon the mountain side like liquid from a damaged container (*saxa adsidue instillant*). The εἰκών may plausibly be attributed to Aeschylus himself[317] but not the inelegance of its expression[318] or (with certainty) all its details.[319] About the μεταφοραί no deductions seem possible. As often as Cicero translated a μεταφορά straight from his original he ignored one or substituted another or added one quite absent; at *TD* II. 20–2 *corpore exanclata atque animo*[320] (~ καὶ χερσὶ καὶ νώτοισι μοχθήσας), *tuque caelestum sator, dolorum...torquent uertices, taetra mactata excetra, e Tartarea tenebrica ...plaga*[321] (~ ὑπὸ χθονός); at *TD* III. 18 *decore atque omni me orbatum laude* (~ μ' ἀσύφηλον...ἔρεξεν); at *TD* III. 29 *molem... mali*[322] (~ κακῶν ὁδούς); at *TD* III. 59 *sic iubet Necessitas*[323] (~ ἀναγκαίως δ' ἔχει); at *TD* III. 71 *cum fortuna mutata impetum* |

315. As blood congeals the protein fibrinogen turns into fine threads of fibrin (called ἶνες by Greek biologists) which entangle the blood cells, contract and form a firm mass binding the clot.

316. See Aesch. *P.V.* 94 and schol., Hygin. *Astrol.* II. 15, who make it 30,000 years.

317. Like the other Attic tragedians Aeschylus drew a great deal of imagery from seafaring (see D. van Nes, *Die maritime Bildersprache des Aischylos* (Groningen 1963)). The mooring image is applied differently to Prometheus at *P.V.* 965 ἐς τάσδε... πημονὰς καθώρμισας and quite similarly to Hercules at Eurip. *Heracl.* 1094–7... δεσμοῖς ναῦς ὅπως ὡρμισμένος | νεανίαν θώρακα καὶ βραχίονα and to Andromeda at Aristoph. *Thesm.* 1105–6 παρθένον...ναῦν ὅπως ὡρμισμένην (parody of Euripides). For the method of mooring the poets had in mind see Hom. *Il.* I. 436.

318. Euripides' neat εἰκὸς σφαδάζειν ἦν ἂν ὡς νεόζυγα | πῶλον χαλινὸν ἀρτίως δεδεγμένον (fr. 821. 3–4) becomes in Cicero's clumsy hands *esset dolendi causa, ut iniecto eculei | freno repente tactu exagitantur nouo* (*TD* III. 67).

319. For Cicero's tendency to specify generalities in his original see above, p. 100. For the sailor's fear of the open sea at night, however, see Aesch. *Suppl.* 764–70. The strip of water between Sicily and the toe of Italy was notoriously dangerous (cf. Thucyd. IV. 24. 5, Virg. *Aen.* III. 410–32 et al.) but not necessarily the *fretum* referred to; the Euripus and the Hellespont had their dangerous winds and currents.

320. Cf. Pacuv. *tr.* 290 *non potest Melanippe hic sine tua opera exanclari labos*, Acc. *tr.* 91 *cladesque exanclarem impetibiles*.

321. Cf. Enn. *tr.* 201 *caeli...plagas*, Lucr. V. 31 *Bistoniasque plagas*.

322. Cf. Lucr. III. 1056 *tanta mali tamquam moles*.

323. Cf. Acc. *tr.* 481 *ueter fatorum terminus sic iusserat*.

conuertat[324] (~ ὅταν δὲ δαίμων ἀνδρὸς εὐτυχοῦς τὸ πρὶν | †μάστιγ᾽†
ἐρείσῃ τοῦ βίου παλίντροπον); at *Diu.* II. 63–4 *pectoris orsus,
uestita est classibus Aulis* (~ ἐς Αὐλίδα νῆες... ἠγερέθοντο), *foliorum
tegmine saeptos* (~ πετάλοις ὑποπεπτηῶτες) *taetro mactatas dente,
tot... exanclabimus annos*[325] (~ τοσσαῦτ᾽ ἔτεα πτολεμίξομεν). Memory of older poetry rather than a creative imagination was
probably responsible. Traditional phrases constantly diverted his
mind from the Greek text before him. Soph. *Trach.* 1076–8 καὶ
νῦν προσελθὼν στῆθι πλησίον πατρός, | σκέψαι δ᾽ ὁποίας ταῦτα
συμφορᾶς ὕπο | πέπονθα became *accede, nate, adsiste, miserandum
aspice euisceratum corpus laceratum patris*, quite probably with the aid
of Ennius, *tr.* 58 *quid ita cum tuo lacerato corpore miser*[326] and 309
ipse summis saxis fixus asperis, euisceratus.[327] Ennius, *tr.* 315
priusquam oppeto malam pestem mandatam hostili manu[328] would
have helped turn Soph. *Trach.* 1056–8 καὶ διέφθαρμαι δέμας | τὸ
πᾶν, ἀφράστῳ τῇδε χειρωθεὶς πέδῃ | κοὐ ταῦτα λόγχῃ πεδιάς...
into *sic corpus clade horribili absumptum extabuit,* | *ipse inligatus peste
interimor textili.* | *hos non hostilis dextra*... With regard to the
speech from Aeschylus' Προμηθεὺς λυόμενος one can only point out
that Lucretius had already used the phrase *uirum...suboles,*[329] that
Cicero himself had used the phrase *socio tui sanguinis* in a speech,[330]
that Ennius had used the phrase *effudit uoces* in an epic poem,[331] that
Cicero had spoken of time as a spinning woman in an epic poem,[332]
and that most of the old epic and tragic poetry known by Cicero is
now lost.[333] Aeschylus' contribution to the imagery and phraseology
of the Latin senarii might therefore be quite a small one.

324. Cf. Anon. rhet. *Herenn.* IV. 24 *omnis impetus fortunae se putant fugisse.*
325. Cf. Enn. *tr.* 90 *illum exanclaui diem.*
326. Other parts of Cassandra's speech are quoted by Cicero at *Diu.* I. 66,
I. 114, II. 112.   327. Quoted by Cicero at *TD* I. 107.
328. Quoted by Cicero at *TD* II. 38.
329. IV. 1232. At *Pseud.* 892 Plautus uses the word, perhaps paratragically,
of a cook's many assistants. The nearest parallel I can find in Attic tragedy
is Eurip. *El.* 15 θῆλύ τ᾽ Ἠλέκτρας θάλος.
330. *Dom.* XXV. Cf. Ov. *Trist.* IV. 5. 29 *diligat et semper socius te sanguinis.* The
chorus of Aeschylus' Προμηθεὺς δεσμώτης refers to the Titans as Prometheus'
ξυνομαίμονες (v. 410).
331. *Ann.* 540. Cf. Cat. LXIV. 125, *fudisse... uoces,* Ter. *Ad.* 769 *tu uerba
fundis hic, Sapientia?* (paratragedy).
332. *Diu.* I. 19 *omnia fixa tuus glomerans determinat annus* (from *de consulatu suo lib.* II).
333. Other phrases with parallels in older Latin poetry are *Iouisque numen* (Acc.
tr. 646), *Iouis satelles* (Cic. *Mar.* fr. ap. *Diu.* I. 106) and *amore mortis* (Lucr. V. 179).

There can be no certainty that even the facts of Prometheus' confinement and torture in the Προμηθεὺς λυόμενος were represented exactly by Cicero.

Cicero often, as we have seen,[334] allowed his philosophical context or a memory of old Latin poetry to divert his attention from the Greek verses in front of him. He was also capable of outright error. Whereas, for example, Sophocles conceived of the shirt of Nessus donned by Hercules as a vampire consuming the flesh and blood of a young and healthy living person and threw out the unusual and striking phrase ἐκ δὲ χλωρὸν αἷμά μου πέπωκεν[335] as part of the total image, Cicero remembered the conventional epithets applied in poetry to the blood issuing from lung wounds or congealed on corpses[336] and wrote *decolorem sanguinem omnem exsorbuit*; Sophocles' continuation of the image with δαίνυται γὰρ αὖ πάλιν, ἤνθηκεν, ἐξώρμηκεν[337] he simply ignored.[338]

Religious notions foreign to Roman society which the older poets had failed to domesticate made Cicero helpless. Thus Homer's οὓς μὴ Κῆρες ἔβαν θανάτοιο φέρουσαι[339] became *qui non funestis liquerunt lumina fatis*.[340] Sophocles' κοὐδεὶς τροπαῖ' ἔστησε τῶν ἐμῶν χερῶν[341] became *nec quisquam e nostris spolia cepit laudibus*,[342] doubtless because the practice of setting up a monument on the battlefield decorated by armour taken from the defeated enemy[343] had never been followed by the Italian tribes and had long fallen into disuse among the Greeks.

334. See above, pp. 77 ff.
335. *Trach.* 1055–6. Cf. Eurip. *Hec.* 126–7 τύμβον στεφανοῦν αἵματι χλωρῷ (it is a question of the maiden Polyxena), Virg. *Aen.* v. 295 *uiridique iuuenta*. The source of the idea is perhaps in Hom. *Il.* vi. 146.
336. Cf. Aesch. *Ag.* 1020 μέλαν αἷμα, *Eum.* 980, Soph. *OR* 1278–9, *Trach.* 717, *Ai.* 376, 919, Eurip. *El.* 318, *Hec.* 537, *I.A.* 1114, Enn. *tr.* 310 *sanguine atro*, Virg. *Aen.* iii. 622.
337. *Trach.* 1088–9. Cf. Aesch. *Eum.* 265 (of 'Ερινύες) ῥοφεῖν ἐρυθρὸν ἐκ μελέων πέλανον.
338. With *dolorum anxiferi torquent uertices* he imported a metaphor quite absent from the Sophoclean verses; see above, p. 102. Where errors are concerned the difficult subject matter of Aratus' Φαινόμενα caused him to make many (pointed out by Turnebus, *Aduers.* viii 18, xxviii 30, Scaliger, *M. Manili Astronomicon libri V* (Paris 1579), passim, H. Grotius, *Syntagma Arateorum* (Leiden 1600), pp. 128ff.). 339. *Il.* ii. 303.
340. *Diu.* ii. 63. Cf. Naev. *tr.* 28 *ubi bipedes uolucres lino linquant lumina*.
341. *Trach.* 1102. 342. *TD* ii. 22.
343. See K. Woelke, *Bonn. Jahrbb.* 129 (1911), 131ff.

The practices and beliefs of Roman society itself often pushed their way into Cicero's versions, sometimes through the medium of the older poetry, sometimes, perhaps, through his own imagination.[344] I cannot, for example, see why he turned Sophocles' ἄλλων τε μόχθων μυρίων ἐγευσάμην[345] into *multa alia uictrix nostra lustrauit manus*[346] unless he thought of the Nemean lion, the Lernaean Hydra and the rest as *monstra* indicating the presence of *scelus* in the places they infested.[347] The Roman augur's concern for the appearance of the first light of day helped Euripides' εἰ μὲν τόδ᾽ ἦμαρ πρῶτον ἦν κακουμένῳ[348] become *si mihi nunc tristis primum inluxisset dies*.[349] The sign which appeared to the Achaeans sacrificing at Aulis was interpreted by the Homeric Calchas[350] as *in toto* objectively favourable. Cicero's context made him emphasize the unfavourable part of the sign[351] and traditional Roman attitudes to such signs helped him with the required emphasis. A Roman augur would have interpreted the Achaean τέρας as an *augurium oblatiuum* and thus as necessarily indicative of evil to come;[352] the snake inspired fear,[353] particularly when it appeared at an altar or in a temple.[354] Cicero translated Homer's account not only using the technical terms of Roman sacrifice

344. He had become a member of the college of augurs in 53 (see Plut. *Cic.* xxxvi) and was proud of his knowledge of the augural discipline (see *Brut.* 1, *Phil.* ii. 4, *ND* i. 14), even writing a book *de auguriis*.

345. *Trach.* 1101.   346. *TD* ii. 22.

347. All misbirths among men and domestic animals were certainly so regarded (see Cic. *Diu.* i. 93, i. 98, i. 121, *ND* ii. 14 and the notes of A. S. Pease). Among wild animals snakes at least caused religious foreboding (see below, n. 354). Lucretius had referred sarcastically to the monsters slain by Hercules as *portenta* (v. 37).

348. Fr. 821. 1.

349. *TD* iii. 67. Cf. Acc. *tr.* 583–4 *quianam tam aduerso augurio et inimico omine* | *Thebis radiatum lumen ostentum tuum* (~ Eurip. *Phoen.* 4–5 ὡς δυστυχῆ Θήβαισι τῇ τόθ᾽ ἡμέρᾳ | ἀκτῖν᾽ ἔφηκας), Cat. viii. 3, Hor. *Sat.* i. 9. 72. For *tristis* as a technical term in divination see Cic. *Diu.* ii. 36 (*exta*), ii. 69 (*ostentum*), Liv. ix. 38. 15 (*omen*), xxv. 16. 1 (*prodigium*).

350. *Il.* ii. 299–330.

351. *Diu.* ii. 63. See above, p. 82.

352. See R. Bloch, *Les prodiges dans l'antiquité classique* (Paris 1963), pp. 13ff., 84ff.

353. See *TLL* ii 53. 49ff., s.v. *anguis*.

354. Cf. Ter. *Phorm.* 707, Liv. i. 56. 4, xxviii. 11. 1–2, xli. 21. 13, Val. Max. i. 6. 8, Julius Obs. xxviii, xlvii, Granius Licin. p. 13. 3ff. It was a *haruspex*, not an *augur*, who interpreted the snake at Sulla's sacrifice as a favourable sign (Cic. *Diu.* i. 72, Val. Max. i. 6. 4, August. *Ciu.* ii. 24).

and divination where they were roughly equivalent to those used by Homer[355] or in harmony with his general intentions,[356] but also introducing a detail of Roman sacral practice[357] and attributing to the Achaean sacrificers the terrified state of mind historical Romans would have had in similar circumstances.[358] He had the sign itself described in Latin terms implying divine disfavour and human horror.[359]

One can accordingly question on purely general grounds whether Aeschylus in the Προμηθεὺς λυόμενος really had the Titan nailed to the mountain through his joints, with the Ἐρινύες for company, visited by the eagle only every other day, and desiring the embrace of Θάνατος. There are also particular grounds which raise suspicion.

It is odd that after an allusive εἰκών – *religatum asperis | uinctumque saxis, nauem ut horrisono freto | noctem pauentes timidi adnectunt nauitae* – and with even more allusive references to the binding of his limbs and the wedging through of his chest to follow – *uinclis constrictus Iouis...atque haec uetusta saeclis glomerata horridis | luctifica clades nostro infixa est corpori* – Prometheus should give so many details of the method of his incarceration as he does with

355. Cf. *auguris ut nostri Calchantis fata queamus | scire ratosne habeant an uanos pectoris orsus* ∼ ὄφρα δαῶμεν | ἢ ἐτεὸν Κάλχας μαντεύεται, ἦε καὶ οὐκί (the reference to *pectus* may import the philosophical distinction [Plat. *Tim.* 72] between irrational vision and rational interpretation), *portentum* ∼ σῆμα, *diuom placantes numina tauris* ∼ ἔρδομεν ἀθανάτοισι...ἑκατόμβας, *portenta dedit* ∼ ἔφηνε τέρας, *edidit haec* ∼ τὼς ἀγόρευε, *iam matura uidetis* ∼ νῦν πάντα τελεῖται.

356. Cf. *mirabile monstrum | uidimus* ∼ θαυμάζομεν οἷον ἐτύχθη. Elsewhere Cicero emphasizes that the Achaeans actively perceived both the sign and its fulfilment (*uidimus* ∼ ἐφάνη, *auis...mactatas...uidetis* ∼ κατὰ τέκνα φάγε στρουθοῖο καὶ αὐτήν, *matura uidetis* ∼ πάντα τελεῖται). Roman signs had to be seen to be valid (see Cic. *Diu.* II. 77, Plin. *HN* XXVIII. 17).

357. Cf. *fumantibus aris | aurigeris diuom placantes numina tauris* ∼ ἱερούς κατὰ βωμοὺς | ἔρδομεν ἀθανάτοισι τεληέσσας ἑκατόμβας. For the Roman practice of gilding the horns of *hostiae* see Liv. XXV. 12. 13, Plin. *HN* XXXIII. 39, Serv. Virg. *Aen.* IX. 624, Aur. Vict. *De uir. illustr.* LXXXIV. 2. The presence of analogues for *fumantibus aris* in Lucretius (VI. 752) and Catullus (LXIV. 393) suggests that some episode in Ennius' *Annales* may have affected Cicero's translation quite extensively (cf. also Hes. *Theog.* 557 θυηέντων ἐπὶ βωμῶν).

358. Cf. *timidi stantes mirabile monstrum | uidimus* ∼ ἑσταότες θαυμάζομεν οἷον ἐτύχθη.

359. Cf. *immani specie tortuque draconem | terribilem* ∼ δράκων ἐπὶ νῶτα δαφοινός, | σμερδαλέος (for *immanis* in a phrase of ominous associations cf. Cic. *Pis.* XXXI), *taetro mactatas dente* ∼ κατὰ...φάγε (for *taeter* of prodigies cf. Liv. XXII. 9. 8).

Saturnius me sic infixit Iuppiter,
Iouisque numen Mulciberi adsciuit manus.
hos ille cuneos fabrica crudeli inserens
perrupit artus; qua miser sollertia
transuerberatus castrum hoc Furiarum incolo.

His previous visitors were allowed to rest content with the evidence of their eyes.[360] But even odder are the differences between the details of the Ciceronian senarii and those of the scene enacted at the beginning of the Προμηθεὺς δεσμώτης. Here Ζεύς was absent and two of the children of Στύξ,[361] Βία and Κράτος, held Prometheus to the mountain while Ἥφαιστος fixed him with clasps set around his limbs and joints[362] and a wedge of adamant driven between the bones of his chest-cage.[363]

The mountain had no regular inhabitants.[364] In the Ciceronian senarii *Iuppiter* himself has replaced Βία and Κράτος[365] while *Mulciber* has pinned Prometheus with wedges through his joints.[366] The site of the incarceration is a primitive collection of dwellings[367] occupied by *Furiae*.

I should guess that Cicero interpreted a number of Aeschylean generalities with Roman relegation and crucifixion in mind. An offended *paterfamilias*[368] or magistrate[369] could banish a man

360. Cf. *P.V.* 92–7, 113, 119, 141–2, 168–9, 175–6, 304–6, 438, 991–1006. To Io's request σήμηνον ὅστις ἐν φάραγγί σ' ὤχμασεν (618), Prometheus answered simply βούλευμα μὲν τὸ Δῖον, Ἡφαίστου δὲ χείρ.

361. See Hes. *Theog.* 385.

362. Cf. vv. 54–6...πρόχειρα ψάλια...βαλών νιν ἀμφὶ χερσὶν ἐγκρατεῖ σθένει | ῥαιστῆρι θεῖνε, πασσάλευε πρὸς πέτραις, 60–1 ἄραρεν ἥδε γ' ὠλένη δυσεκλύτως:: καί τήνδε νῦν πόρπασον ἀσφαλῶς, 71 ἀλλ' ἀμφὶ πλευραῖς μασχαλιστῆρας βάλε, 74 σκέλη δὲ κίρκωσον βίᾳ, 76 ἐρρωμένως νῦν θεῖνε διατόρους πέδας.

363. *P.V.* 64–5 ἀδαμαντίνου νῦν σφηνὸς αὐθάδη γνάθον | στέρνων διαμπὰξ πασσάλευ' ἐρρωμένως.

364. *P.V.* 2 ἄβροτον εἰς ἐρημίαν, 270 τυχόντ' ἐρήμου τοῦδ' ἀγείτονος πάγου.

365. For Ζεύς tying enemies up see Aesch. *Eum.* 641.

366. *Artus* sometimes stands for the limbs in poetry, but never, so far as I can see, for the trunk. The link usually seen with *P.V.* 64–5 is therefore illusory.

367. For *castrum* cf. Festus, p. 430. 34 *Saturnii quoque dicebantur qui castrum in imo cliuo Capitolino incolebant*, Serv. Virg. *Aen.* vi. 775 (*castrumque Inui*) *castrum autem ciuitas est...in Plauto 'castrum Poenorum'*. The often alleged link with *P.V.* 31 ἀτερπῆ τήνδε φρουρήσεις πέτραν and 141–4 δέρχθητ', ἐσίδεσθ' οἵῳ δεσμῷ | προσπορπατὸς τῆσδε φάραγγος | σκοπέλοις ἐν ἄκροις | φρουρὰν ἄζηλον ὀχήσω is illusory. 368. See Cic. *S. Rosc.* XLII, *de Off.* III. 112, Liv. VII. 4. 4.

369. See Cic. *Sest.* XXIX.

from his normal abode to some distant and unpleasant environment. In 186 the Capuan religious agitator Minnius Cerrinius was imprisoned at Ardea[370] and in 63 Julius Caesar had proposed that Lentulus and the other Catilinarians be kept in bonds in Italian municipia.[371] From at least the year 217 onwards[372] various malefactors, including *sacrilegi*,[373] could be hung up to die with nails piercing the flesh in strategic positions.[374] Citizens rarely suffered this punishment, but when one did a magistrate would supervise and a lictor perform the actual hanging-up.[375] Manilius depicted Andromeda's imprisonment as a crucifixion and both Lucian[376] and Ausonius[377] Prometheus' imprisonment likewise. Interestingly, the text of the Προμηθεὺς δεσμώτης carried by the Medicean codex had v. 438 corrupted to ὁρῶν ἐμαυτὸν ὧδε προσηλούμενον.

The Ciceronian *Furiae* must be the eagle and the *pestes anxiae*. Aeschylus could hardly have referred to these even metaphorically as Ἐρινύες. The children of Νύξ[378] dwelt normally in the underworld[379] and did not deal with such offences as those committed by Prometheus. Indeed they belonged to that set of powers in the universe to which even Ζεύς was subject and were regarded by the Aeschylean Prometheus practically as allies.[380] The *Furiae* of Roman poets, however, are sometimes the Ἐρινύες[381] but often mere spirits of destruction.[382] At *Aen.* III. 252 Virgil called the

370. Liv. XXXIX. 19. 2.

371. Cic. *Catil.* IV. 7–8, Sall. *Catil.* LI. 43.

372. See Liv. XXII. 33. 2 for the first recorded case. Crucifixion was certainly not one of the normal practices of fifth-century Athenian society (see K. Latte, *RE* Suppl. 7 (1940), 1606, s.v. *Todesstrafe*).

373. See Ulp. *Dig.* XLVIII. 13. 6–7 (the phrase *in furca suspendisse* is a Christian alteration).

374. For the breaking of flesh in crucifixion see Cic. *Verr.* IV. 26, Sen. *Dial.* VII. 19. 3, Lucan, VI. 545–9, Plin. *HN* XXVIII. 46, John, *Euang.* XX. 25, Artemidorus, II. 56. Archaeological evidence now exists on the details of Roman practice: see N. Haas, *Israel Exploration Journal* 20 (1970), 49ff., P. Ducrey, *MusH* 28 (1971), 183ff.

375. See Cic. *Rab. perd.* XV.   376. *Prom.* I.   377. XII. 10. 9.

378. Aesch. *Eum.* 321ff., 416ff.

379. Hom. *Il.* IX. 571f., XIX. 259f., *Od.* XX. 78, Aesch. *Eum.* 72f., 115, 395f.

380. *P.V.* 511–20.

381. Cf. Lucr. III. 1011, Cic. *S. Rosc.* LXVI–LXXI (referring to plays about Orestes and Alcmeon).

382. Cf. Enn. *tr.* 56. Cicero's political enemies are often labelled *furiae* (*Dom.* XCIX, CII, *Pis.* VIII et al.).

Harpy Calaeno a *Furia*. One cannot therefore know what lies behind Cicero's *castrum hoc Furiarum incolo*. It could as well be a memory of the punishment of Ixion or Tityos as anything in the text of the Προμηθεὺς λυόμενος.[383]

Hermes' prophecy in the Προμηθεὺς δεσμώτης, vv. 1024–5 ἄκλητος ἕρπων δαιταλεὺς πανήμερος | κελαινόβρωτον δ' ἧπαρ ἐκθοινήσεται, is not completely lucid in what it says and offers no explanation of how the liver-supply will be maintained through the centuries. According to Hesiod[384] and the mythographers[385] the eagle dined every day and the liver grew every night. The Ciceronian senarii state clearly that dinner is provided only every other day and suggest that injected air[386] is responsible for the regular restoration of the damaged organ. In the fourth century certainly, and perhaps as early as the mid-fifth, philosophers had ideas about the liver forming itself from solidified blood[387] and about the gods of heaven being nourished by vapours excited from the earth by the sun's heat.[388] Aeschylus may have himself rationalized the saga and provided a full day's sunshine as well as two chilly nights between each visit from the eagle in order to promote full restoration of Prometheus' liver. It is more likely that Cicero unconsciously imposed what was current philosophical doctrine and what he perhaps imagined to be the doctrine of Pythagoras, Aeschylus' supposed philosophy teacher.

The furthest departure from the assumptions of the Προμηθεὺς δεσμώτης occurs in the verses

383. Horace seems to know a story setting the consumption of Prometheus' liver in the underworld (*Ep.* XVII. 67; cf. *Carm.* II. 13. 37, II. 18. 34).

384. *Theog.* 525.

385. Cf. Apollod. I. 7. 2, Hygin. *Fab.* 144, *Astrol.* II. 15, Fulgent. *Myth.* II. 6.

386. I.e. πνεῦμα; *inflatus* always has an active sense (Cic. *Brut.* CXCII, *Ac.* II. 20, *Diu.* I. 12). No adequate parallel is provided by Dio Chrys. VIII. 33 (quoted by Davies and others). Homer's Sarpedon is revived by the breath of the North Wind (*Il.* V. 696–8). Bion's Aphrodite expresses a desire to kiss the dying Adonis and thus have his departing breath flow into her liver (*Epit.* XLV–XLIX).

387. Cf. Arist. *Part. anim.* II. 1, [Hippocr.] *Carn.* 8 (VIII. 594).

388. Cf. Cic. *ND* II. 40, II. 83, II. 118, Plin. *HN* II. 10, 102, Sen. *Nat.* VI. 16. 2, Sext. Emp. *Adu. math.* IX. 71–3. Corollary with this was the view that respiration did more than cool the concocting blood (see Cic. *ND* II. 134, Galen, *Us. part.* VII. 9).

> sic me ipse uiduus pestes excipio anxias
> amore mortis terminum anquirens mali
> sed longe a Leto numine aspellor Iouis.

In the Προμηθεὺς δεσμώτης Prometheus is the immortal god of the ancient saga, his immortality something determined by Μοῖρα[389] and fully accepted.[390] The words εἰ γάρ μ' ὑπὸ γῆν νέρθεν θ' Ἅιδου | τοῦ νεκροδέγμονος εἰς ἀπέραντον | Τάρταρον ἧκεν...[391] express a dislike of being maltreated in the sight of others rather than a desire for death. His reaction to the threats of Hermes, εἴς τε κελαινὸν | Τάρταρον ἄρδην ῥίψειε δέμας | τοὐμὸν ἀνάγκης στερραῖς δίναις· | πάντως ἐμέ γ' οὐ θανατώσει,[392] makes plain that his death is inconceivable. The Latin Prometheus is imagined more as an ordinary mortal who would prefer death to the continuation of his agony and is yet deliberately kept alive by his tormentor. He lies in wait like a hunter[393] to trap some disease[394] which will stop his breathing.[395] He invites the embrace of Death[396] but is pushed away[397] because of a decision taken by Jupiter. Many who have written about the character of the Aeschylean Prometheus and the religious argument of the trilogy[398] have based upon the Latin verses speculation about a change in Prometheus' attitude to his situation and a merging of Μοῖρα and the will of Ζεύς, of the old order and the new. There is a less exciting and more probable explanation. Cicero could with difficulty represent the idea of an immutable destiny independent of the will of gods[399] but Zeno and his successors regularly

389. See v. 933 ᾧ θανεῖν οὐ μόρσιμον. Cf. vv. 511ff., 753ff.

390. See vv. 98ff., 183ff., 258.   391. Vv. 152-9.   392. Vv. 1050-3.

393. For *excipio* as a hunting term cf. Caes. *BG* vi. 28. 4, Hor. *Carm.* iii. 12. 12.

394. For *pestis* in this sense see Enn. *Ann.* 559, Liv. iv. 25. 3. For diseases as independent entities see Hes. *Erg.* 90–104, Virg. *Georg.* iii. 471, iii. 552, *Aen.* vi. 275; as beast-like beings Soph. *Phil.* 265-6, 706, 743-4, 758-9, 807-8.

395. For the active sense of *anxius* see Lucr. iii. 993, vi. 1158, Cic. *TD* iv. 34.

396. According to Hesiod Θάνατος was a fatherless child of Νύξ (*Theog.* 212). For *Letum* as some kind of person cf. Lucr. i. 852, Virg. *Aen.* vi. 277–8.

397. Cf. Plaut. *Amph.* 1000, *Merc.* 115, Titin. *tog.* 47.

398. E.g. G. Thomson, *Aeschylus. The Prometheus Bound* (Cambridge 1932), p. 19.

399. Livius Andronicus' translation of Hom. *Od.* iii. 237–8 ὁππότε κεν δὴ μοῖρ' ὀλοὴ καθέλῃσι τανηλεγέος θανάτοιο as *quando dies adueniet quem profata Morta est* (cf. Latte, *Röm. Rel.* p. 53 n. 1) seems to have had no effect on later Latin poets. Acc. *tr.* 534–6 †eum doctus† *Prometheus clepsisse dolo poenasque Ioui fato expendisse supremo* is a little obscure. At *TD* i. 115 Cicero turns κεῖται μοιριδίῳ θανάτῳ with *potitur fatorum numine leto*.

identified both the Μοῖρα and the Ζεύς of the poets with their own εἱμαρμένη.[400] Cicero was also capable of representing a totally human and defiant Titan, but again the Stoic philosophers he knew considered that a person not completely his own master could not be εὐδαίμων[401] and might with full propriety give up his life.[402] His theme in the second book of the *Tusculanae dis-putationes* was grief and pain beyond a person's power to control and the cast of his argument a Stoic one.[403] The divinity of Prometheus was irrelevant to, perhaps inconsistent with, the argument. All in all, Cicero is likely to have attended more to this argument than to the archaic patterns of thought in the verses which his source quoted in support of it.

400. Cf. Cic. *ND* I. 40, Tertull. *Apol.* XXI. 10, Schol. Hom. *Il.* VIII. 69, Schol. Hes. *Theog.* 211.

401. Cf. Cic. *Parad.* II. 17.

402. See above, p. 85.

403. See above, pp. 83ff.

A New Look at the Manuscript Tradition of Catullus

D. F. S. THOMSON

DURING the anti-clerical fury of the French Revolution the custodian of the library at the Abbey of St-Germain-des-Prés took to its ruined and roofless tower such treasured manuscripts as he thought most worthy of preservation; preservation from the rain which beat night and day upon the now dangerously broken stairs where he strove unsheltered to sleep and to guard his books, and from the rage of the mob who would have sought his life had they not supposed the place to be deserted because uninhabitable. In the end, at no small cost to his health, he saved for us *inter alia* the Codex Sangermanensis (G) of Catullus. Yet this tale of peril, almost of disaster, is for all its drama not unique in the history of these poems; for if to some the story faintly recalls the return to Verona of the sole surviving Catullus, long hidden 'beneath a bushel', there may be others who will reflect on the discovery, by the sort of accident that happens only to the prepared, of a third cardinal manuscript to be set beside O and G, the Codex Romanus (R) in the year 1896, together with certain Homeric battles over its importance which ensued.

It has always been the fate of Catullus, not only to live dangerously so to speak, but to attract to himself the attention of minds fertile in humanistic accomplishment. To take only the earliest period, the shade of Petrarch seems to haunt the origins of G and R, and the personality of Coluccio Salutati broods over the emendation and diffusion of their readings. About the very end of the fourteenth century, as we shall see, another equally great reputation lent prominence to, and drew distinction from, the use of the Codex Romanus. A few years before the discovery of R, Robinson Ellis had drawn attention to the resemblance between G and a manuscript in the Library of St Mark's in Venice, known nowadays as M.[1] It is interesting to speculate on

1. See Appendix 1.

[113]

the question what status would today be accorded to M if R had not yet emerged from the shadows of the Vatican; for in fact M is a copy, as close as its writer could manage to make it – and he had none other to check it by – of R itself. The scribe of M was a very young man, hardly proficient in Latin as yet, employed at Florence (where he had recently arrived from the country) in the service of the Chancellor of that city, owner of R for perhaps thirty years, Coluccio Salutati; the date was in, or shortly after, the year 1400. He tried out three different styles of writing in the course of the transcription, changing in mid-page to a second style to which he adhered until he equally abruptly abandoned it for a third. The fact is not devoid of significance, since he was to become one of the leading patterns and exponents of the new humanistic book-hand (his text begins with a colored initial C in the fully humanistic manner). Years later, as it would seem, he went over his own manuscript again, once more with no intention but that of following as faithfully as possible what he found before him in R, incorporating Coluccio's corrections and variant readings as far as possible. A certain number of the many *deteriores* appear to derive their R-like readings from his manuscript rather than from R itself; not surprisingly, perhaps, in view of the prestige which later came to be attached to the name of M's scribe: Poggio Bracciolini.[2]

That in spite of the fact that M's hand appears three times in R itself it should never have seriously occurred either to W. G. Hale (R's discoverer) or to B. L. Ullman (Hale's chosen successor in textual matters concerned with Catullus) that M might be Poggio's work, is very surprising. It is tempting to attribute this obliviousness towards M to the running battle, which lasted many years, between Hale and M's champion, K. P. Schulze, who had been prompted by Ellis's notice of M to publish a series of readings from that manuscript in *Hermes* for 1888.[3] Schulze bitterly and repeatedly attacked the credentials of R; with some success, because Hale never gave anything like a full picture of R's contents and – astoundingly – never published a collation. It may be therefore that M was subconsciously eliminated from

2. See A. C. de la Mare and D. F. S. Thomson, 'Poggio's Earliest Manuscript?', *Italia medioevale e umanistica* (forthcoming).

3. See Appendix 1.

Hale's memory while he concentrated on his long and ultimately unfinished task of tracing the affiliations of later and less important manuscripts, with the declared intention of reconstructing the entire tradition. In 1928 Hale died at his desk, his collations of the *codices deteriores* of Catullus lying open before him.[4] Meanwhile, one vital fact had apparently eluded the attention of Hale himself and of the many young scholars, members of his 'seminary' on the manuscripts of Catullus (several of whom were to win great distinction later): namely, that the composition of M – and also, to a much lesser degree, of Laur. 36.23 – provides the essential key to the dating of various stages in the process of correction, including the addition of variant readings, which R underwent at the hands of Coluccio. The same fact is also serviceable to us in deciding questions, often delicate enough to defeat Hale and his most expert pupils, whether a very slight change in R – a mere erasure, say, or the addition of an expunging dot – should be credited to R himself (for if it was not there to be imitated by M, it must be a *late* addition by Coluccio); or whether again a similarly slight correction in R should be attributed to Coluccio or to the hand which, in the late fifteenth century, added those variants and corrections which, in my published collation of R, I designate by the siglum R³.[5] In the latter case, of course, it is obvious that a probable ascription to R³ attaches to corrections which we can see in R, but which Poggio, at his careful second recension (M²), could not.

The evidence that M was copied directly from R, without inspection of G or of any other manuscript of Catullus, is so strong as to be overwhelming: (1) The metrical notes in M correspond exactly with those in R, save for the fact that against poem 11, M has *Genus metri* preceding *faleuticum endecasillabum*, whereas R has not. (This divergence is fully explained by Hale in *CP* 3 (1908), 252–3; it does not in effect constitute an exception.) In G, on the other hand, the metrical notes differ widely from those in M.

---

4. The best and fullest account of Hale's life available to classical scholars is, I think, to be found in the obituary article 'William Gardner Hale 1849–1928' which appeared in *CP* 23 (1928), 278–9 over the initials C.D.B. (Carl D. Buck).

5. D. F. S. Thomson, 'The Codex Romanus of Catullus: A Collation of the Text', *Rh. Mus.* 113 (1970), 97–110.

(2) The system of crosses, written in the margin by R in order
to mark apparent errors in the text which seemed to him to
require investigation, is carefully imitated in M, which reproduces
not only the style of the small crosses but their position in the
margins vis-à-vis the lines of poetry to which they refer.

(3) The readings of M faithfully follow those of R. The list
of correspondences given in A. C. de la Mare and D. F. S. Thomson, 'Poggio's Earliest Manuscript?' (*Italia medioevale e umanistica*,
forthcoming) is highly selective. There are, I believe, only three
exceptions, all mentioned in the above-quoted article, with the
following comments in substance: (*a*) xxi. 6 *experibus* GM, *-bis*
OR; but the error seems quite independent – cf. cod. Leid. 76 –
and is perhaps a natural one since (both words being *uoces
nihili*), while *-bis* makes no sense at all, *-bus* at least seems to
offer a familiar kind of ending; (*b*) lxiv. 211 *uiscere* GM, *uisere*
OR, which may be explained by the widely differing habits in
the matter of spelling of humanists at that period ('largely a
matter of individual habit', Hale *loc. cit.* 250: those familiar with
the manuscripts under discussion will readily agree); and lastly
(*c*) xxxix. 12 *lamiuinus* OGM, *lauuinus* R, where R looks so like
lamiuinus as to be deceptive, though Poggio in his second or M²
revision finally perceived the truth.

We may at this point take as established the faithful dependence
of M on R (and early R² = Coluccio. Some indication of the
actual date of these early R² corrections may be obtained from
the fact that v. 8, corrected by Coluccio to read *mi altera da* –
imitated of course by M – appears in this form in a letter of
Coluccio's dated to 1392–4). Similarly faithful imitation of R²
(late) by M² (Poggio again) may also be taken as established. It
is time to turn to the Sangermanensis (G), in view of the
commonly accepted derivation of both G and R from a lost copy
(X) of the lost Verona manuscript. It would be quite easy to
show that – to take last things first – the hand known as G²
depends wholly on M² and hence (indirectly, not directly) on
R–R²; but the evidence of this has been quite well mustered by
Hale, and need hardly be repeated or amplified. As for G itself
in its original form, Giuseppe Billanovich has with considerable
probability identified its scribe as Antonio da Legnago, chancellor
of Cansignorio della Scala, which means that it was written at

Verona in 1375.[6] R, on the other hand, was copied in Florence, in the scriptorium of Coluccio to whom it belonged. Its scribe was a professional, who put right his own slips of the pen, but fails to show a scholar's interest in 'improving' the text; this task was left, or reserved, for Coluccio himself. Plainly the writer of G can have had no knowledge of R; that the reverse is also true is generally admitted, and requires little demonstration. It is now accepted doctrine that the similarities between G and R arise from their common origin in X.

Hale and Ullman came to accept the view that Coluccio first commissioned G to be written in Verona, then found its text unsatisfactory upon inspection, and caused R to be made in its place. This would imply that both X and G found their way to Florence, but G arrived there first. However, for reasons that will appear presently, I find it preferable to suppose that both indeed came to Florence, but X preceded G. The question is not as unimportant as perhaps it may seem; for it affects the status of certain series of variant readings which appear to occur both in G and R (if we do not accurately distinguish what has been contributed by the various hands) and which scholars have been led too readily to take as representing original variants in X, if not in V (the lost Verona manuscript) itself.

Let us for a moment look at R, bearing in mind that R^2 made two recensions, which we may call R^2 'early' and R^2 'late'. Examination of these two recensions shows a difference, based on the distinction between *variants*, or alternative readings (whether or not based on the authority of a second manuscript: sometimes they are due to conjecture) and *corrections*, due to the scribe's belief that the manuscript before him is actually corrupt. In R^2's first recension, not unnaturally perhaps, the stress is upon corrections. There are about 186 of these: all obvious, except perhaps two. By contrast, R^2 'late' shows only about 12 corrections in the strict sense. *Per contra*, R^2 'late' reveals about 104 *variants*; in R^2 'early', there had been scarcely 24 of them; and the contrast is even more marked in the last 17 of R's 37 folios, for there we find only 6 R^2 'early' variants against 51 R^2 'late' variants. As to these six, they in no way suggest that the

6. 'Dal Livio di Raterio al Livio del Petrarca', *Italia medioevale e umanistica* 2 (1959), 103–78, esp. 160ff.).

hand that inserted them had knowledge of any other manuscript, such as G: the single agreement is obvious and, I believe, co-incidental.[7] Indeed with very few minor exceptions, explicable on special grounds, there is no single instance where we *must* posit some reason for agreement between R and the original text of G: except in the following group. In G (fols. 1–7) there are ten variants shared with R^2 'late'.[8] If these were in X, and R^2 saw X, then since R^2 was already looking for variants in his first recension, why did he not adopt them in his 'early' period? These are in fact the only variants, given as such, in G's original hand. Presumably G inherited them from X, since they also appear in R – such has been the critical argument hitherto. But one may then well suppose that these were the only variants offered in X itself, and if so the overwhelming majority of R^2 variants were invented. All of R^2's early variants do in fact suggest this by their nature. It does seem therefore that R^2 either had access to no other manuscript, during his early recension, than the one he was correcting, or chose to neglect one that he might have seen. (Was the first recension a rapid run-through with the firm intention of returning to the task with X, say, in hand?) Later, R^2 called for *some* manuscript (either X or G, on the evidence thus far) and, relying on it, inserted those R^2 'late' variants which agree with those we see in G. Since Cod. Laur. 36.23, written about 1400,[9] has a purely R/R^2 text – showing not a single agreement with G against R, and indeed no R^2 'very-late' readings either – it does not seem that G was easily to be consulted in Coluccio's scriptorium at that date, or perhaps even later, at the time when Poggio made his thorough (M^2) recension of the text of his own manuscript, M. G was, then, brought presumably from some obscurity, and rather late, after Coluccio's death in 1406, so that the G^2 additions could be made in it by a scribe as devoted to his model, M/M^2, as Poggio himself had been to what he saw before him in R/R^2.

7. See fol. 36 r (c. 2: al. *ueronensum*).

8. See Max Bonnet, *Revue critique d'histoire et de littérature*, no. 4, 27 January 1877, where these variants by the first hand of G are separately described.

9. See e.g. R. A. B. Mynors, *OCT*, preface, p. vii: *fortasse saeculo quarto decimo exeunti ascribendum*, and the unpublished manuscript notes on the fly-leaf of the collation made and revised by W. G. Hale's students and kept at Chapel Hill in the library of the Department of Classics, U.N.C.

I conclude (1) that R² probably did not see G himself at any time (at least the evidence points the other way); (2) that R² used X – not G – in his later recension, and drew from X the ten 'inherited' variants mentioned above, and quite possibly many of his *late*-period variants also, which do not appear in G for the simple reason that G stopped (we do not know why he stopped) inserting X's variants after fol. 7 – perhaps under the urging of haste, or of pressure from Florence to finish the job at Verona? (3) that R²'s *early* variants have nothing to do with G or X, but are (so far as we can see) inventions, of a fairly obvious sort, by a scholar who was unaware, perhaps, that X offered variants at all.

Overall, as we have seen, R²'s variants show very little agreement with G (first hand); but they do offer some remarkable agreements with O; such agreements are always R² 'late', and especially occur in the last seventeen folios.[10] It looks as if R² had a manuscript of the type of O brought to him latterly. Was it O itself? If O was kept at Florence along with the (R² version of) R, then we could explain the scattering of O-readings among the minor manuscripts of the central tradition, derived essentially from R, which Zicàri has both observed, and used as a basis for arranging those manuscripts into groups.[11]

One further corollary is this: if the variants in R were copied from, and may be assumed to represent, variants existing in X, and if no further variants were added to X between the copying of G and X's migration to Florence, then it would appear that G entered only a few of the variants he found in X, and gave up doing even this after his own fol. 7. A word may also be added concerning O. Because of the lack of agreement between the GR variants and those few variants which O exhibits, it is hardly without diffidence that we can suppose the GR variants to be an inheritance from V itself; we must rather consider whether some of them at least may not have been entered in X by a person who read it, whether or not he found another manuscript in Verona to be a source of variants. If we remember that G

---

10. E.g. on fol. 29 r (LXVI. 86): *indignatis* O, al. *indignis*, al. *indignatis* R².

11. See M. Zicàri, 'Ricerche sulla tradizione manoscritta di Catullo', *Bollettino del comitato per la preparazione dell'Edizione Nazionale dei Classici Greci e Latini* N.S. fasc. 6 (1958), 79–99.

was copied in the year after Petrarch died, and remember also
Petrarch's habit of adding notes and conjectures to manuscripts
he used, it is not beyond the bounds of possibility that a considerable
number of improvements in the text of Catullus, transmitted to
us largely by Coluccio Salutati, is the work of Petrarch himself.
Whether Petrarch actually owned a manuscript of Catullus is
still a matter of some dispute,[12] but certainly Coluccio was in
touch with Petrarch's circle of friends – one of whom (Gaspare
de' Broaspini) was also a close friend of the copyist of G – in the
year 1375, and the Propertius from Petrarch's library, requested
by Coluccio in that year, actually reached Coluccio four years
later from the hand of Petrarch's literary executor, Lombardo
della Seta. An attempt, at any rate, to obtain a Catullus from
the same source was made at the same time by Coluccio.[13]

Among the late variants added by Coluccio in R, there are, as
I have already remarked, some that introduce (prefixed by 'al.')
the readings we find in O. Now, we have seen that whereas in
his 'early R²' recension Coluccio seems to have been more or
less content to correct the text of R *suo Marte*, in his later revision
he called upon the help of other manuscripts: at least X, which
he does not seem to have used systematically (and perhaps not
at all) before, and possibly also a manuscript of the O tradition –
was it O itself? – which could possibly have been the Catullus
(with the poet's name spelled with a single *l*, as in O and also
apparently in V) which we find recorded in Milan in 1390.[14]

12. *Pro*: B. L. Ullman, *Studies in the Italian Renaissance* (Rome 1955), p. 195,
and 'The transmission of the text of Catullus', *Studi in onore di Luigi Castiglioni*,
vol. 2 (Florence 1960), pp. 1025–57, esp. pp. 1043ff. *Contra*: Umberto Bosco,
'Il Petrarca e l'umanesimo filologico (postille al Nolhac e al Sabbadini)',
Giorn. Stor. Lett. Ital. 120 (1942), 65–119, esp. 108–16. Bosco's arguments do
not quite convince me, but they are supported by the authority of M. Zicàri,
'A proposito di un altro Catullo', *Rendiconti dell'Istituto Lombardo di Scienze
e Lettere, classe di lettere*, vol. 85, fasc. 2 (1952), 248ff., esp. 254.

13. See B. L. Ullman, 'The transmission of Catullus', pp. 1045ff.

14. See F. Novati, 'Umanisti genovesi del sec. XIV', *Giornale Ligustico di
Archeol. St. e Lett.* 17 (1890), 40; quoted by M. Zicàri, 'Ricerche sulla tradizione',
p. 99 n. 27. According to information kindly supplied to me by the author
of the latter article, the owner of this Catullus was in Verona about the year
1387. It might also seem appropriate if I were to quote the conclusion of
his note, *à propos* of the Visconti library at Pavia: 'la famosa biblioteca, che
proprio in quegli anni [sc. 1385–9] (ved. Sabbadini, *Scoperte ecc.*, II, 125), si
arrichiva di prede sottratte anche a Verona e a Padova, fra le quali non
è forse ardito supporre che si potesse trovare una copia di O'. For the spelling

If this was indeed of 'O type', and made its way to Florence about 1400, it might have been taken into fairly frequent use for checking manuscripts copied in Florence, the usual base of which was, as their readings demonstrate, the splendidly legible R. Such use of an O-type manuscript would at least conjecturally explain the scattering of O-readings that affects the early fifteenth-century tradition of Catullus, beginning with Bononiensis 2621 (1411/12) and Parisinus 7989 (1423). The latter manuscript brings us back to Poggio; for it is the famous codex Traguriensis, and contains the *Cena Trimalchionis* and other fragments of Petronius, which were the fruits of Poggio's travels in England, it would seem, and in Cologne.[15]

The effect perhaps, and certainly the intention, of this summary discussion has been in the first place to invite exploration of many questions it has raised but cannot, within its limits, hope to solve; and in the second place to emphasize the debt, a debt greater than has been hitherto acknowledged, that we owe, in matters concerning the text of Catullus, to the care and toil of Coluccio Salutati.

APPENDIX I. THE DISCOVERY OF R AND ITS PLACE IN THE HISTORY OF SCHOLARSHIP

Clear and succinct accounts of the discovery of R have at various times been given by Hale and Ullman, and its is hardly necessary to do more than summarize these and refer to the list of Hale's published articles compiled by Ullman and included in Ullman's *The Humanism of Coluccio Salutati* (Padua 1963), p. 193.[16] In 1896, the moment should have been opportune.

of the poet's name in the Pavia manuscript, and the relation of that spelling to V (and of course to O, by-passing G and R), see B. L. Ullman, 'The transmission of Catullus', p. 1045.

15. See Appendix II.

16. See especially the articles in *CR* 10 (1896), 314; *TAPA* 28 (1897), liii–lv; *AJA* N.S. 1 (1897), 33–9; *Hermes* 34 (1899), 133–44; *TAPA* 53 (1922), 103–12. The list given by R. G. C. Levens in M. Platnauer (ed.), *Fifty Years of Classical Scholarship* (Oxford 1954) is not quite complete, omitting articles in *AJA* (1897) (see above) and *CP* 1 (1910), 56. Mr Levens is inaccurate also in one detail: the codex was not finally obtained by 'ringing the changes' on a catalogue number; on the contrary, this proved, by Hale's own repeated admission, to be a waste of time (*AJA* (1897), 37; *TAPA* 53 (1922), 109). The

Lachmann in 1829 had struggled to establish a sound text on the basis of D and another Berlin manuscript; but he as signally failed here as he succeeded with the text of Lucretius, for his manuscripts were worthless. It was Baehrens who, accepting Ellis' indications of the extremely high value to be set on O, showed beyond doubt that of all manuscripts then known – at the date, that is, of his text-edition, 1876 – only O and G would serve as a foundation for Catullus. Twenty years spent in the digestion of Baehrens' arguments ought to have sufficed to prepare the scholarly world for the absorption of a twin and supporter to G in the shape of a new-found R. Most unfortunately, Schulze, acting upon another suggestion of Ellis to the effect that the codex Marcianus (M) might repay further study, had adopted this manuscript (M) with a fostering and indeed possessive zeal, and by an article on its readings in *Hermes* (1888),[17] established for himself a considerable reputation as its exponent. But alas for Schulze! The manuscript about to be reborn was to prove to be the source and the immediate source of everything in his cherished Marcianus.[18] The rumor that such was its general character was to him, therefore, bound to be at the least highly exciting; a psychological probability for which Hale made totally insufficient allowance, with the consequences which we shall presently observe. Hale's other blind spot lay in his failure to realize the deep attachment he would have to overcome on the part of German scholars to D; not because of its merits, but because of their veneration for the name of Lachmann which had become attached to it. It was urgently necessary, therefore, that he should produce all the evidence on which rested his incautiously announced discovery of the third major manuscript and in some ways the most important of all.

It was because Hale was already familiar with O and G, as well as having a broad acquaintance with the minor manuscripts, that he was able to realize at once what a prize he had secured. He perceived at once that R had been in the possession of

codex was in fact located by calling for the *inventario* of the Ottoboni collection and glancing at numbers adjacent to the false one, namely 1809 (for '1829'). It is well to note how manuscripts may be lost – and found.

17. 'Der Codex M des Catull', *Hermes* 23 (1888), 567–91.

18. As Hale demonstrated in *Hermes* 34 (1899), 141 and esp. *CP* 3 (1908), 256.

Coluccio Salutati, and related it tentatively to Coluccio's search for Catullian manuscripts in Verona and Padua at Petrarch's death, attested in certain letters from Coluccio's *epistolario* as edited by Novati.[19] He noted the large number of alternative readings in R, and later discovered that those in the earliest of its correcting hands were added by Coluccio himself. The acumen which discovered so much so soon is almost beyond praise. But frustration lay ahead.

In July 1896 Hale wrote:[20] 'The results of my collation will appear in Vol. 1 of the Papers of the American School next winter...At my request the Vatican will publish a complete facsimile, which will appear at the same time.' In 1897:[21] 'I plan...to publish a volume. This volume will contain the collation of R, G and O...and the collation will accompany a continuous restored text of the "lost Verona MS"', and 'The Vatican will publish a facsimile...' In the following year, however, he writes in a somewhat different strain:[22] 'The date of the announcement now seems remote...busy cares...have left me little time for the very considerable labor of the preparation of my collation for print.' Meantime, the world of scholarship waited in vain for the full evidence upon which Hale's discoveries were to be convincingly seen to rest; and three things happened. First, Robinson Ellis, with Hale's knowledge and permission, made a visit to Rome for the purpose of satisfying his curiosity by noting the readings of R in the margins of his copy of the 1893 Baehrens–Schulze Catullus (but had refrained from using his knowledge);[23] secondly, A. E. Housman's ferocious review of this same Baehrens–Schulze volume ('Mr Schulze's ignorance of how things are done and his inability to learn...No vestige of these corrections [by Baehrens] survives in the monument reared to their author's memory by the Oedipodean piety of Mr

19. I. 170, 207, 222.   20. *CR* 10 (1896), 314.
21. *TAPA* 28 (1897), liii–lv.
22. *CR* 12 (1898), 447–9.
23. Ellis' notes of the readings of R are now in the possession of Mr R. G. C. Levens, who kindly put them at my disposal for study. Though they do not amount to a full collation of the manuscript, the notes have in several places been useful for checking my own. R[2] identifications were checked with Ullman's thesis, *The Identification of the Manuscripts of Catullus cited in Statius' edition of 1566* (Chicago 1908), and with Merrill's 1923 Teubner Catullus.

Schulze')[24] had time to exert its full effect on Schulze's equanimity; and thirdly, Schulze himself seized his pen and, in the thirty-third volume of *Hermes*,[25] fired the opening salvoes of a violent battle. He complained bitterly of Hale's long silence and of his failure to show why R was to be considered superior to his beloved M and to all others save O and G; and at the same time announced that he had solved the problem for himself by collating R at the Vatican in the spring of that year (1898) and proving to his own satisfaction that, since it agreed so largely with M, it was of little independent value. In reply to this Hale in *Classical Review* for 1898[26] offered an answering article, which he said would be published presently in *Hermes* (it appeared in the next volume)[27] and again referred to 'the collation, which I hope will appear before many months.' Hale dismissed some of Schulze's more palpable errors, e.g. by spelling out the external evidence for a fourteenth-century dating of R; and ended by promising to make (with the aid of students) complete collations of a considerable number of the *minor* manuscripts; 'this done, I propose to publish a continuous restored text of the Verona Ms.' Schulze's reply was a further complaint of delay on Hale's part, and of Hale's 'very irritated tone'.[28] Unwisely, Schulze gave a series of what he alleged to be the readings in R, collected by himself, to prove that R was a manuscript 'of no exceptional worth'. Most of these, as Hale had no difficulty in showing (and as inspection of the manuscript confirms) either are simply erroneous or confound the original hand with hands of perhaps a century later.

Hale's extended reply to Schulze, in German this time, appeared in *Hermes* vol. 34 (1899).[29] After a particularly valuable introduction on the use of different manuscripts by the principal Catullian scholars from Baehrens onwards, Hale patiently restated the problem, and went on to convict Schulze both of misreading the manuscript and of failing to draw the proper conclusions from the evidence, especially that appertaining to M's agreements with R. He showed how and why R ranked with O and G although it was independent of both; and further why he believed the *deteriores* (including M) to derive largely from R itself.

24. *CR* 8 (1894), 251–7.   25. *Hermes* 33 (1898), 511–12.
26. *CR* 12 (1898), 447–9.   27. *Hermes* 34 (1899), 133–44.
28. *B. Ph. Woch.* (1899), 442–5.   29. See note 27.

In June 1902 Ellis, whose patience and scholarly good manners in leaving the field to Hale are publicly acknowledged in Hale's writings (e.g. *CR* 20(1906), 160), went to Rome again. This time he noted a series of readings with a view particularly to R's relation to M, and in the second place to other *Vatican* manuscripts, to one of which Ellis had previously drawn attention; but he still made no public allusion to the fact of his two collations – a fact, it seems, known only to Ehrle, Hale and Hale's students. In 1904, Ellis published his Oxford Classical Text of Catullus; and in the same year, Schulze, largely ignoring Hale's previous comments, tried once again to exalt M above R in value.[30] Then came a lull until, in an article in *Classical Review* for 1906 entitled 'Catullus Once More',[31] Hale remarked: 'No one can regret more deeply than I do my enforced delay' and added some fresh observations on R, e.g. 'There are eight hands at least... Many of the double readings of G and R were in V (e.g. R *al' mauli* 68. 11 restores for us the original *Manli*). If today all Mss of Catullus but one were to be swept from the world, R would best deserve to remain... A new collation of G is necessary... G was (probably) corrected on R.' Among these suggestions there was one which had to be retracted two years later, namely that O was likely to have belonged to Petrarch. In the latter year, 1908, Hale gave details of the activities of his students in collating the *deteriores*, a comparison of which among themselves and with the major manuscripts must, he now thought, precede the 'reconstruction of the lost Verona Ms' which was to justify his high opinion of R. It will be observed that Hale had by this time shifted completely the ground of his delay in producing for public inspection a collation and facsimile of R. Further, he is apt to blame the reluctance of scholars to accept his assertions about the superiority of R for imposing on him the necessity of investigating a multitude of secondary manuscripts as a first priority.[32] As a result of this shifting of ground, some distrust of his perfectly correct conclusions was inevitable, even had Schulze, for example, been less obtuse and unyielding. What is distressing, to those who believe in the sovereignty of reason

---

30. *Woch. f. kl. Phil.* (30 November 1904).
31. *CR* 20 (1906), 160–4.
32. *CP* 3 (1908), 232–6; *TAPA* 53 (1922), 103–12.

and persuasion in the world at least of scholarship, is the deliberate
and long-enduring adherence to manifest error in the face of
rational argument and common sense which made Hale's task
so difficult and robbed his discovery of some deserved laurels.

APPENDIX II. CODEX PARISINUS 7989; WITH REMARKS ON CODEX BONONIENSIS 2621

The first (and more important) of these, which I shall call P,
is the only representative of the stage of correction designated
by the symbol β in Mynors' *OCT*; similarly B, as I shall call
it, is the sole representative of Mynors' α. It is only when one has
made clear, as I hope my own published collation of R will
have done, that P antedates many of the readings denoted by
a small r in the *OCT* that one can speak usefully of P's place in
the tradition. I shall be brief at this point, as I hope to supply
confirmatory detail, and an ampler discussion, elsewhere.

P stands at a nodal point in what M. Zicàri ('Ricerche sulla
tradizione', pp. 88–91 and table, p. 80) has called the 'Σ'
tradition: it is in fact the head of Zicàri's 'B' group, standing as
a milestone between Σ and σ. The first thing it tells us is that in
1423, when it was written, manuscripts of Catullus were not
plentiful; not only was the Catullus part a late arrival, following
the Tibullus and Propertius (which show knowledge of each
other, of Ovid and of Petrarch but never of Catullus), but, to
take an example, whereas at Propertius III. 11. 35 no less than
seven different readings are quoted which can now be linked
to manuscripts of quite diverse traditions (the first two of them
to manuscripts of the A class, the third and fourth to some in
the μυρ tradition, the fifth to NΔ, the sixth and seventh to sources
unknown today), nothing comparable to this can be found anywhere in the Catullus part, even though the scribe of P was a
cultivated scholar with a genuine power of discrimination and
a desire to seek out the best available reading; in fact analysis
of the readings of P shows that he is principally dependent on
(1) R + R^2 (or a copy; but not 'R^2 very late', since for example
he shows at LXVI. 86 R^2's first correction *indignis*, but not his
second correction *indignatis*, which is not in Laur. 36.23 (c. 1400)
either; (2) a manuscript similar to B. In addition, there are

correspondences with O, of moderate number: apart from those very few which could have been mediated to P by R, I have counted some 50 to 60 links between O and P which are not mediated through any channel we know of. (We have already observed signs of an O-connection in the later readings of R^2, and briefly discussed the possibility that an O-type manuscript was available in Florence, where P was written.) What is quite notably absent is the shadow of G: indeed only *one* reading in P has G as its only indicated source, namely xv. 16 *nostrum*, for *nostrorum* R *cett.* This of course completely eliminates G as the indirect progenitor of the part of the tradition of which P is (as Zicàri has shown, 'Ricerche sulla tradizione') the fountain-head, and reinforces Hale's and Ullman's view of the central importance of R.

There are in P also 22 (not I think 23, as Zicàri suggests) readings belonging to Zicàri's Σ tradition. Finally, there is a group of readings which, up to P's date, must be regarded as unique; which is not to say that they are inherited from some unknown source: three-quarters of them are palpable emendations, or attempts at emendation – presumably emanating from P himself, since his marginal notes betray the emendator's mind and outlook. The rest are either errors or point to an unknown cause or source: only five at most seem to me to fall within the latter category, and any or all of these may be errors too. It may be remarked how free from the phenomenon of sheer error P's manuscript is: in which respect he is at the opposite pole from B, who teems with mistakes and *lapsus calami*. Not that P absolutely does not commit these, but he is alert to them and corrects them himself – almost always.

There is a definite, recurring pattern in P's relation to B (written about eleven-and-a-half years before P) which expresses the relation of both of them to R. It will be found, as a rule, that where B = R, P = R^2. It may seem that where R^2 gives a variant, overwhelmingly the choice of B is for the original reading in the text. This is in accordance with his character: cautious, fulfilling to the best of his very limited ability his function as a transcriber, which he seems to have interpreted as a licence to ignore additions and variants. By contrast, P is careful and judicious at the same time, and also bold in adopting

good corrections – or leaving corrections alone, if the old text
seems to him better. This explains why almost exactly twice as
many β (P) as α (B) corrections have found their way into the
apparatus of the *OCT*, for instance. So unreliable is B, despite
his early date, that some of his 'good' readings appear to have
arrived in his text by accident; one never feels this about P. The
procedure of P leads one to believe that the choice between R
and R² readings is not made by P himself, but by a predecessor;
which, if true, implies that P used R indirectly. It may be that
B did the same for reasons of which the following is an example:
at LXVI. 86 (a line we have already discussed) R has *indigetis*; so
has G; B shows *ingetis*; R² corrects to *indignis*, but there is no
sign of this in B (although B in many places does agree with R²);
P, though he adopts R²'s *indignis*, is (as above remarked) unaware
of R²'s last correction *indignatis* (= O).

Headings, gaps and omissions in P

The headings (some sixty of them) have the following relation
to those suggested for the archetype of the main 'V' tradition
in *OCT* (pp. xiv–xv):

P agrees with archetype:	38 times
'No'	18 times
'Not quite'	6 times
	62

In P the introductory verses are attributed to Catullus himself;
P is the earliest extant MS to do so. See, on this attribution,
M. Zicàri, 'Ricerche sulla tradizione', p. 90 and n. 21.

The gaps in P help to fix its relationship to O and to R, G and
B. P contains XCII. 3–4, thereby agreeing with O and not with
GR; on the other hand, it does not omit LXIV. 330, as O does.
It also contains LXI. 149–53, omitted by B; and it contains
LXI. 142–6; thus R², not R. On the other hand, it places LXI. 189–93
after 198, in which it is without a known forerunner.

Blank spaces equaling one line are left (originally) by P at
v. 9 (*rest. in marg.*) – there is no gap here in R, but there is in
G – ; LXV. 9 (no gap in R); LXVIII. 47 (blank space in R, with
deficit in left margin). In the three lines XXXI. 11–13, P obviously
had difficulty in reading his exemplar, for there are despairing

dashes covering the extent of about a word each: this means
that P's exemplar could not have been R or B as they stand,
though his text here otherwise agrees with theirs, for the readings
they offer are perfectly clear. It should be added that in poem
LXII, where the word *Puelle* appears in the margin of R in R²'s
hand at vv. 6, 11, 20, 32 and 39, P has .P. (= Puelle) oniy at
20, 32 and 39; whereas the word *Iuuenes*, appearing in R² at
vv. 26 and 49 only, appears in P (as .Iu.) at vv. 26, 36 and 39.

Towards a fresh interpretation of Horace *Carm.* III. 1

EDMUND T. SILK

THE admirable new commentary on the first book of Horace's Odes by Nisbet and Hubbard opens with the intriguing sentence, 'The Odes of Horace are too familiar to be easily understood.'[1] In the opinion of the present writer, *Carm.* III. 1 is a fine example of what Mr Nisbet had in mind. None of Horace's poems can be more familiar than the first 'Roman' ode, and there is a huge literature dealing with all the Roman odes. Yet some obvious questions remain unsolved and even unasked. Part I of this paper was directly inspired by Mr Nisbet's intimation that students of Horace have become inattentive readers of Horace. Both the question there raised and my answer to it will probably be controversial. Part II is a reopening of a case that I presented in an earlier volume of *Yale Classical Studies*.[2] In that publication I raised objections to the identification of *Necessitas* (III. 1. 14) with 'Death the Leveler'. Since my objections appear to have escaped the notice of editors and commentators hitherto, I am presenting them once more in a revised and expanded form.

I. THE INAUDIBLE SONG OF THE MUSES
(III. 1. 1–4)

The first 'Roman Ode' begins:

> Odi profanum vulgus et arceo.
> favete linguis: carmina non prius
> audita Musarum sacerdos
> virginibus puerisque canto.

In all the discussions of this famous stanza, as far as I can discover, the question has never been asked, whether the phrase *carmina*

---

1. *A Commentary on Horace: Odes Book I* (Oxford 1970), p. xi.
2. 'Notes on Cicero and the Odes of Horace', *YCS* 13 (1952), 145–58.

non prius audita could mean anything but 'poems that have never been recited or published before'. That is to say, students and commentators seem generally to have assumed that the phrase contains a poet's expression of pride in achievement. He is announcing quite literally that he is herewith publishing poems that have never been recited, or he is announcing the publication of a new kind of poetry. Heinze appears to have taken the phrase quite literally as 'neue Lieder'.[3] Wickham[4] thought Horace might have been echoing this phrase when he later wrote:

> Hunc [sc. Alcaeum] ego, non alio dictum prius ore, Latinus
> volgavi fidicen. iuvat immemorata ferentem
> ingenuis oculisque legi manibusque teneri. (*Ep.* 1. 19. 32-4)

The most recent comment on *carmina non prius audita* appears to be that of Professor Gordon Williams, who takes the phrase to be Horace's announcement of something quite new in Latin poetry, namely political lyric.[5]

If one asks the question whether Horace, in using the phrase *carmina non prius audita*, can have had in mind anything beside an expression of pride in accomplishment, it seems to be that the answer should be 'yes'. Horace explicitly says in this opening stanza that he is turning in disgust from one audience and hopefully appealing to another. At least a case can be made, it seems to me, for seeing in *carmina non prius audita* the cause of the poet's disgust as well as his reason for turning to the younger generation. I venture to render the phrase, 'a poet's message that has hitherto fallen upon deaf ears'.

In spite of the superficial plausibility of the prevailing interpretation of III. 1. 1-4 as an expression of the poet's pride, there are serious objections to be made to it. In the first place the

---

3. *Q. Horatius Flaccus, Oden und Epoden* (Berlin 1930), p. 251.
4. *The Works of Horace* 1 (Oxford 1896), p. 187.
5. *The Third Book of Horace's Odes* (Oxford 1969), p. 3. Part of Williams' comment on III. 1. 1-4 reads as follows, 'It is a proud announcement in the manner of an announcement at the mysteries, by which the poet declares first those whom he does not address (the general mass of the people), then his chosen audience (boys and girls) – representatives of a new generation: this choice of audience prepares the reader for a certain didactic element in the poetry. Finally, the poems will be totally original (2-3): the poet is conscious that no one has ever yet brought poetry directly into the field of contemporary politics.'

Roman Odes can scarcely be described as Horace's first political lyrics, whether you calculate chronologically or review the poems in their published order. The Roman Odes may be Horace's most ambitious, most remarkable, most impressive, extensive, and most concentrated expression of his philosophical, religious and political sentiments, but it cannot be said that such topics are treated by Horace for the first time in the Roman Odes. While there is nothing quite like the Roman Odes elsewhere in Horace, these poems are rather an Horatian synthesis than a new revelation. They are a restatement in the grand style of characteristic Horatian views. The Roman Odes gather light, as it were, from all quarters of Horace's work and focus it intensely upon a limited area. The *vulgus*, it is true, has never been given the opportunity or the privilege of enjoying the concentrated experience here offered to youths and maidens, but somewhere in the Satires, in the Epodes, and in the first two books of the Odes the Roman people, either collectively or singled out as individuals, has been appealed to, dramatically exhorted, sternly reproved, benignly mocked or ridiculed under thin disguises of myth or allegory. The Roman people has in one way or another been shown most of the shapes of its vice and abundant images of virtue. In other words, the Roman people or the *profanum vulgus* could long since have heard the wisdom of the Muses relayed to them in the songs of the sacred bard – had they been listening! We may recall that at the very beginning of his lyric volume the *vates* broadly hinted his misgivings about the *vulgus* and intimated that probably nobody could hear the song of the Muses but possibly himself:

> me doctarum hederae praemia frontium
> dis miscent superis, me gelidum nemus
> Nympharumque leves cum Satyris chori
> secernunt populo, si neque tibias
> Euterpe cohibet nec Polyhymnia
> Lesboum refugit tendere barbiton. (*Carm.* i. i. 29–34)

Objection to the prevailing interpretation of iii. i. 1–4 as an author's boast does not by itself support my view that what Horace is really doing in this proemium is turning his back on an audience that had failed to get his message and inviting the

attention of one that may be able to hear and understand. Positive
support for my interpretation should presumably begin with a
review of the occurrences of *audire* in the sense of 'hear and
understand'. In the *pro Cluentio* Cicero says to his hearers: *etsi
a vobis audior ut numquam benignius neque attentius quemquam auditum
putem* (63). *Audire* in this sense is not rare. There are examples in
Livy and other writers. More to our purpose, however, are
examples in Horace's own work. One thinks at once of the lyre
of Orpheus that was heard by the trees. In the consolation to
Virgil Horace says

> quid? si Threicio blandius Orpheo
> auditum moderere arboribus fidem... (*Carm.* 1. 24. 13–14)

Then there is the case of Vesta's deliberate deafness to the prayers
of the Vestals:

> ...prece qua fatigent
> virgines sanctae minus audientem
> carmina Vestam? (*Carm.* 1. 2. 26–8)

On another occasion the poet is jubilant because the gods have
given ear to his prayer for revenge:

> Audivere Lyce di mea vota, di
> audivere Lyce... (*Carm.* iv. 13. 1–2)

The most striking instance of the use of *audire* to refer to the
capacity of an audience to hear that which is normally inaudible
occurs at the beginning of the fourth Roman Ode:

> Descende caelo et dic age tibia
> regina longum Calliope melos
> seu voce nunc mavis acuta
> seu fidibus citharave Phoebi.

At this point the poet presumably turns to the choir of youths
and maidens and asks

> Auditis? an me ludit amabilis
> insania?

The poet feels that he himself has caught the sound and, in
hearing it, he feels transported to the groves of the blest:

> audire et videor pios
>   errare per lucos, amoenae
>   quos et aquae subeant et aurae.

As far as language is concerned, the phrase *carmina non prius audita* can surely be taken to mean a poet's message that up to the present moment has been inaudible or unheeded. A more compelling reason for this rendering of the phrase is the fact that it fits the rhetorical posture or the dramatic role of the poet in all his political poetry. If we review briefly the poems in which Horace affects to be addressing the Roman people, the image we get of the poet is that of the *vates* deeply concerned, earnestly exhorting his countrymen to save the state but at the same time plagued by an anxiety that promises to become despair. *Quo quo scelesti ruitis (Epod. 7)?* is the cry of one desperately trying to check a disaster he fears is already beyond control. The frustration of the *vates* is elaborately set forth in Epode 16:

> Altera iam teritur bellis civilibus aetas,
>   suis et ipsa Roma viribus ruit...

Rome, that no enemy could conquer, is collapsing of herself. With heavy irony the poet urges those of his fellow citizens who will (i.e. the *melior pars*) to abandon Rome as it is, sail away and make for the Isles of the Blest where Jove has reserved a place for the good, the just and the virtuous:

> Iuppiter illa piae secrevit litora genti,
>   ut inquinavit aere tempus aureum;
> aere, dehinc ferro duravit saecula, quorum
>   piis secunda vate me datur fuga. (63–6)

The *vates'* mood of anxiety and pessimism is more indirectly but just as vehemently expressed in Ode 1. 2 (*Iam satis terris*) and 1. 3 (*Sic te diva potens*) in which a prayer for Virgil's safe journey to Greece ends in a horrifying vision of Romans as latter-day Titans on the point of storming Heaven:

> Nil mortalibus ardui est:
>   caelum ipsum petimus stultitia neque
> per nostrum patimur scelus
>   iracunda Iovem ponere fulmina. (37–40)

Anxiety verging on despair is the dominant note in what most people since Quintilian have called the 'Ship of State' (I. 14). Recent commentators[6] refuse to see political allegory in the prophecy of Nereus (I. 15), but the tone and tenor of Nereus' warning to Paris are strikingly similar to the other poems cited so far; in fact, Nereus' warning is not unlike that of Juno in the third Roman ode, where the idea of another 'Trojan war' explicitly refers to the situation of Rome. The hymn to Fortune (*O diva gratum quae regis Antium* I. 35) is a bitter poem filled with a mixture of faded hope and near-despair like that which I have seen in the previously mentioned poems. The poems of Book II are chiefly addressed to and concerned with individuals, but *Iam pauca aratro iugera* (II. 15) is a jeremiad in much the same tone as the other poems that we have reviewed. There is some of the same spirit in II. 18 (*Non ebur neque aureum*).

This brief survey has brought us back to the Roman odes. But, before returning to the *carmina non prius audita* we should note that Horace still is playing the role of the *vates* near desperation in *Carm.* III. 24 (*Intactis opulentior*).

The poet has, then, figuratively come before the people many times with pleas, prophecy, warning and cries of despair. He has heard the Muses' message, but he has not been able to make others hear it. So he now makes a final effort to secure a receptive audience.

The foregoing contains the substance of my case for a fresh interpretation of *carmina non prius audita*, but there is something more to be said about Horace's playing the role of the frustrated *vates*. Horace's playing of this role has, I think, controlled the order in which the Roman Odes are arranged. As the series begins, Horace writes with a comfortable didactic poise (III. 1). In the second and first half of the third ode the poet's mood is one of exuberance and soaring confidence. Then, as Juno begins her speech, images of challenge, vaulting hope and limitless possibility are matched by those of weakness, fear and defeat. Even as the poet strains his ear to catch the heavenly music (III. 4) doubt and misgiving return. Doubt turns to incredulous disgust and ultimate despair, as the poet makes a swift descent from celestial ecstasy via the decadence of evolution to the terrible reality of modern Rome.

In all the efforts to analyze the Roman Odes and determine

6. Nisbet and Hubbard, *Commentary*, pp. 188ff.

their relationship to each other, little attention, as far as I know, has been paid to the movement of the poet's mind or the succession of his moods as a major factor in the fusion of a series of autonomous works into an organic and meaningful whole, with beginning, middle and end. The plot of the drama is in the question: can unspoiled youth hear the message of the Muses that its parents and forefathers had failed to hear? The tragic conclusion of the action is that youth cannot hear it either. Students of Horace scarcely need to be reminded, of course, that the terrible pessimism of Horace in the Roman Odes and the other poems that present the image of the frustrated *vates* is not final and irrevocable. As the prayer to 'Mercury' at the close of *Carm.* I. 2 and the Bacchic ecstasy of III. 25 (*Quo me Bacche rapis tui plenum*) make clear, the pessimism is destined to receive ultimate rhetorical relief at the hands of a *deus ex machina* in the person of Caesar. But that rhetorical happy ending has nothing to do with the problem of the *carmina non prius audita*.

The foregoing may seem to have been a rather massive attack upon a small question. But, if there is any validity in the argument that I have presented, the question was not so small. For interpreted one way, *carmina non prius audita* are merely literary novelty; taken the other way the phrase alerts readers to the special place of the Roman Odes in Horace's political poetry as a whole.[7]

Two passages of Cicero make interesting collateral reading for anyone that has followed my discussion thus far. It is also quite within the realm of possibility that they may have been in Horace's mind during the composition of the Roman Odes. The first is the little-read *Paradoxa Stoicorum*. This slight work addressed to Marcus Brutus consists of a preface, in which Cicero urges the utility of the Stoic paradoxes to the orator who can adapt them for presentation to popular audiences. This is not easy to do, for

7. My colleague Professor A. T. Cole has pointed out to me that Ovid's portrait of Pythagoras at the beginning of the fifteenth book of the Metamorphoses may owe something to Horace's picture of the frustrated prophet. Pythagoras, of course, is represented as endeavoring to instruct his audience in the mysteries of the natural universe as a preliminary step to the teaching of ethics. The phrase that Ovid uses (*Met.* xv. 60–75) to characterize Pythagoras' teaching: *non et credita* (referring either to the difficulty of Pythagoras' theme or the unresponsiveness of his audience) has certainly a curious resemblance to Horace's *carmina non prius audita*.

despite the fact that the paradoxes are *verissima* and *maxime Socratica,* they are so far removed from the intellectual experience of the *vulgus* that they are not readily understood. Cast into settings of common life and daily experience these forbidding truths become very effective indeed. So Cicero proceeds to take six paradoxes and 'toss them into commonplaces', to show Brutus what he means. It is, if nothing more, at least an interesting coincidence that passages of the six Paradoxes remind one of the Roman Odes and parts of the Satires of Horace. Certainly Cicero and Horace made use of some of the same *loci communes,* for both have the noble Regulus, who though an exile was not really an exile at all, and both have the planter whose vines have been beaten by the hail. A comparison of the *Paradoxa* with the Roman Odes is also of value, because it helps to sharpen our awareness of the progressive character of the Roman Odes to which I have drawn attention. The *Paradoxa* is a series of six short independent essays more or less mechanically juxtaposed. Odes III. 1–6 are six independent poems dealing with some of the same Stoic themes as the *Paradoxa* but made into a cohesive whole by their order, which reflects the growth of a poet's thought and feeling from hope through anxiety to despair.

The other passage of Cicero suggested as collateral reading is the *Somnium Scipionis.* It is brought to mind by Horace's treatment of the idea of a heavenly music not commonly audible on earth. It will be recalled that, after his father has foretold the brilliance and the perils of his career and after the elder Africanus has shown the younger the place reserved in heaven for the great spirits of earth, Africanus the younger becomes curious to know the source of the remarkable sound that is filling his ears. He is told that it is produced by the perfect harmony of the celestial spheres. This perfect music has, in fact, been reaching the earth always, but men over the ages have become deaf to it. The deafness of men to the heavenly music is like that of those people in Africa who live close to the Cataracts of the Nile. That great roar of the waters has filled their ears for so long that they can no longer hear it. Africanus the younger is impressed but, as his grandfather notes, he cannot keep his attention fastened upon things in heaven but gradually allows his gaze and his mind to turn back to things on earth.

II. NECESSITAS AND DEATH THE LEVELER

regum timendorum in proprios greges,
reges in ipsos imperium est Iovis,
 clari Giganteo triumpho
  cuncta supercilio moventis.

est ut viro vir latius ordinet
arbusta sulcis, hic generosior
 descendat in Campum petitor,
  moribus hic meliorque fama

contendat, illi turba clientium
sit maior; aequa lege Necessitas
 sortitur insignis et imos:
  omne capax movet urna nomen. (III. 1. 5–16)

In these stanzas, the three following the proemium, Horace
marshals representatives of the great and powerful of this world
before Necessitas, who is busy casting lots. For some time it has been
assumed by students of Horace that Necessitas with her urn is
intended to represent 'Death the Leveler', who reduces to naught
the ambitions of men.[8] As far as I have been able to discover, only
two voices have ever been raised in opposition to this identification
and neither recently. Orelli took it for granted that Horace
intended Necessitas to stand for Ἀνάγκη or Εἱμαρμένη.[9] Medley[10]

---

8. Typical expressions of this view are those of Williams (above, n. 5),
Third Book of Horace's Odes, p. 284, and *Tradition and Originality in Roman
Poetry* (Oxford 1968), pp. 586–7; R. Heinze, *Q. Horatius Flaccus*, p. 250, and
Wickham, *Works of Horace*, p. 186. Hendrik Wagenvoort, *De Horatii quae
dicuntur Odis Romanis* (Leiden 1911), was reminded by the gallery of folk
before Necessitas of the similar gathering of souls in the Myth of Er; nevertheless
he had no doubt that Horace's *Necessitas* represented Death. Since my purpose
is to oppose an opinion that is current at the present time, I shall not undertake
to make a complete census of opinion in the past. My one hope, however, is
that I may not have missed any Horatians who should be honored by inclusion
in the next two notes with Orelli and Medley.

9. Io. Caspar Orellius, *Q. Horatius Flaccus*, ed. minor tertia, 1 (Zürich 1802),
ad loc.

10. John Green Skemp, M.A. and George Watson Macalpine (eds.),
Interpretations of Horace by the late William Medley, M.A. (Oxford 1910), p. 102.
Medley's analysis of III. 1 as a whole is very interesting. I quote part of his
commentary on verses 14–24: 'So the word picture, with its panelled cameos,
is complete and Horace strikes once more his familiar note. Through all the
differences and varieties of human lot exhibited on this stage where men play

simply observes that the hierarchy is facing the urn of destiny. It seems to me that Orelli and Medley had the right of the matter and that the preference for 'Death the Leveler' is the result of inattentive reading of Horace.

The identification of Necessitas as Death the Leveler is so plausible that its attractiveness to students of Horace is easy to understand. All society, with its inequalities, rivalries, ambitions and frustrations has been drawn up, as it were, in review awaiting the outcome of Necessitas' casting of lots. In an ode of Horace what could be the outcome of such a lot-casting be but the frustration of all ambitions by death? Is it not quite natural to see in these lines simply a characteristic variant of the situation Horace has made unforgettable in the lines to Dellius (*Carm.* ii. 3. 21 ff.):

> divesne prisco natus ab Inacho
> nil interest an pauper et infima
>   de gente sub divo moreris,
>   victima nil miserantis Orci.
>
> omnes eodem cogimur, omnium
> versatur urna serius ocius
>   sors exitura et nos in aeternum
>   exilium impositura cumbae.

It makes no difference to Death whether we are bluebloods or peasants, rich or poor; we all in turn receive our place in Charon's boat. Horace does not mention Necessitas by name as officiating in the lottery that determines the priority of Charon's passengers,[11] any more than he does in the similar passage in

their parts, acting life's tragedies and comedies, where petty ambitions work out their successes or their failures, see, rising high above and over-arching the whole scene, like the vault of heaven where reigns the King of kings, a lex suprema which is aequa lex. Necessitas, the Greek Ἀνάγκη, a giant figure dark and dread, ever lying in the background of classic thought – Destiny – that which must be – ever overshadows, not mortal men alone and their petty pursuits, but even the desires and volitions of the gods themselves. To this dread power supreme the poet refers the issues of all these human competitions for place and power. 'Destiny' it is that allots to each his station – highest, lowest, distinguished or obscure: *sortitur insignes et imos*. There stands her symbol, the mighty urn. And this urn of Destiny in which is found the lot of every man, is ever being shaken – *movet* – and there leaps out the lot of each.'

11. Orelli appears to assume that Ἀνάγκη or Εἱμαρμένη is conducting the lot-casting in *Carm.* ii. 3.

Carm. II. 14, where he reminds Postumus of the approach of inevitable death (*Carm.* II. 14. 5ff.):

> non si trecenis quotquot eunt dies,
> amice, places inlacrimabilem
>   Plutona tauris, qui ter amplum
>   Geryonen Tityumque tristi
>
> compescit unda, scilicet omnibus,
>   quicumque terrae munere vescimur
>   enaviganda sive reges
>   sive inopes erimus coloni...

In two other passages Necessitas is explicitly referred to as closely associated with Death and, in fact, scarcely distinguishable from Death. In I. 3. 29ff., describing the unfortunate results of Prometheus' exploits, Horace says

> post ignem aetheria domo
>   subductum macies et nova febrium
> terris incubuit cohors
>   semotique prius tarda necessitas
> leti corripuit gradum...

The other passage in which Necessitas is closely associated with Death is *Carm.* III. 24. 1–8:

> Intactis opulentior
>   thesauris Arabum et divitis Indiae
> caementis licet occupes
>   terrenum omne tuis et mare publicum:
> si figit adamantinos
>   summis verticibus dira Necessitas
> clavos, non animum metu,
>   non mortis laqueis expedies caput...

Necessitas and Mors are clearly depicted here as performing distinct functions; still death is the outcome for the rich man and the tone of this passage is much like that of the lines quoted from Book II.

The passages that have been cited so far emphasize the inevitability of Death. But Death is also just, in so far as showing no partiality in the choice of victims, as *beatus Sestius* is reminded in *Carm.* I. 4. 13–14:

> Pallida Mors aequo pulsat pede pauperum tabernas
> regumque turris, o beate Sesti.

Readers of Horace familiar with the passages we have just reviewed can scarcely avoid being reminded of them when turning to lines 5–16 of the first Roman Ode. And it may be that Horace intended that they should – at least until they realize that the poet in III. 1 is thinking along lines that are on a higher plane than that of a Cynic–Stoic *topos* regarding the worthlessness of riches, high birth, power, and fame in the face of inevitable death. At all events, despite the plausibility of the identification of Necessitas in *Carm.* III. 1 with Death the leveler, there are, in my opinion, serious objections to it. Even the most convinced holders of the view that Necessitas of the *aequa lex* represents Death cannot maintain that Necessitas *is* death. She is a close associate of Death at times. She makes Death inevitable and irrevoc-able: in modern parlance, Necessitas is the 'finalizer'. But Necessitas can have other associates and finalize other things besides death. Even in Horace she appears on one occasion as the associate of Fortune and is equipped and ready to render irrevocable the decisions of that whimsical power. The hymn to Fortune says (I. 35. 17ff.):

> te semper anteit saeva Necessitas,
> clavos trabalis et cuneos manu
> gerens aena, nec severus
> uncus abest liquidumque plumbum.

Necessitas drives the stake or pours the lead and renders Fortune's acts irrevocable. If we look for examples of Necessity in such a role outside of Horace, we are likely to think first of Necessity in 'the Myth of Er'. Here Necessity (Ἀνάγκη) is called the mother of the Fates. The process by which men's destinies are determined in the Myth of Er is rather elaborate. If reduced to its essentials, however, it consists of the choice of a way of life, a kind of astrological integration of this choice into the world order, and the rendering of the choice irrevocable. Lachesis and Ananke have their own roles in the drama of the

Myth of Er, but, to all intents and purposes, by the time the souls arrive *in luminis oras*, it may be said their lots have been determined by Fate.

Other examples can probably be found in which Necessity is in the act of giving finality to matters not connected with death. But Horace's Ode to Fortune and the Myth of Er provide sufficient evidence of Necessitas' versatility to relieve us, when reading lines 5–16 of *Carm.* III. 1, of the necessity of concluding that the folk lined up before Necessitas can have been brought there for only one purpose, namely to receive sentences of death. The sentences could just as well be more varied, involving any of the ills of life which Fate, Fortune, or Destiny have it in their power to inflict: death, loss of friends and family, loss of material goods, or perhaps, as will be suggested at a later stage in my argument, the inevitable consequences of wrongdoing. Horace would then be presenting us at the beginning of this poem with a mind's-eye picture of the universe such as he appears to have had when writing at least two other passages. The first occurs in *Carm.* II. 17, where Horace endeavors to give Maecenas some astrological reassurance about the approach of death. Whatever happens, the two friends, he insists, cannot be separated:

> me nec Chimaerae spiritus igneae
> nec, si resurgat, centimanus Gyas
> divellet umquam: sic potenti
> Iustitiae placitumque Parcis...(13–16)

Such is the verdict of Justice and Fate. The other passage reflecting Horace's concept of the administration of the universe comes at the beginning of the first Satire:

> Qui fit, Maecenas, ut nemo quam sibi sortem
> seu ratio dederit seu fors obiecerit illa
> contentus vivat...?

Although it may be objected that Horace's terms are not precisely alike in these cases, it does not seem unreasonable to me to maintain that, to Horace the poet–theologian, Jove and Necessitas, Justice and the Parcae, and Ratio and Fors stand for much the same thing. At any rate it seems unlikely that at the beginning of a piece like *Carm.* III. 1, where Horace clearly is presenting us with a mind's-eye view of the cosmos, he would depart from his usual theology and divide the administration of the universe between Jove and Death the Leveler!

So much for probabilities. An unanswerable objection to Death the Leveler is, in my opinion, the fact that such a concept or motif is out of place here since it has no relevance to the theme of III. 1. It is true that the comparative worthlessness of material things enters into the thinking behind *Carm*. III. 1, but this poem goes beyond such thinking. Death the Leveler is the ultimate bogyman to be summoned to dissuade from the pursuit of goods and riches those who would not appreciate philosophical arguments in disparagement of the temporal treasures. III. 1 does not really have anything to do with death but with life. Its subject is the spiritual or psychological torment experienced by those who transgress the laws of Justice in pursuing what are popularly regarded as the good things of life. Injustice is the poet's primary target; the comparative worthlessness of material things emerges as a kind of corollary to the primary proposition, as it appears that material goods even when acquired provide no solace for either the torment of injustice or the very desire of which they have been the object. To define justice and depict the furies that pursue the unjust is an intellectual undertaking on a higher plane than that on which Scrooge could be frightened by Marley's ghost or Sestius be jolted into sense by a spectre.

Proof that the subject of III. 1 is justice *versus* injustice is given by the poet's selection of his first *exemplum*. By Cicero's time – and Horace almost certainly borrows the Damocles story from Cicero – Dionysius appears to have become the symbol of injustice. Short of saying in bald prose *iniustus beatus esse non potest*, there was no way a poet could express this truth more explicitly than by recalling the famous tyrant's own dramatic demonstration that the acquisition of power and luxury beyond measure – and such acquisition is impossible without injustice – produces for the luckless possessor not peace and happiness but fear and torment from which there is no escape.

There is no place for Death the Leveler in any consideration of the relationship of justice and injustice to *beata vita*. *Beata vita* subsists on *virtus* which is contented with itself. Amid such considerations, nothing can be terrifying but the loss of *virtus*. And thus mere natural death that sooner or later must come to all can scarcely be of any concern to those to whom it is irrelevant.

The replacement of 'Death the Leveler' by Fate or Fortune in the dramatis personae of *Carm.* III. 1 should relieve Horatian critics of a certain embarrassment. With Necessitas as Fate or Fortune we have a poem that is not only lucid and philosophically consistent but a work that is artistically intelligible as an Horatian production. With Death the Leveler we are forced to concede that in this, if in no other work, Horace made no effort to avoid inconsistency and unnecessary, meaningless complexity. No analysis of the poem known to me, that is based on the interpretation of Necessitas as Death the Leveler, succeeds in making of *Carm.* III. 1 a *simplex et unum*. In fact, the most recent such analysis that I have read is far more complex and much more difficult to understand than the poem itself.[12]

12. Williams (above, n. 8), *Third Book of Horace's Odes*, pp. 586–7.

Tibullus: Elegy I. 3

C. CAMPBELL

ONE of the most frequent errors made by critics who would defend Tibullus' poetry is the acceptance of the very standards of judgement which led earlier critics to attack it. Because they continue to ask the same, wrong questions about a poem, they should not be surprised to arrive at the same, wrong answers. The resulting conflict between an intuitive admiration for Tibullus and a negative judgement based upon the observation of apparent flaws has led even his staunchest defenders to make statements like the following:

> La malchance de notre poète, c'est que, chez lui, les imperfections apparaissent au premier regard, alors qu'il faut quelque examen pour discerner les perfections.[1]

> The price of such disciplined artistry may be a lack of depth and internal movement, but the reward is lucidity and harmony of emotional colours.[2]

Even a lenient judge must conclude that perfections which are concealed from the average reader by a host of flaws, or technique so refined that it produces shallow and static poetry can hardly be characteristic of a first-rate poet. Yet Quintilian names Tibullus first of the elegists,[3] and we are loath to disagree.

One example of a critic asking the wrong question is Elder, when he discusses Tibullus' methods of achieving unity in his poems. This discussion should be viewed against a backdrop of those critics who called Tibullus an *Ideenflüchtiger*[4] or saw only loose connections between the 'episodes' of a poem.[5] In defense Elder says:

1. L. Catin, *BAGB* (1960), 530.
2. J. B. Elder, 'Tibullus: *Tersus atque Elegans*', *Critical Essays on Roman Literature: Elegy and Lyric* (Cambridge, U.S.A. 1962), p. 79.
3. Quintilian, *Inst.* x. 1. 93.
4. J. van Wageningen, *Neue Jahrb.* xxxi (1914), 350.
5. Kirby Flower Smith (ed.), *The Elegies of Tibullus* (New York 1913), p. 92: 'In short the most characteristic feature of our poet's rhetorical

It is by such means that the general, overall unity of an
elegy is achieved. The individual sections may seem, superficially, to have little or no connexion with one another. But
closer study will show that through a common style of
writing, through smooth transitions and adroit repetitions
of words and images, and above all through the fact that
'behind the scene' of every section is present the same
figure, Tibullus being tortured in love – that through these
devices the poet has ingeniously succeeded in knitting all
the diverse parts of his elegy into a firm oneness.[6]

Elder's error lies in his implicit acceptance of the charge of
inconsistency ('The individual sections...little or no connexion
...'). In effect, rather than asking, 'How are the sections
related?', Elder has asked, 'How does Tibullus impose unity
upon essentially unrelated episodes?' As a consequence, the
'unity' he succeeds in demonstrating is as superficial as the lack
of connection he seeks to disprove.[7]

This critical problem has immediate application to elegy I. 3.
Numerous scholars have attempted to show how this poem fits
together, some, like Jakoby, by attempting to supply a reason
for its episodic character,[8] others, like Eisenberger, by attempting
to enter the poet's mind and reconstruct the unexpressed transitions between the episodes.[9] What these critics share is a depen-

exposition is that it proceeds by parallelism, comparison, contrast, by statement
and counterstatement, desirable and undesirable, negative and positive, running off from time to time into variations which seem to halt like eddies in
a flowing stream, albeit the stream continues to flow steadily onward until it
reaches the end.'

6. Elder, '*Tersus atque Elegans*', p. 103.

7. R. Hanslik, in his article 'Tibulls Elegie I. 3', *Forschungen zur römischen
Literatur* (Festschrift K. Büchner, herausgegeben von W. Wimmel, Franz
Steiner Verlag, Wiesbaden 1970), goes to the other extreme, asking the
question 'How does this poem exhibit that Alexandrian "Chinese-box"
structure which we have come to expect?' Elder asks how Tibullus imposes
unity upon disconnected material; Hanslik imposes a ready-made structure
with little regard for the material itself.

8. Felix Jakoby, *Rh. Mus.* 60 (1905), 78: 'Der Dichter liegt auf seinem
Krankenlager und vor seinem geistigen Augen ziehen "wie im matten Fieber-
traum" einzelne Bilder vorüber.'

9. H. Eisenberger, *Hermes* 88 (1960), 197: 'Wir haben versucht, uns in
die Seele Tibulls einzufühlen und ihm so auf dem Wege, den er in diesem
Gedicht innerlich zurücklegt, zu folgen. Es scheint uns, dass dieser Weg aus

dence upon some external factor, be it the poet's fever, his *Gefühlsgründe* or his technique, to explain the coherence of the poem. I think I can show how elegy I. 3 has an inner coherence which is more functional than decorative, illuminated and enhanced by the external 'devices' Elder has listed above, but not created by them. In this way I hope to show that, far from requiring my excuses or apologies, the poem is quite able to speak in its own defense.

The first step, however, is to ascertain the linear development of the poem, and for this purpose, I propose to adopt temporarily Elder's definition of unity and his technique for demonstrating it.[10] The content of the individual sections and the transitions between them may be summarized as follows:

I am dying.	1	lines 1–10: The poet, who has accompanied Messalla on a voyage, now lies ill and alone in a foreign land. He prays that he will not die, because he has near him neither mother nor sister to attend his funeral nor Delia...
I should never have left home; the gods should have prevented me.	2	lines 11–22:...who had consulted all the gods to be sure of his safe return, while he had used every pretext to delay his departure. He concludes that he should never have left, implying that the gods should have prevented him. [The transition is accomplished by a switch from what his mother and sister *would* do at his funeral to what Delia *did* do before his departure.]
But since I did leave and they didn't stop me, at least *now* Isis	3	lines 23–8: All that consultation of the gods was useless. Now Isis should come to help him. [The transition is

seiner menschlichen und dichterischen Eigenart verständlich geworden ist, dass die Gedanken, die Tibull bewegten, aus dem Gefühlsgründe seines Wesens, aus seinem lyrischen Wertempfinden in natürlicher Folge hervorgetreten sind und dass demgemäss sich die Motive zu einem sinnvoll gestalteten Kunstwerk verbinden.'

10. Elder, *'Tersus atque Elegans'*, pp. 97ff.

should help...(I am
dying.)

centered about the word *nunc*, which
marks the contrast between both the
past and the present and what he should
have and has in fact done].

...so that I may   4
come home.

lines 29–34: (Isis should help) so that
Delia may fulfill her vows upon my
return and I may once again worship
the ancestral Penates and the ancient
Lar. [The transition to the homecoming of the future is accomplished
by the conjunction *ut*.]

There was a time   5
when I couldn't
have left.

lines 35–48: But it would be even
better to have lived in the Saturnian
Age when I *could* not have left home.
[The transition is accomplished in two
ways, by the logical bridge from *ancestral Penates* and *ancient Lar* to a
description of that antiquity, and by
quam bene which marks the shift from
'I should not have left' to 'I could not
have left.']

But that time is   6
gone. This is why
I am dying.

lines 49–56: But now we live under the
rule of Jove, and voyages and death
are inevitable. I am guiltless; I am
dying because of an inevitable journey.
[Again the transition is marked by
nunc, now in contrast to *then*, 'but as it
is' in contrast to *quam bene*.]

But I will continue   7a
to live and love in
the Elysian Fields.

lines 57–66: (I may die) but I will
continue to love in the Elysian Fields,
where everyone goes who dies while
he is in love. [The transition is marked
by *sed me*; *sed* implies the contrast
between the end of earthly existence
and the beginning of life-after-death
in the underworld.]

| But the enemies of love are punished in Hell; may my enemies be so punished! | 7b | lines 67–82: (others may die) but they will be punished as they deserve in the traditional underworld. May anyone who defiles my love or tries to take advantage of my absence be so punished. [The transition is marked by *at* which contrasts the rewards of the Elysian Fields with the punishments of the *scelerata sedes*.] |
| But you be chaste, Delia; I will come to you. | 8 | lines 83–94: But you, Delia, be chaste; resist my enemies (*quicumque*). Sit at home spinning and listening to the old woman. As you are falling asleep, I will come to you. May that day come! [Again *at* marks the transition; the contrast is between those who would tempt Delia and Delia who is not tempted.] |

If we use Elder's summary as a checklist, we can see that, in his terms, this poem does achieve linear unity. Each section has the same style: clear, unforced, *tenuis*. The transitions are smooth, clearly marked by syntax and diction, especially by disjunctive conjunctions or emphatic time expressions. Words and images are repeated in such a way as to link the various sections: *undas* and *ignotis terris* in lines 1–3 and 37–9; *via* in lines 14, 36, 50; time expressions in 27, 49, 89; *precor* in 5, 83, and 93. And the subject which underlies each section is indeed Tibullus and his confrontation with death.

This method, however, has failed to answer some important questions. Why does the poem end where it does? The vision of homecoming is not, of itself, a natural conclusion; if it were, the poem could have ended at line 35. If the logic of the poem is merely linear, nothing prevents the poet from knitting one row after another until he simply runs out of yarn. Why has the poem taken *this* direction and what has the poet achieved in his poem? Why is the underworld imagined as a Golden Age for lovers? This startling departure from tradition certainly demands explanation.[11] A fresh approach to the poem will, I think, answer these questions while suggesting some further answers to the general questions, 'how does this poem work' or 'what does this poem mean?'

The poem divides into two parts, 11–34 and 35–82, framed by an introduction, 1–10, and conclusion, 83–94. The introduction poses the problem, death. Each of the two central parts represents an attempt to solve that problem, to understand the reason for death and thereby to accept it. The first is unsuccessful, for death remains something without reason, to be avoided if only one knew how. The second is apparently successful; the poet is resigned to dying, and from that resignation he obtains the hope which enables him, in the concluding lines, to transcend death. The end is an answer to the beginning, an answer which was obtained in the course of the poem.

The problem posed by the introduction is not simply how one is to face death, but how Tibullus, the elegiac lover–poet, is to face death under these special circumstances. He prays that death will hold off because he is alone; the loneliness of death is more terrifying than death itself. By line 10 this fear has become still more specific: the lover does not want to die away from his mistress.

The poet first attempts to encompass this problem in the familiar terms of the elegiac world. The mistress and lover frame the first major part (11–34): *illa* (11) and *ipse ego* (15); *mea Delia* (29) and *at mihi* (33). This familiar elegiac world lies necessarily in the past (11–20) where the poet engages in the elegiac *topos*

11. The combination of Golden Age motifs with the description of the Elysian Fields in a specifically elegiac context is original with Tibullus. Eisenberger's comments here are instructive (p. 193): 'Das Elysion ist in der frühgriechischen Literatur bekanntlich die Stätte, an die einzelne Heroen nach ihrem Tode auf Grund ihrer Verwandtschaft oder Verbundenheit mit einer Gottheit versetzt werden, um dort ein zweites, seliges Dasein zu geniessen; der Gedanke, dass ein solcher Ort einem Menschen von schuldlos-reiner Lebensführung zuteil wird, tritt unter orphisch-pythagoreischem Einfluss erst bei Pindar und Plato auf. In den Resten der alexandrinischen Dichter findet sich kein Vorbild Tibulls. Er hat hier offenbar aus den alten Elementen völlig Neues gestaltet: an die Stelle der Heroen oder der "Guten" treten die, die der Tod aus einem Leben der Liebe plötzlich hinweggerissen hat (V. 65); ihnen ist unter Amors Leitung inmitten üppig prangender und splendender Natur ein neues, ungetrübt schönes Dasein in Gemeinschaft mit ihren Geliebten beschert.'

of 'The Departing Lover', perhaps best exemplified by Propertius 1. 6. But where Propertius is imagining how Cynthia would react, Tibullus must recall how Delia did react. Propertius can say, 'I shall not go.' Tibullus can only say 'I should not have gone.' The elegiac world of the past holds no clue to how the elegiac lover–poet should face death when he is separated from his mistress, because once separated from her, he is also separated from that world. The conclusion 'I should not have left' does not lead to understanding and acceptance in the form of 'I offended *Amor*; I am dying for my sin; I deserve to die.' Rather it leads to an affirmation of guiltlessness with respect to non-elegiac gods in the form of 'Isis has no cause for complaint; where is Isis now?' The standards of behavior which made sense within the elegiac circle must now be broadened to include a world where lover and mistress cannot always be together. In this broader context, the poet finds death still undeserved, still to be avoided rather than accepted. The result of seeing that 'I should not have left' is simply to restate 'I must get home.' The poet has not moved perceptibly from his original situation or from his original understanding of that situation.

Our sense of having completed one movement of the poem is structurally reinforced. From the present of the introduction the poet has moved through past (11–22), present (23–8) and future (29–34), with an implicit return to the present of the opening lines. The future is imagined as an extension of the elegiac past; the mistress and lover will, as before, make their separate religious observances. This future is, however, dependent (*ut*) upon a change in the present (*nunc, dea, nunc succurre mihi*). Present, past and future are linked in a circle which returns inevitably to its beginning.

The second movement (35–82) commences with an attempt to break that circle by a retreat to an even more distant past, the Saturnian Age, a time when journeys were not possible. Its opening section is parallel in time to 11–22: *ante* (10) and *priusquam* (35). The thematic link is provided by *vias* (14 and 36). We are invited to compare the elegiac world before the journey with the Golden Age world before any journey. We are further invited to contrast the present of the introduction with the past of the Golden Age: *nondum...undas...nec ignotis...terris* (37–9) and *undas...ignotis...terris* (1–3). The suggested link between the Golden Age and the world of elegy is further reinforced by depicting the Age of Saturn in terms of another elegiac *topos*: the conflict between the life of the country and the life of *negotium* and *militiae*.

But where the elegiac world only produced the useless response 'I must return home', the Saturnian Age produces acceptance: *fac lapis...stet* (54). Death is now seen as the inevitable consequence of the world-order: *nunc Iove sub domino*. Where before the poet was intent upon avoiding death, now he sees that the *via* is death (*nunc leti mille repente viae*); and that the only way to avoid either is to return to the Golden Age of Saturn. This section (49–56) parallels 23–8 in time (*nunc* 23, 26, 26 and 49, 50, 50, 53) and is linked by the address to divinity and the emphasis on ritual purity. The essential contrast, however, is unmistakable. Now Tibullus prays, not to avoid death in return for rituals piously completed, but to be granted a tomb. *Immiti morte* (55) is now seen as the result of *immiti arte* (48), a fundamental aspect of the current era. Following Messalla has become, not an error of choice, but an act of inevitable necessity: *nunc mare* (50) and *mari* (56).

The next segment of the poem (57–66) is a fulfillment of structural and thematic expectations already established. From past and present we move to a future which is again an extension of the past. This future is a regeneration of the Golden Age after death, corresponding in time to the return to the elegiac world of 29–34. The combination of Golden Age themes, elegiac world and the Elysian fields now makes real sense. Rather than being a whimsical twist to tradition, it is the natural outgrowth of what has preceded. First, the implication of accepting an Ages-of-Man theory of human development is that the Golden Age will return; this is clear both in Hesiod and in Vergil's Fourth *Eclogue*. From the standpoint of a world-cycle, the Golden Age, as well as the beginning of the cycle, is also the next step after the Age of Jove at the end of the cycle. But from the standpoint of the individual life-cycle, the underworld is the next step after death. Lastly, the suggestion (in lines 35–48) that the Golden Age is a parallel to the elegiac world is a preparation for their explicit identification in lines 57–66. These three separate lines of thought meet and combine in the vision of the Elysian Fields as a Golden Age paradise for lovers. It is no longer necessary to avoid death in order to return to the elegiac world of love. Instead death is seen as a direct prelude to an ideal elegiac world. Venus, rather than disappearing with death, replaces Hermes as the guide to a new life of perpetual love.

The transformation of the Elysian Fields demands a corresponding transformation of Tartarus. Cereberus is portrayed in elegiac terms: *excubat ante fores.* Ixion is punished for his violation of Juno, and the Danaids *Veneris quod numina laesit.* It is to this realm that Tibullus condemns all his enemies in love.[12] Tartarus is the reverse of the Elysian Fields, the second half of the contrast between the lover and the man of *negotium* and *militiae.* This relationship is clearest in the parallel couplets 65–6 (*illic est, cuicumque rapax Mors venit amanti, | et gerit insigni myrtea serta coma*) and 81–2 (*illic sit quicumque meos violavit amores, | optavit lentas et mihi militias*). The black death (*Mors atra, nigras manus,* lines 4–5) which the poet feared for himself at the beginning of the poem has now been reserved for his enemies (*nocte profunda, flumina nigra, niger Cerberus, atro viscere,* lines 67–76). The poet himself now has nothing to fear.

In the concluding section (83–94), the vision of homecoming returns, this time not as a future which can only be reached through a change in the present (*succurre...ut*), but as a future which the present does not touch (*tunc veniam*). What is essential to a grasp of this passage is the recognition that it does not matter whether the poet imagines himself as returning to Delia physically, as a living man, or spiritually, as a shade or dream of a shade. He leaves both options open, but seems to imply the second. He will appear as the girl falls asleep: *tunc veniam subito.* When he comes he wants no word to precede him, but to appear

12. Here is an important area where Hanslik's insistence upon the 'Chinese-box' structure has led him to what I feel is a fundamental misinterpretation of lines 21ff., as well as lines 67ff. The earlier passage, with its mention of Tibullus' 'einmalige Schuld' is made a pendant to the later discussion, and the two are seen as symmetrically placed around the imaginary epitaph of 55–6. The parallel which Hanslik finds between these two passages is suspect, because Tibullus specifically confines his enemies to Hell and excludes himself from this punishment. Furthermore, it is questionable whether a poet who is seeking the sort of structure that Hanslik assumes would 'balance' a passage of two lines with one of sixteen.

caelo missus. And her tousled hair and bare feet, as if roused from bed, also indicate the dream-like nature of this imagined home-coming. So too does the rapid movement from the dark through the lamplight (*lucerna*) to the brilliant imagery of dawn (*Aurora nitentem | Luciferum roseis candida...*), which contrasts so sharply with the blackness of the opening lines. In effect, Tibullus has transcended death; alive or dead he shall go on loving and he will return.

Now a schematization of the structure of the poem can show that, beneath the linear progression, there lies an integrated whole, a real unity of subject which would exist even if the linear unity were taken away.

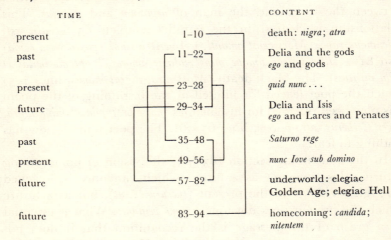

TIME		CONTENT
present	1–10	death: *nigra*; *atra*
past	11–22	Delia and the gods *ego* and gods
present	23–28	*quid nunc* . . .
future	29–34	Delia and Isis *ego* and Lares and Penates
past	35–48	*Saturno rege*
present	49–56	*nunc Iove sub domino*
future	57–82	underworld: elegiac Golden Age; elegiac Hell
future	83–94	homecoming: *candida*; *nitentem*

Here we can see that the temporal progression provides a source of movement for the poem, while thematic collocations and verbal links or contrasts provide cohesion. It is instructive to note that this poem does not readily fall into the kind of numerical pattern of the *Eclogues*.[13] Here structure is not decorative but the real skeletal support of the poem. The poem hangs together not because of a common style, clear transitions, skillful but random repetitions and single underlying subject, but because the material is so organized that it cannot fall apart.[14]

13. O. Skutsch, 'Symmetry and sense in the Eclogues', *HSCP* 73 (1969), 153ff.

14. According to this structural analysis, line 56 cannot be the center of the poem, as has often been maintained (cf. above, n. 12). It is probably a

The critic must be careful not to mistake his own failure for that of the poem or poet. In my opinion, much of the unfavorable or confused judgement about Tibullus' poetry is the result of just such a mistake: ill-conceived questions, not bad poetry, have produced ill-founded judgements. In my analysis of elegy I. 3, I have tried to show how appropriate questions can yield meaningful answers. In light of these answers, I must conclude that elegy I. 3 is an unqualified poetic success.

mistake even to look for a 'central line' in a poem such as this, where the themes are so intricately woven that no one line can be singled out for special distinction.

Notes on Livy IX

R. M. OGILVIE

I T IS easy to belittle the contribution which technology can make to the appreciation of the classics but in one field at least, the compilation of Concordances, progress has been sensational. For over 200 years scholars have promised to produce a Concordance of Livy. No less than fourteen ventures have been advertised during that period – and have foundered. Now at last in Packard's monumental *Concordance*[1] scholars of Livy's text and style have the tool for which they have waited so long. It is, of course, a tool conditioned by its own limitations: it is not analytical; it does not classify; and it accepts standard editions without considering textual difficulties. Nevertheless some indication of its value may be gained from the frequency with which its evidence is used in the following reconstruction of certain passages of Livy Book IX.

The manuscript tradition for that book is the same as that for the rest of the Decade.[2] The Mediceus (M), supported by Gelenius' citations of a closely related manuscript, represents one tradition of the Nicomachean edition, except for chapters 9 to 14 where it appears that a quaternion in M's original was lost and was restored from the λ branch. The second tradition is divided into two independent branches π, most faithfully witnessed by the Paris (P) and Upsala (U) manuscripts, and λ, most faithfully witnessed by the Codex Thuaneus (T). The Oxford manuscript (O) represents the π branch contaminated with the λ branch. It follows that wherever M and λ or M and π agree against π or λ, they must preserve the closest approximation to Nicomachus' text. We should, therefore, reconstitute the text by assessing the agreed readings of M and λ (or π) and establishing

1. David Packard (ed.), *Concordance to Livy* (4 vols., Harvard University Press 1968).

2. See *CQ* 7 (1957), 68ff. The introductions to volumes 1 and 2 of the Oxford Classical Text of Livy by Conway and Walters still offer the fullest information on the manuscripts. On M, however, one should consult also G. Billanovich, *Italia Medioevale e Umanistica* 2 (1959), 103ff.

what, if anything, is wrong with them. The isolated readings of
π or λ have no authority; if they are right, they are right by
accident or by conjecture. My aim is to review some passages
where it seems to me that, on the evidence supplied by Packard,
the editors of Livy VI–X in the Oxford Classical Text series have
made wrong decisions. Although in no sense a mechanical writer,
Livy did demonstrably develop a vocabulary which tended to
repeat itself in stock situations. Such repetitions help an editor
to decide what is Livian usage, although the possibility of unique
and unexpected turns of phrase must never be excluded. The
text printed is, in all cases, that of the latest edition of the Oxford
text, edited by Conway and Walters.

    4.5   his condicionibus paratum se esse foedus cum consulibus
          ferire.

his *OT*   iis *MPU*

    iis must have been Nicomachus' reading, and is to be ex-
    pected in O.O.

    4.7   cum diu silentium fuisset nec consules...hiscere possent,
          L. Lentulus, qui tum princeps legatorum...erat, 'patrem
          meum' inquit....

    All primary manuscripts have *qui tum*; they also all read
possent tum L. Lentulus, except for M which has *possentium
L. Lentulus*. Nicomachus, therefore, had the repeated *tum*.
Editors have deleted either the first (Conway and Walters)
or the second (Drakenborch). But both seem idiomatic. For
cum...tum cf. XXXIV. 5. 1 *cum pauca adiecissent, tum L. Valerius
...ita disseruit*; et al. saep. For *qui tum princeps...erat* cf.
XXVII. 11. 11 *quem tum principem Romanae civitatis esse*; et al.
saep. Livy is not averse to such repetitions: see on 16. 8
below and the examples in my note on 1. 14. 4. The shape
of the sentence can be compared with XXXVIII. 11. 4. *si qui
eo tempore ex iis capti essent qui tum hostes erant*.

    4.14 hic omnes spes opesque sunt quas servando patriam
          servamus, dedendo ad necem patriam deserimus [ac pro-
          dimus].

M (and also, independently, O) omits the words *ac prodimus*.
There is, therefore, a straight choice between M and πλ.
The paired phrase is rhetorically more impressive and seems

guaranteed by II. 54. 8, II. 57. 4, XXVI. 6. 17, XXVI. 13. 19,
XXXV. 38. 2, et al.

5. 13 tum a consulibus abire lictores iussi paludamentaque
detracta; tantam ⟨id⟩ inter eos qui paulo ante [eos] exsecrantes
dedendos lacerandosque censuerant miserationem fecit.

id *suppl. Drakenborch* inter eos *O*: inter ipsos *cett.* eos *del. Walters*

There are two problems here. (1) Nicomachus read *inter
ipsos...eos* and there is no call to alter that reading. *inter
ipsos* means 'the very people who previously...', and *eos* refers
to the consuls. Cf. XXVIII. 4. 1 *laeta et ipsis qui rem gessere urbis
eius expugnatio fuit et imperatori*. (2) Drakenborch supplied *id*
as the subject of *fecit*, whereas Gronovius had earlier removed
the punctuation after *detracta* and read *fecerunt* with *lictores
iussi paludamentaque detracta* as the subject. Drakenborch's
supplement is preferable and is supported by such passages
as XXVI. 11. 13 *tantum id interest veneritne*.

6.2 [Ofillius] A. Calavius Ovi filius.

The evidence of the manuscripts here is confused but can
be tabulated briefly.

Ofillius *M*
Ofillius *A* Calavius Ovi filius π
Ofilius Calavius Ovi filius λ

M (which here probably represents a secondary tradition;
see above) also has a marginal note '*Ofilii Calavi primatis
capuensium sententia* which may be ancient. M's own reading
is plainly the result of haplography. The manuscript evidence
points to the true reading as being λ's *Ofilius Calavius Ovi
filius*, for the form of which cf. 9. 12 *C. Pontium Herenni filium*.
The names are all attested from the Campanian area: for
Of(f)ilius cf. *C.I.L.* x 1049 (it is very common), for Calavius·
cf. *C.I.L.* x 1090 (Nuceria), 2202 (Puteoli), 3787 (Capua),
for Ovius cf. 26. 7; *C.I.L.* x 4264–6; Münzer, *R.E.* 'Ovius'.
The problem is that both *Ofilius* and *Calavius* are *nomina* and
we expect a *praenomen*. There is, however, evidence of an
Oscan *praenomen Upfals*[3] which would be latinized as *Ofilus*
and *Of.* does indeed occur as an abbreviated *praenomen*.[4]

3. F. Bücheler, *Rh. Mus.* 39 (1884), 316; W. Schulze, *Zur Geschichte latei-
nischer Eigennamen* (Berlin 1933), p. 452.
4. R. S. Conway, *Italic Dialects* (Cambridge 1857).

There are other cases in Livy of rare *praenomina* being corrupted (presumably by Livy himself or his sources) into more familiar *nomen*-forms, e.g. Mettius (for Metius) Fufetius, Turnus Herdonius.

10.10   illum legatum [fetialem].

The same adjectival use of *fetialis* with *legatus* occurs in 11. 11, forming a typically Livian 'unconscious repetition'. It is reinforced by 11. 8 *hoc fide, hoc foederibus, hoc fetialibus caerimoniis dignum erat*, where *fetialis* is again adjectival. Cf. also Varro (*de Vita Pop. Rom.* 11) ap. Non. Marc. 529. 24M *faetiales legatos res repetitum mittunt quattuor*.

13. 8   quae regio si fida Samnitibus fuisset aut pervenire Arpos exercitus Romanus nequisset aut interiecta [inter Romam et Arpos] penuria rerum omnium exclusos a commeatibus absumpsisset.

Tanaquil Faber deleted *inter Romam et Arpos* as a gloss – rightly since the words are quite inapposite and in Livy *interiectus* is qualified by a dative not by *inter* with the accusative. However, as Luterbacher divined, *interiecta* itself must also be deleted since *interiectus* is always used of places that are interposed, not abstract entities such as scarcity.[5] For the expression here cf. xxviii. 35. 2 *causando corrumpi equos inclusos in insula penuriamque omnium rerum et facere ceteris et ipsos sentire, ad hoc equitem increscere desidia*.

14. 5   signa inde ferre iussit.

Gronovius, following the reading of the edition of 1470, argued that *ferri* should be read against the manuscripts. The linguistic evidence is decisive:[6] *ferri* is always used in this phrase except where an object for *iussit* is either expressed or clearly understood, as in xxxi. 21. 14, xxxiv. 48. 9.

16. 8   eadem nocte portam...aperuerunt armatosque clam hoste in urbem acceperunt.

hoste is Gelenius' reading for which the manuscripts have *nocte*; there is no proof that Gelenius found it in his manuscript and *nocte* was clearly in Nicomachus' text. *clam hoste* does not occur in Livy, *clam nocte* is regular: cf. ii. 3. 7, x. 27. 4, xxiv. 30. 2, xxiv. 40. 3, xxiv. 45. 1, xxvii. 5. 18. The only

5. Packard, *Concordance*, vol. 2, p. 1273.
6. Ibid. vol. 2, p. 593.

objection to it is the repetition of *nocte* (with *nocte* and *noctis* in the preceding sentence as well) but the objection is insufficient. See 4. 7 above.

17.2 quibus saepe tacitus cogitationibus volutavi animum.

tacitus *P*   tacitis *MUOT*

Conway and Walters defend their choice of *tacitus* by Virg. *Ecl.* IX. 37 but cf. Livy XXVI. 28. 10 *silentium ortum et tacita cogitatio quidnam egissent.*

19. 7 arma clupeus sarisaeque illis.

post illis *add.* id est hastae *codd.*

Editors, at least as early as Gelenius, have deleted the words *id est hastae*. But were they justified? On the two other occasions that Livy uses *sarisa* he feels obliged to explain it: XXXVII. 42. 4 *praelongarum hastarum – sarisas Macedones vocant*; XXXVIII. 7. 12 *praelongae hastae, quas sarisas vocant. id est* is similarly written to explain an unfamiliar Greek term in XXXIV. 26. 3 and XLI. 20. 7 and its use to refer to only one of a pair can be paralleled by XXVII. 32. 4 *inter Aetolos et Tralles – Illyriorum id est genus.*

19. 16 nunquam ab equite hoste, nunquam a pedite, nunquam aperta acie, nunquam aequis, utique nunquam nostris locis laboravimus: equitem sagittas, saltus impeditos, avia commeatibus loca gravis armis miles timere potest.

ab equite hoste and *equitem* (for which UO read *equidem*) are clearly contradictory and incompatible. Editors have approached the problem from different angles. Some, like Dobree, observing that the Romans had been defeated by enemy cavalry (e.g. at Carrhae), deleted *nunquam ab equite hoste* (a Livian phrase; cf. IV. 33. 7) and kept *equitem*, but stylistically this is unacceptable in such a rhetorical context, as Anderson observed in his edition (p. 242). The first sentence is clearly constructed as a bi-colon

$$\begin{Bmatrix} nunquam\ ab\ equite \\ nunquam\ a\ pedite \end{Bmatrix}\ \text{followed by a } tricolon\ auctum$$

$$\begin{Bmatrix} (1)\ nunquam\ aperta\ acie \\ (2)\ nunquam\ aequis \\ (3)\ utique\ nunquam\ nostris\ locis. \end{Bmatrix}$$

Others have deleted or emended *equitem* – a better approach. But some of the emendations proposed (e.g. *loricatum equitem, sagittas* Anderson; *equitum sagittas* Stroth, Conway) also overlook the clear rhetorical structure of a *tricolon auctum* in

$$\left\{ \begin{array}{l} (1)\ \textit{sagittas} \\ (2)\ \textit{saltus impeditos} \\ (3)\ \textit{avia commeatibus loca} \end{array} \right\}$$

Deletion, however, leaves the connection between the sentences too abrupt. The natural emendation is *etenim* and a very similar corruption occurs in the manuscript F of Tertullian, *Apol.* XLI. 1 *utique enim* for *etenim*.

27. 13   maius quam pro numero auxilium advenerat fortes viri. So the manuscripts, except that M reads the plural *advenerant*, and the corrector of P adds ∞ (= *mille*) after *advenerat*. Walters obelizes *fortes viri* doubting whether the words are a gloss or whether they conceal a deeper corruption for which he proposes *advenerat – advenerant mille fortes viri -* . The words are certainly a gloss: for, although *fortes viri* is a Livian phrase (v. 36. 5, x. 13. 8, XXI. 44. 8) *mille fortes viri* would be untrue since the reinforcements were 1,200 in number (27. 12) and neither *fortes viri* nor *mille fortes viri* can be construed with *auxilium*, since *auxilium* is elsewhere used proleptically only at XXVII. 47. 7 *vereri ne serum ipse auxilium venisset*; and, where it is defined, it is defined not by an apposition but by a genitive (XXIII. 29. 4, XXV. 29. 8, XXXVII. 50. 3).

28. 4   eo se...et Samnitium omnis multitudo et Nolana agrestis contulerat. The text is that of Gelenius (or his manuscript). The manuscripts have been inaccurately cited: M read *nolani agrestes contulerant*, T read *nolani agrestes* but the scribe himself corrected *contulerat* to *contulerant*, PUO agree on *contulerat* but differ on the preceding words, P having *nolani agrestas*, U *nolani agrestes*, and O *nolani agrestis*. The agreement of M and T points to the true reading *Nolani agrestes contulerant*. Where *agrestis* is used with a topographical adjective, it is always in the plural in Livy, standing for a substantive: cf. 36. 12 *agrestium Etruscorum*, I. 22. 3, XXX. 7. 11. The

closest parallel to the Oxford text would be XXI. 25. 3 *non agrestis modo multitudo sed ipsi triumviri Romani.*

29. 11   nec nomen tantum Potitiorum interisse sed censorem etiam [Appium]...luminibus captum.

Appium is in all the manuscripts, except F which is of no authority. The name is needed to balance *Potitiorum.*

31. 6   quaereretur locus si qua licentia populando effusus exercitus excipi ac circumveniri posset.

Packard offers no analogy for the use of *populando effusus* in the sense of *ad populandum effusus* (XXI. 57. 3). Crevier's emendation *populandi* seems inevitable especially in view of XXII. 3. 9 *ab effusa praedandi licentia.*

34. 15   familia imperiosissima [superbissima].

imperiosissime superbissima   *M*: imperiosissima et superbissima   πλ

There is no justification for deleting *superbissima* which is the *mot juste* for the Claudian family (cf. 34. 22, 34. 24, et al. saep.). πλ preserve the right reading.

34. 24–5   et, nisi Aemiliae legi parueris, in vincula duci iubebo nec, cum ita comparatum a maioribus sit ut comitiis censoriis, nisi duo confecerint legitima suffragia, non renuntiato altero comitia differantur, ego te, qui solus censor creari non possis, solam censuram gerere nunc patiar.

nunc patiar *ed. Par.* 1510: non patiar *codd.*

If the manuscript reading is taken strictly, *nec...non* (*patiar*) should cancel out and give a positive. Hence editors have either emended *nec* to *atque* or tackled *non* by emendation or by deletion (Aldus). *non patiar* is, however, a forceful and favoured conclusion to a statement; cf. III. 71. 4 *errare ego populum in hac causa non patiar*; VI. 38. 8 *vim tribuniciam a se ipsa dissolvi non patiar.* We should, perhaps, consider the possibility that the two negatives reinforce rather than eliminate one another, a possibility made all the easier by the length of their separation. The phenomenon is discussed by Kühner–Stegmann;[7] cf. e.g. Plaut. *Epid.* 532 *neque, ea nunc ubi sit, nescio*; Livy XLIII. 13. 1 *non sum nescius ab eadem neglegentia qua nihil deos portendere vulgo nunc credant neque*

7. *Lateinische Grammatik* (Hannover 1962), vol. 1, pp. 827–8.

nuntiari admodum nulla prodigia in publicum neque in annales referri.

36. 2   consulis frater – M. Fabium, Caesonem alii, C. Claudium quidam...tradunt –

This is Gelenius' text where the other manuscripts agree on *fratrem m̄. fabium.* This passage is an important one because with the received reading Livy could be held to have consulted at least three sources, as Klotz argues.[8] There is, however, no parallel for the linguistic phenomenon of writing A, B *alii,* C *quidam.* Where Livy uses *alii* and *quidam,* it is always to distinguish two, and two only, alternatives, as in VII. 22. 3 *quidam Caesonem, alii Gaium praenomen Quinctio adiciunt,* IV. 46. 11, IX. 41. 14, XXX. 24. 11, XLV. 10. 14. The true text must have been *consulis frater – Fabium Caesonem alii* or *consulis frater – eum Fabium Caesonem alii* (Perizonius) and the corruption in the manuscripts was caused by the assimilation of *frater* to the following accusatives. For the inversion of *nomen* and *praenomen* (Fabius Caeso for Caeso Fabius) see my note on III. 1. 1.

38. 7   itaque armis virisque ad obterendum C. Marcium consulem concurrunt.

obterendum was an early conjecture for the manuscript *obtinendum.* It is by no means certain. *obterere* is inappropriately strong in this context: it means 'to grind down' and is usually linked with such verbs as *sternere, calcare* etc. (cf. XXVII. 41. 10, where R's *opteneri* is an easier dittography than the corruption assumed here; XXXIV. 2. 2; XLIV. 42. 6), or used to describe the effects of large animals such as elephants (XXX. 33. 15, XXXVII. 43. 10). The expected sense is no more than 'to gain control of' which could be conveyed by *obtinendum*: cf. XXIV. 21. 4 *cum ceteri ex coniuratis ad exercitum obtinendum remansissent.*

39. 4   nam et cum Umbrorum exercitu acie depugnatum est; fusi tamen magis quam caesi hostes, quia coeptam acriter non tolerarunt pugnam; et ad Vadimonis lacum Etrusci...dimicarunt.

Three objections have been raised to this difficult sentence. (1) *nam* has no connection with the preceding paragraph; (2)

8. *Mnemosyne* 6 (1938), 96ff.

the defeat of the Umbrians appears to be contradicted by 41. 8 where they are described as *gentis integrae a cladibus belli nisi quod transitum exercitus ager senserat*; (3) the mention of the battle of Lake Vadimo is an anticipation of the battle of 283 B.C. None of these objections is adequate.

(1) Before *nam* M preserves the remains of a word *etrurae* (sic: corrected to *etruriae* by a corrector) and P² inserts *interea res in etruria gestae* after *pugnam* (as also do U and F). Such supplements represent independent transcriptions from the fragmentary archetype,⁹ where for instance a line was damaged or omitted and restored in the margin, and must be judged to have ancient authority. An analogous case in Book IX is the restoration at 5. 10. Since *res gestae* is not used by Livy without qualification, it is probable that he wrote *interea res in Etruria prospere gestae* which would be very susceptible to loss by homoeoteleuton. The connection made by *nam* is then regular; cf. v. 10. 2 *multa domi militiaeque gesta; nam et bellum multiplex fuit*...; XXIV. 41. 1 *in Hispania varie res gestae; nam priusquam Romani*...; XXVI. 39. 20 *nequaquam pari fortuna per eos dies Tarenti res gesta; nam ad quattuor milia hominum*...; XXXV. 22. 5 *et in utraque Hispania eo anno res prospere gestae; nam et C. Flaminius oppidum expugnavit*...*et M. Fulvius*...*proelia fecit.*

(2) The contradiction between 39. 4 and 41. 8 is only apparent since 41. 8 presupposes earlier Roman activity in Umbria and 39. 4 is merely a characteristic exaggeration of a non-engagement.

(3) The duplication of the battle of Lake Vadimo is to be explained as a chronological confusion, since 309 B.C. is one of the Varronian 'dictator years', rather than a textual error. So Salmon, rightly.¹⁰

Walters notes that the words of the whole passage *Livium longe potius quam glossematorem sapiunt*. Detailed analysis confirms this. For *acie depugnatum* cf. VII. 14. 5, XXIX. 36. 4; for the *fusi/caesi* dichotomy cf. VI. 2. 12, et al. saep.; for *tolerarunt pugnam* cf. XXIII. 45. 7, XXVII. 13. 1. Other remedies are thus unnecessary. W. B. Anderson, for instance, in Appendix 3 of

9. L. Voit, *Philologus* (1936), 309ff.; Billanovich, p. 111 n. 9.
10. E. T. Salmon, *Samnium and the Samnites* (Cambridge 1967), p. 243.

his excellent edition of Book IX rejected *interea res in Etruria gestae* as without authority and regarded *nam...Vadimonis lacum* as a commentator's interpolation to explain 39. 11 *ille primum dies*. Earlier editors (cf. Madvig),[11] had been content to reject *interea...gestae* but to accept *nam...Vadimonis lacum* as an inexplicable inconsistency.

39. 10 ut semel dedere hi terga, etiam ⟨ceteri⟩ certiorem capessere fugam.

certiorem was read by the manuscripts; *ceteri*, inserted here by Walters, was conjectured by Harant who proposed *ceteri item* instead of *certiorem*. *certam (certiorem) fugam* is not found in Livy (or indeed, as far as I can tell, elsewhere). Therefore *ceteri* should be correct, preferably without the pointless *item*. Cf. e.g. XXII. 60. 18 *hos cives patria desideret quorum si ceteri similes fuissent, neminem...civem haberet.*

45. 17 unum et triginta oppida intra dies quinquaginta... ceperunt.

triginta (*vel* xxx) *MPO*: xl *P²Uλ*

There is, as far as manuscript authority goes, really a straight choice between thirty and forty and the latter seems supported by the parallel account of Diodorus xx. 101. 5 τετταράκοντα πόλεις ἐν ἡμέραις ταῖς πάσαις πεντήκοντα. The fact that one cannot actually identify more than thirteen Aequan settlements is, of course, irrelevant.

11. J. N. Madvig, *Emendationes Livianae* (Copenhagen 1877), p. 183.

Structure and meaning in the prologues of Tacitus

A. D. LEEMAN

I. INTRODUCTION

A LITERARY work of art, or a more or less self-contained part of it, can be analysed with the help of the categories of unity and variety, or, otherwise expressed, constancy and progress, or theme(s) and variations. Such an analysis will take into account both the component parts or elements of the work in themselves, and their function in the whole. It can contribute to a better insight into the artistic composition and the full meaning of these elements. By 'full meaning' I understand their meaning at different levels, their undertones and overtones. It may also help to read 'between the lines' without losing ourselves in vain speculation. In the case of an author like Tacitus who made 'emphasis' (in the ancient rhetorical meaning) a major device, an effort to read between the lines is a prerequisite for any serious reader.

If we now turn to Tacitus' prologues, we first realize that they answer to the description of 'more or less self-contained parts' of his works. In the second place their literary 'situation' is completely different from that of the historical *narratio*, and more akin to that of the title of the work. In a way, they can be defined as extended titles, insofar as they too contain information on the author and the subject. In the prologue, the author presents this information in a personal address to his reader, whereas in the *narratio*, the author of a historical work disappears more or less behind his work and lets the events mostly speak for themselves – at least, that is the fiction.

A *narratio* could do without a *praefatio*: a *praefatio* without a *narratio* would be an absurdity. To the average Roman reader the prologue was of secondary importance; but for the modern student of literature, who is looking for motives and backgrounds and is aware that he has to do his job at a 2000-year distance, the importance of those prologues is paramount.

In the case of Tacitus, we possess four prologues, namely those of the *Agricola*, the *Histories*, the *Dialogus de oratoribus* and the *Annals* – the *Germania* being without prologue for some obscure reason (ethnographical writings like those of Strabo and Pomponius Mela do have prologues). The prologue of the *Dialogus* enables us to measure the impact of literary tradition as a pre-formative element in a given prologue. It is very different in character from the other three prologues, and very close to those of the Ciceronian dialogues, especially the *de oratore*, in the following respects. In the first place a certain person, to whom the dialogue is dedicated, is mentioned; secondly, in a fiction which to us is very strange but ultimately goes back to the Platonic dialogue, the discussion is presented as a 'real' conversation which took place at a certain place and time, the author's task being merely to reproduce it from his memory.

From this observation we may expect that the other three prologues, too, will show pre-formative elements belonging to the tradition of historical writing. I must stress, here already, that these traditional ('diachronic') elements are at the same time structural ('synchronic') elements functioning within the prologues of Tacitus; and their functionality is intensified by the fact that the Roman reader more or less expected to find them.

Whereas Herodotus' short prologue presents a number of such elements *in nuce*, Thucydides' prologue is immensely more sophisticated and shows the author keenly aware of the problems involved. In Rome, Sallust is represented by two extensive prologues (*Catilina, Iugurtha*) and by considerable fragments of the prologue of his most influential work, the *Historiae*. These highly-strung and ambitious prologues are in striking contrast to Livy's manner – relaxed, balanced, modest. The traditional elements as they are found in these four authors – studied as paradeigmata in the oratorical curriculum as it appears from Quintilian, *Inst.* x. 1 – can be summed up as follows:

(1) information about the author: his name, his career, his personal pretensions and ambitions;

(2) information about the subject: its nature and importance;

(3) information about the author's approach to his subject and his conception of historiography in general: *memoria, veritas, documentum*;

(4) information about the author's conception of history;

(5) a summary of earlier events, i.e. what is called the 'archaeology' in the case of Thucydides.

These basic elements occur in ever varying formulation,
combination and emphasis; and one or two of them may even
disappear altogether. Every historian has his own special preoccupation and idiosyncrasy. Thus every individual prologue is
at the same time traditional and personal. As is so often the case
in Roman literature, the originality lies in the personal variations
and adaptations of traditional elements, rather than in the introduction of completely novel elements. A close reading of Tacitus'
prologues will subsequently reveal these personal variations within
their structure. Here, it seems more suitable to look at novel,
completely Tacitean elements revealing Tacitus' idiosyncrasies
not as a historian, but as a writer and a thinker. For this, we
shall turn once more to the prologue of the *Dialogus*. Here, the
non-traditional element is the antithesis between the Republican
past with its oratorical greatness, and the Imperial present with
its oratorical decline. To be sure, Tacitus was not the first to
have realized or treated the problem of oratorical decline. On
the contrary it was a much debated question (Seneca Rhetor,
Petronius, the *Auctor de sublimitate*, Quintilian); but only in Tacitus
does it figure as a basic element in his prologue. A glance at the
three historical prologues confirms that the antithesis between
past and present is a basic element there as well. Just as Tacitus'
possibilities as an Imperial orator were treated and questioned
in the prologue of the *Dialogus* in a direct confrontation with those
of the Republican orators, so Tacitus' historiography is confronted
with that of his predecessors in the historical prologues. Tacitus
is so much of a historian, even in his *Dialogus*, that he realizes
his own 'historicity', both as an orator and as a historian; and
he draws his conclusions and accepts the implications of his own
historical position. The relevant terms in the four prologues show
a marked parallelism:

Dialogus: *priora saecula – antiqui/nostra aetas – horum temporum*
Agricola: *antiquitus – apud priores/nostris temporibus – nunc*
Histories: *prioris aevi/postquam bellatum apud Actium*
Annals: *veteris populi Romani/temporibus Augusti, Tiberii* etc.

Thus we seem to have discerned a basic preoccupation of Tacitus

which has left a profound mark in the structure of his historical
prologues, alongside the traditional elements.

II. MODERN STUDIES

The prologues have not yet received the attention they deserve.
It is significant, e.g., that in Borszak's *R.E.* article they are
barely mentioned at all,[1] and that Syme's *Tacitus*[2] devotes less
than one page (out of 807) to them. Nor are the remarks in
Mendell's *Tacitus, the Man and his Work*[3] very penetrating.
Courbaud, it is true, had devoted a long chapter of his book[4] to
the prologue and its history, but he does little more than repeat
the points of Fabia's curious invective against the *Histories'*
prologue and of Boissier.[5]

Structural studies of the prologues can be said to have started
only within the last decade. In his *Studien zur römischen Literatur*
vol. 4, Büchner published a highly debatable paper with conclusions very different from those in Heubner's extensive *Histories*
commentary – the first commentary to devote attention to these
questions.[6] Heubner's ideas on the prologue were subjected to
severe criticism by Drexler and Steinmetz.[7]

In the same volume of his *Studien* we find Büchner's paper
'Das Proömium zum Agricola des Tacitus'.[8] Unfortunately, the
recent commentary by Ogilvie and Richmond does not bring
us much further than pointing out some *topoi*.[9] Also confined to

1. *Suppl.* XI (1968), pp. 373ff.
2. (Oxford 1958).
3. C. W. Mendell, *Tacitus, the Man and his Work* (New Haven–London
1957), pp. 109ff.
4. E. Courbaud, *Les procédés d'art dans les Histoires de Tacite* (Paris 1918).
5. Ph. Fabia, 'La préface des Histoires de Tacite', *REA* 3 (1901), 41–76;
G. Boissier, 'Opinion de Tacite sur les historiens qui l'ont précédé, Hist. 1. 1',
Journal des Savants (1900), 548–55.
6. K. Büchner, 'Das Proömium zu den Historien des Tacitus im Zusammenhang seiner Proömien', *Studien zur römischen Literatur*, vol. 4 (Wiesbaden
1964), pp. 43–60; H. Heubner, *P. Cornelius Tacitus, die Historien, Kommentar*
(Heidelberg 1963).
7. H. Drexler, 'Die Praefatio der Historien des Tacitus', *Helikon* 5 (1965),
148–50; P. Steinmetz, 'Die Gedankenführung des Proömium zu den Historien
des Tacitus', *Gymn.* 75 (1968), 251–61.
8. First published in *WS* 69 (1956), 325–43.
9. R. Ogilvie and I. Richmond (eds.), *Corneli Taciti de vita Agricolae* (Oxford
1967).

such topical elements are the relevant passages in Janson's *Latin Prose Prefaces*, in which only the preface to the *Dialogus* is treated at some length, and that only from the author's point of view.[10]

The most convenient collection of topical parallels is found in Avenarius, *Lukians Schrift zur Geschichtsschreibung*, especially chs. D and G.b.[11]

If the *Annals* prologue is slightly better off in modern literature than its brothers, it is mostly because of the extraordinary interest of chs. 2–15, not because of ch. 1, which like the first chapter of the *Histories* will receive most of our attention here. There are some perfunctory remarks in Walker,[12] and there is little in Koestermann's comprehensive commentary, though this scholar has made good points in his paper, especially on the general structure of chs. 1–15.[13] The same passage is dealt with by Wimmel, with views on ch. 1 that were challenged subsequently by Schillinger-Häfele.[14]

We hope to show that a structural treatment of the prologues along the lines sketched in our introduction may yield information about Tacitus' aims and intentions, and about the constructive powers, both intellectual and artistic, of his mighty mind. We shall start 'half-way' with the *Histories* prologue, and then continue with the most simple, yet in some ways most difficult prologue – that of the *Annals*. Finally, we shall make some remarks on the prologue of the *Agricola*, which, though to a lesser degree than that of the *Dialogus*, belongs to a different genre.

III. THE PROLOGUE OF THE HISTORIES
(ESP. CH. 1)

The *praefatio* may show various degrees of independence from the *narratio*, both in its structural relation to what follows, and in its thought. In a similar way, the inner structure of a prologue

10. T. Janson, *Latin Prose Prefaces, Studies in Literary Conventions* (Stockholm 1964), pp. 60–4.

11. G. Avenarius, *Lukians Schrift zur Geschichtsschreibung* (Meisenheim 1956).

12. B. Walker, *The Annals of Tacitus* (Manchester 1952, 1960²).

13. E. Koestermann 'Der Eingang der Annalen des Tacitus', *Historia* 10 (1961), 330–55.

14. W. Wimmel, 'Roms Schicksal im Eingang der taciteischen Annalen', *Ant. u. Abendl.* 10 (1961), 35–52; U. Schillinger-Häfele, 'Zum Annalen-proömium', *Hermes* 94 (1966), 496–500.

may constitute one indivisible unit, or may be split up into sub-units. Tacitus' technique differs in his three historical prologues. Those of the *Agricola* (chs. 1–3) and of the *Histories* (chs. 1–11) are structurally independent from the *narratio*, whereas the *Annals* prologue (ch. 1) is linked with the *narratio* proper (chs. 16ff.) by a transitional passage (chs. 2–15). In their inner structures, the *Agricola* prologue and that of the *Annals* form single units, whereas the *Histories* prologue is clearly divided into three sub-units.

Even a casual reader feels that ch. 2, *opus aggredior*, and ch. 4, *ceterum antequam destinata componam*, constitute new beginnings, and he can easily observe that ch. 1, chs. 2–3, and chs. 4–11 are independent sub-units, each of which could be missing without destroying the meaning of the other sub-units. This reader would also feel that the end of ch. 11, *hic fuit rerum Romanarum status, cum Servius Galba iterum Titus Vinius consules inchoavere annum sibi ultimum, rei publicae prope supremum*, is the gloomy announcement of the beginning *narratio* – though only an attentive reader will notice the cyclic return to the very first sentence of the prologue, *initium mihi operis Servius Galba iterum Titus Vinius consules erunt.*

As our attention will be focused on ch. 1, I will first make some perfunctory remarks on the second and third sub-unit. The second unit is an extensive and gloomy characterization of the subject. Thus it corresponds with element 2 of our list of five topical elements of the historical prologue, and is to be compared with Sallust's succinct statements in his *Cat.* iv. 4, *nam id facinus in primis ego memorabile existimo sceleris et periculi novitate*, and, slightly more elaborately, in *Iug.* v. 1–3:

> bellum scripturus sum quod populus Romanus cum Iugurtha rege Numidarum gessit, primum quia atrox (!) variaque victoria fuit, dehinc quia tunc primum superbiae nobilitatis obviam itum est, quae contentio divina et humana cuncta permiscuit eoque vecordiae processit, ut studiis civilibus bellum atque vastitas Italiae finem faceret. Sed priusquam huiusce modi rei initium expediam, pauca supra repetam, quo, etc.

The last sentence corresponds with the beginning of ch. 4 (third sub-unit) in Tacitus, *ceterum antequam destinata componam, repetendum videtur, qualis*, etc., which shows us again the traditionality of such forms: Sallust and Tacitus go on with the events leading up to the proper subject, in other words our element 5. There is also a difference. In the *Iugurtha*, this *repetitio* belongs already to the *narratio* (chs. 5–17, until the first *digressio*), just like the 'archaeology' of the *Catilina* (chs. 6–13), which is purposely separated from the prologue (chs. 1–4) by Catiline's biography in ch. 5. In Tacitus' *Histories*, however, chs. 4–11, the third sub-unit, is part of the prologue proper. This corresponds to the structural technique of Sallust's *Histories* (fr. 1, 1–18M), whereas in the *Annals* Tacitus will partly return to the technique of the Sallustian monographs.

The nearest to our element 4 – information about the author's views on human history – is found at the end of ch. 3, *adprobatum est non esse curae deis securitatem nostram, esse ultionem*, which to me seems to be more than an effective epiphonema of the second sub-unit. The similar phrase *deum ira*, recurring in *Hist.* II. 38 and *Ann.* IV. 1. 2 (*deum ira in rem Romanam*), also suggests the conception of a tragic doom in Roman history so familiar in Augustan poets (Horace and Virgil). Moreover in his description of the fate of his heroes Tacitus often employs tragic categories like *hybris* and *peripeteia*, e.g. in the case of Seianus (*Ann.* IV. 39, *nimia fortuna socors*) and also of Tiberius. In the *Histories* a passage like that describing Vitellius' death (ch. 84) has a strongly tragic ring.[15] This attitude, ultimately going back to Hellenistic historians, has been represented in Rome by Sallust, again, who, both in his description of Catiline and Jugurtha, and in his view of Roman history, can be called a 'tragic' historian.[16]

Thus we are left with elements 1 and 3 – information about the author and about his approach to his task. We expect to find them in ch. 1, and our expectations are indeed fulfilled: for its content could be described adequately in that way, at least from the topical point of view. Ours is the structural point of view, and that demands a close reading of the chapter, sentence by sentence.

HISTORIAE, I. 1:

(1) Initium mihi operis Servius Galba iterum Titus Vinius consules erunt. (2) nam post conditam urbem octingentos et

15. See my *Orationis Ratio* (Amsterdam 1963), p. 351.
16. See my paper 'Formen sallustianischer Geschichtsschreibung', *Gymn.* 74 (1967), 108–15.

viginti prioris aevi annos multi auctores rettulerunt, dum
res populi Romani memorabantur, pari eloquentia ac
libertate: postquam bellatum apud Actium atque omnem
potentiam ad unum conferri pacis interfuit, magna illa
ingenia cessere; (3) simul veritas pluribus modis infracta,
primum inscitia rei publicae ut alienae, (4) mox libidine
adsentandi aut rursus odio adversus dominantes: ita neutris
cura posteritatis inter infensos vel obnoxios. (5) sed ambi-
tionem scriptoris facile averseris, obtrectatio et livor pronis
auribus accipiuntur; quippe adulationi foedum crimen
servitutis, malignitati falsa species libertatis inest. (6) mihi
Galba Otho Vitellius nec beneficio nec iniuria cogniti.
dignitatem nostram a Vespasiano inchoatam, a Tito auctam,
a Domitiano longius provectam non abnuerim: sed incor-
ruptam fidem professis neque amore quisquam et sine odio
dicendus est. (7) quod si vita suppeditet, principatum divi
Nervae et imperium Traiani, uberiorem securioremque
materiam, senectuti seposui, rara temporum felicitate, ubi
sentire quae velis et quae sentias dicere licet.

(1) *Initium...erunt.* This phrase, taken up, as we have seen, at
the end of the prologue, indicates the beginning of the period
to be treated, A.D. 69. The final year is only given implicitly, in
the last part of the chapter. Tacitus' purpose is not so much to
define his subject as to argue that he had to start here, *nam...*
Some of his readers may have noticed that he had changed his
mind since he announced a history beginning in A.D. 91 at the
end of the *Agricola* prologue. Many of his readers were no doubt
reminded of the similar very direct way in which Sallust had
begun his *Historiae, res populi Romani M. Lepido Q. Catulo consulibus
ac deinde militiae et domi gestas composui* (fr. 1M). It is as if Tacitus
implicitly announces a work in the grand manner of Sallust.[17]

(2) *nam post...cessere.* This sentence has puzzled many commentators. The 820 years must comprise the whole Republican
period plus the first 99 years of the Empire; however in that case
there appears to be a contradiction between the *eloquentia* and
libertas of historical writing during these years and the phrase
magna illa ingenia cessere referring to historians after Actium. More-

17. Steinmetz, 'Die Gedankenführung...'.

over in this case the conclusion could only have been that Tacitus himself had to start with Actium. Büchner[18] tries in vain to improve the situation by striking the semicolon after *memorabantur* and conceiving *pari eloquentia ac libertate* as an indication of Republican historiography. In the first place *res populi Romani* is an effective and emphatic indication in itself, just as in *Ann.* 1. 3. 7 *quotus quisque reliquus, qui rem publicam vidisset*; we remember Cicero's definition of *res publica* as *res populi* (*Rep.* 1. 25. 39 [41]). In the second place *pari eloquentia ac libertate* may serve as a characterization of Republican historiography, but it cannot serve as its definition. In my opinion, the difficulty of the sentence-structure and its meaning can be solved by a better view of the ablative *pari eloquentia ac libertate*. This is usually taken either as an *ablativus qualitatis* going with an ⟨*auctores*⟩ (not, of course, *multi auctores*), or as an *ablativus modi* going with a ⟨*rettulerunt*⟩. However, it is much better to take it as an *ablativus absolutus*, which seems to be confirmed by a striking parallel in *Germ.* xxviii. 3 *quia pari olim inopia ac libertate eadem utriusque ripae bona malaque erant*. Thus the words get a much greater independence as one of the many instances of an *ablativus absolutus* at the end of a main clause in Tacitus. Structurally the words are balanced by *magna illa ingenia cessere*, just as the temporal *dum* sentence is balanced by the temporal *postquam* sentence. Now *magna illa ingenia* is completely detached from *multi auctores*, and we realize that in the latter words it is only the quantity, and in the first words it is only the quality that is implied. All contradiction and incongruity have disappeared. There were many historians before 69 B.C., even under the Empire, but there were scarcely any *magna ingenia* after Actium. Thus there was a good reason for Tacitus to take up this last period at some later time – as indeed he did in the *Annals*; but bad authors were better than practically no authors at all, and the most urgent need now was for a history of the Flavians. Tacitus expresses his meaning not only clearly but with all desirable qualifications.

As the expression *pari eloquentia ac libertate* apparently carries a heavy weight, it is to be expected beforehand that it will play a main role in the thematic structure of the whole chapter. Therefore it is important to realize its full meaning. Now the

18. Büchner, 'Das Proömium...'.

expression brings to the mind – not to Heubner's, who omits it
in his commentary! – Cicero's theory of historiography in the
de oratore II. 62:

> videtisne quantum munus sit oratoris historia? Haud scio
> an flumine orationis et varietate maximum [= eloquentia]
> ...quis nescit primam esse historiae legem, ne quid falsi
> dicere audeat? Deinde ne quid veri non audeat? Ne quae
> suspicio gratiae sit in scribendo, ne quae simultatis? [= liber-
> tas]

The historian must possess eloquence in his *ratio verborum*; in his
ratio rerum he must speak the truth – he must dare to speak the
truth and nothing but the truth, for ἀλήθεια and παρρησία, *veritas*
and *libertas*, are closely connected in historiographic theory.[19]
The topical character of this connection is also clear from
Suetonius, *Claud.* XLI. 2: the emperor wanted to start with
Caesar's death, but had to give it up because *neque libere neque
vere sibi de superioribus tradendi potestatem relictam*. In Suetonius,
however, *libertas* had a slightly different meaning, namely the
liberty granted by the outer circumstances to speak the truth,
not the inner moral courage to speak it. We should be aware
than an objective aspect of *libertas* is also present in our expression
pari eloquentia ac libertate, which in its context evokes the sphere
of political, Republican freedom. Yet another aspect of *libertas*
appears in the prefaces of Sallust and Livy: it is freedom from
personal bias and outer influence. As Sallust puts it at the end
of his prologue, *Cat.* v *mihi a spe metu partibus rei publicae animus
liber erat*, and Livy, *praef.* 5 *omnis expers* (= *liber*) *curae* (preoccupation), *quae scribentis animum, etsi non flectere a vero* (!) *sollicitum
tamen efficere posset*. This is the kind of freedom alluded to in
Cicero's demand for absence of *gratia* (partiality) and *simultas*
(malice). We shall meet it later in Tacitus' chapter.

To *veritas* and the various shades of *libertas* another related
concept can be added. In the beginning of his *Panegyric* (ch. 1. 6)
Pliny expresses the wish that *omnibus quae dicentur a me libertas,
fides, veritas constet tantumque a specie adulationis absit gratiarum actio
quantum abest a necessitate*. The second half again alludes to freedom
from personal bias and outer influence. In the first half we find
the notion of *fides* coupled with *veritas* and *libertas*. *Fides* indicates

19. Lucian, *Quomodo hist. conscr.* XLIV; Avenarius, *Lukians Schrift...*, pp. 40–6.

loyalty to the truth, with reliability as its result. We shall meet *fides*, too, later in Tacitus' chapter. Now it is significant that in *Annals* IV. 34. 12 the historian Cremutius Cordus, victim of Tiberius, and praised in Seneca's *Consolatio ad Marciam* I. 4 as having possessed *eloquentiam et libertatem* (cf. I. 3, *incorrupta rerum fides*), invoked the example of Livy's relation with Augustus. Livy is characterized by Cremutius as *eloquentiae ac fidei praeclarus in primis*. Apparently, *fides* is not very far from *libertas*, and from *veritas*.

This passage makes it extremely improbable that Syme is right in stating:[20] 'the strictures which Tacitus passes on the historians who wrote on Augustus do not spare the greatest of them; that he had Livy in mind there can be no doubt'. It appears from the passage that Livy was called a *Pompeianus*, a Republican, by Augustus himself. He was a Republican historian '*après la lettre*', and a *magnum ingenium* all right; only, he is not allowed to blur the sharp distinction between Republican and Imperial historians – as he will be in the *Annals* prologue.

I have pointed out the relations between *libertas*, *veritas* and *fides*, which really form one complex, at some length, because they are of vital importance for a correct understanding of the structure of the prologue of the *Histories* as a whole. This will become clear at once.

(3) *simul...alienae.* In his commentary, Heubner warns us against what he thinks is a misunderstanding, namely that *eloquentia* alone is taken up by *magna ingenia*, and *libertate* by *veritas*. This is part of Heubner's view of ch. 1, namely that it consists of loosely connected, shifting thoughts, in which the pair *eloquentia–libertas* disappears altogether in the sequence. His arguments are that *simul* indicates a loose connection and the introduction of a new point; that a lack of *veritas* is said to find its first reason in *inscitia rei publicae* which has nothing to do with frankness; and that Tacitus was obviously influenced by Seneca's words on Cremutius Cordus, where *ingenium* designates that historian's quality as a whole, not just his stylistic achievement.

In the first place, however, direct influence is by no means certain in view of the topical character of the connection *eloquentia–libertas*; moreover, it is only the context which determines whether

20. Syme, *Tacitus*, p. 146.

ingenium means stylistic ability or a writer's abilities in general. Secondly, the *simul* argument can be turned the other way round: to me it seems to take up *pari*, and thus the pair *eloquentia* and *libertas* is taken up in two independent phrases, *magna illa ingenia cessere* and *simul veritas pluribus modis infracta*. The latter is then dichotomized in a well-known Tacitean and Sallustian manner, which is best exemplified by *Cat.* III, *primum–mox*. The argument that *libertas* and *inscitia rei publicae* have nothing to do with one another loses its force as soon as we realize that *libertas* is the readiness and courage not just to speak, but to speak the truth. In order to speak the truth it is essential to know the truth, and to know how to find it. There is no direct connection between *libertas* and *scientia rei publicae*, but they both belong to the *veritas–fides* complex.

What exactly does Tacitus mean by *inscitia rei publicae*? The French scholar Fabia, who wrote an ingenious invective against Tacitus' manner in *Hist.* I. I with the conclusion, 'si cette préface est brillamment écrite, elle est faiblement pensée',[21] has pointed out that Livy, who never held a state-office, was more ignorant than Imperial historians like Cluvius Rufus and Servilius Nonianus, who, like Tacitus himself, did. This makes knowledge of the state dependent upon an active political career, instead of upon a study of the political and constitutional machinery. But that Tacitus indeed means the latter becomes clear from the invaluable digression in *Annals* IV. 32–3, immediately preceding the chapters on Cremutius Cordus' trial, in which Tacitus feels so personally and so deeply involved (esp. IV. 35. 5). In this digression he gives the *raison d'être* of his own work, *in arto et inglorius labor* as compared to the great Republican histories. If one is the historian of a democracy, he argues, *noscenda volgi natura*; an aristocratic history requires historians *senatus et optimatium ingenia qui maxime perdidicerant*; in an analogous way, under the present monarchy – or what amounts to a monarchy: *neque alia re Romana quam si unus imperitet* – it seems useful to investigate the kind of things I do, *haec conquiri tradique in rem fuerit* (33. 1–2). In these somewhat vague words Tacitus seems to suggest that a historian of the Empire must consider it his first duty to study the ruler's psychology, the Imperial mind and its consequences – the *natura*

21. Fabia, 'La préface des Histoires'.

et ingenium unius imperitantis. Within the context of the *Histories* prologue we could paraphrase the idea as follows: the *res publica* is not the *res populi Romani* any more, but a *res aliena*, because a *res imperatoria.* The previous Imperial historians have not realized this sufficiently, and have thus fallen short of their duty – writing history in the full knowledge of the new political truth. *Inscitia rei publicae ut alienae* seems to mean 'ignorance of the commonwealth *as if it were* not theirs any more'; but Tacitus may really mean '*as it is* not theirs any more'. Thus it would be a clear instance of Tacitean emphasis, a figure of speech in which according to Quintilian (*Inst.* IX. 2. 65) one can express things without being allowed to say them in so many words – a new form of *libertas* in an unfree community.[22]

(4) *mox...obnoxios. Libido adsentandi* and *odium adversus dominantes* mark the next stage of deterioration in Imperial historiography, in that the historians fall victim to what Cicero had called *gratia* and *simultas* (*de or.* II. 62), and what Lucian will call χάρις and ἀπέχθεια.[23] In Tacitus the ideas are taken up by *inter infensos vel obnoxios. Libidine adsentandi* instead of *adsentatione* deserves our attention. *Libido, licentia* is a degenerate form of *libertas*, an irrational, unrestrained propensity to do what you like. Structurally, *libidine* is a new variation of the *libertas*-theme. After *aut*, *vel* indicates that it makes no difference whether they are *infensi* or *obnoxii*, because they are one in their lack of *cura posteritatis*. *Ita* is usually taken in the consecutive meaning 'thus, consequently' – *itaque*; but it may be better to take it in the causal meaning 'to that degree', like *adeo* and *tam* in *Agricola*, 1 fin.

The context shows what *cura posteritatis* means, namely, 'to take care to give a truthful account for the enlightenment of posterity'. The same words occur in *Hist.* II. 53. 2 (Otho) *viventem...sola posteritatis cura*, but there they mean 'only caring for what posterity would say of him'. In the *Thesaurus L. L.* two meanings of *cura* are distinguished, namely ἐπιμέλεια and φροντίς; *Hist.* I. 1 is rightly classified under the first meaning, *Hist.* II. 53 under the second one. Gerber–Greef, curiously enough, render *cura* (*s.v.*) in *Hist.* I. 1 in the same way, but explain *posteritas* (*s.v.*) as 'das Urteil der Nachwelt'! The interpretation 'Sorge für

22. On emphasis in Tacitus, see my *Orationis Ratio*, p. 37.
23. *Quomodo hist. conscr.* XXXVIII; cf. Avenarius, *Lukians Schrift...*, pp. 49–54.

'Nachruhm' would introduce a novel element within the thematic structure of the prologue, and is therefore to be rejected.

(5) *sed...inest*. In appearance this is just a curious piece of reader's psychology, very much in the Tacitean manner and in the Sallustian tradition. There is a similar passage of psychological speculation in the prologue of Sallust's *Catiline*, III, where it is functional in a context analysing the difficulties of historiography, in view of the reader's capacity to praise and blame. What are the relevance and the function of the passage in Tacitus? The key-word is *sed*: there is an opposition to the preceding statement that the biased authors of both kinds are alike in their neglect of the historian's primary function, *cura posteritatis*. Now the two kinds are distinguished again, and we could render *sed* by 'yet there is a difference'. Moreover, there is a secondary opposition. Until now attention had been focused on the author; here it is on the reader, the logical subject of *averseris* and *accipiuntur*. No reader will be misguided by *adulatio* (*ambitio*), which reeks of servility, and the vices of the emperors are too well known, if not in their lifetime, at least after their death. Different, and more dangerous, is the effect of *malignitas* (*obtrectatio, livor*), which has the ring of *libertas*, daring frankness – but the ring is false, it is only mock-freedom, and it has to be unmasked, just as all instances of *simulatio* are unmasked by Tacitus.

Thus we are back again to the theme of *libertas*. Whereas *libido adsentandi* was a corrupt form of *libertas*, satisfying personal ambitions but harmless to the reader, the false *libertas* may easily misguide the reader and achieve a cheap success. By the way, the interesting implication is that *libertas* is still what the average reader was looking for – even in an Imperial historian. Tacitus' attitude here is similar to his bitter criticism of the ambitious self-sacrificers, *in nullum rei publicae usum* in his *Agricola* XLII fin. In his view, the historian must neither indulge himself in flattery, nor indulge his readers and his reputation in overdone and unwarranted criticism of rulers, but only seek the truth, between Scylla and Charybdis. There is no independent psychological analysis here, but only a functional analysis of true *libertas* – Tacitus' own *libertas*.

(6) *mihi...dicendus est*. With *mihi* Tacitus switches back to himself and to the first sentence of the chapter. He applies his

analysis of the historian's duties and dangers to his personal situation as a magistrate whose career was favoured by the Flavian emperors, and as the historian of these same emperors. Here, he cannot say what he shall declare in the *Annals* prologue, *sine ira et studio, quorum causas procul habeo*. He could be supposed to have reasons for a too favourable representation of the Flavians; but (*sed*), as a true historian he belongs to those who profess *incorruptam fidem*, a term prepared by *libertas* and *veritas*, and as we have seen belonging to the same complex. As Horace had put it, *iustitiae soror | incorrupta fides nudaque veritas* (*Carm.* 1. 24. 6–7). A similar declaration is found in Sallust's prologue to his *Historiae*, *neque me divorsa pars in civilibus armis movit a vero* (fr. 1, 6M). We are back to our theme again.

One thing in our passage may cause wonder. Together with Vespasian and Titus, Domitian figures as an emperor whom Tacitus might be suspected to have represented in too favourable a light. Indeed, Domitian had favoured his praetorship in A.D. 88, but he also had made him suffer to a degree which we may estimate from the *Agricola* prologue. Nobody expected a trace of *amor* in the *Histories*! However, Tacitus is only dealing with relative *amor*, resulting in a representation of Domitian less unfavourable than he deserves. We cannot but admire the rigorous logic of Tacitus' argument.

(7) *quod si...licet.* From the preceding sentence it could be gathered that Tacitus intended to end his work with the death of Domitian. At the end of the *Agricola* prologue, however, he had promised to write a history comprising both the *memoria pristinae servitutis* and a *testimonium praesentium bonorum* – that is a work beginning with Domitian and ending with the present emperor. Apparently he had changed his mind meanwhile. His readers, including the emperor himself, would expect an explanation. At first sight, however, the words in this passage contain a statement rather than an explanation. If there is an explanation after all, it must be given in the qualifying words *uberiorem securioremque materiam*, and *rara temporum felicitate* etc. – that is either in the character of the subject (*materia*), or in the character of the circumstances (*tempora*), or in both. *Uberior*: richer, and more pleasant to be treated in old age, as an *oblectamentum senectutis*? *Securior*: less perilous, in which there is not the danger that

Pollio ran according to Horace (*Carm.* II. 1); *periculosae plenum opus aleae | tractas et incedis per ignis | suppositos cineri doloso*? Does Tacitus suggest that it is better to leave the safer stuff for later, and to concentrate on the more dangerous subject of the Flavian dynasty now? Now there is a *rara felicitas temporum* – not just happy days, but days in which the freedom of opinion and utterance have been restored, *ubi sentire quae velis et quae sentias dicere licet*: in other words, days of *libertas*, combined, since Nerva, with *principatus, res olim dissociabiles* (*Agr.* III. 1). Here the aspect of *libertas* that comes to the fore is that of political, outer freedom – not frankness, independence, but an objective liberty akin to that of the Republic, the liberty which lies behind the meaning of the phrase *pari eloquentia ac libertate*. This *felicitas temporum* – one of the slogans of the post-Domitian era, and also found in *Agr.* III. 1 – is a rare thing, and the historian must profit from it as long as it lasts by dealing with a subject that needs it. A safer subject may be postponed to a lesser age. In this interpretation, the paragraph becomes an integrated part and a happy conclusion of the chapter, instead of being a kind of encomiastic appendix.

We can guess, but never know, whether Tacitus' declaration and explanation is honest, or no more than a tactful *recusatio*. Did he know already that his next subject, in the *Annals*, would be a yet earlier period instead of the present era? And *senectus* is an ill-defined age...

Let us finally look back, sum up, and conclude. The ever-present theme in the chapter, apart from the first sentence, is *libertas*. Consequently it can be regarded as the basic element of the prologue, and, structurally speaking, the element of constancy. The element of variation and progress has been found in the ever-changing aspects of *libertas* which come to the fore.[24] At the same time it appears that *libertas, veritas, fides* form one inseparable complex, and it is probably better to say that it is this complex which forms the basic theme. As the chapter progresses, the historian's duty is analysed as an obligation to speak the truth for the enlightenment of posterity. In order to fulfil this obligation he must have moral courage to be frank in loyalty

24. For various conceptions of *libertas* see C. Wirszubski, *Libertas as a Political Idea at Rome during the late Republic and early Principate* (Cambridge 1960²).

to the truth and political knowledge of where to find the truth. He must be free from personal ambitions and feelings and outer influence, and he can only publish the results of his work in an atmosphere which guarantees a minimum of political freedom.[25]

The only sentence in which this theme is lacking is the first one. On the other hand the whole analysis of *libertas–veritas* functions as an explanation (*nam...*) of the first sentence. There is certainly a difficulty here, which some scholars have tried to solve by interpolating an idea like ⟨'this is different from what I have announced in my *Agricola*, as you will remember, and my reasons for this change of mind are the following'⟩ (Büchner), or ⟨'as you can see from my words I intend to write in the grand Sallustian manner: the reason for this is the following'⟩ (Steinmetz). However, to me such solutions sound too sophisticated. After all, Tacitus gives a very good reason for his general procedure by first stating that Roman history up to A.D. 69 had been treated by many authors. Then follows a differentiation between the *magna ingenia* of the Republican era and the unsatisfactory historians between 31 B.C. and A.D. 69; but even an unsatisfactory treatment is better than no treatment at all – for the time being. Thus he gives, at the same time, a reason for beginning with A.D. 69 now, and for writing his *Annals* later on (comp. p. 177).

Quite naturally, in my opinion, the purely chronological relation ('I begin where the others leave off') leads to an ideological and polemical relation, anticipated by the distinction between two categories of predecessors – Republican and Imperial historians. The well-known *alii–ego* situation is created. But *nam* is not forgotten. He feels free to write because he has political insight, because he realizes the dangers of external influence but feels morally bound by the primary obligations of the historian. And he feels free to treat his dangerous subject because there is an atmosphere of comparative political freedom just now. Nor is the time element introduced by the first phrase forgotten: *initium mihi – prius aevum – res populi Romani – postquam bellatum apud Actium || mihi Galba Otho Vitellius...Vespasianus...Titus...Domitianus – Nerva–Traianus...senectus.*

25. For an investigation into the philosophical background of this analysis (the four cardinal virtues) I refer to my paper in the *Actes de la XIIe Conférence internationale du comité Eirene* (Cluj 1972).

There is even an inner relation between the chronological and ideological elements. Tacitus can write now about his chosen subject because the historical situation of Republican *libertas* has returned at last, more or less: *dicere verum licet.* Thus it becomes clear why Tacitus, in his version of the traditional *veritas* theme of historiographic theory, has made *libertas* rather than *veritas* the pivot of the complex and of the chapter. It secures the balance in the cyclic development of the prologue.

A last problem arises. In the characterization of Republican historians, *libertas* appears on a line with *eloquentia.* And indeed, Cicero had made *eloquentia* and *veritas* the two main requirements for a true historian. *Libertas* remains throughout the chapter, but *eloquentia* disappears with *magna ingenia.* Did *eloquentia* degenerate as well? It certainly did, though according to Maternus in the *Dialogus* to a lesser degree, *utere antiqua libertate, a qua vel magis degeneravimus quam ab eloquentia (Dial.* XXVII. 3). At the same time, however, we should realize that the classicist generation of Quintilian, Pliny and Tacitus endeavoured to rise to the old classical standards again, in one way or another. The stylistic revival was no doubt keenly felt by their readers, also by the readers of Tacitus' preface; but for obvious reasons Tacitus could not claim to reach the classical level of style again, as he did claim to achieve classical *libertas.* He could not say explicitly that he himself wrote *pari eloquentia ac libertate,* but by linking the two so closely at the beginning, he at least suggested the same link at the end of the chapter by emphasis.

Visible and invisible threads of an almost incredible intricacy compose the texture of Tacitus' prologue. Traditional elements appear in very personal variants, constant elements appear in ever-new variations: but the whole remains a unity – a unity almost as complex as a poem.

IV. THE ANNALS PROLOGUE

The personal prologue of the *Agricola* covers three chapters, that of the *Histories* one long chapter followed by eleven other introductory chapters; the *Annals* prologue consists of one small chapter only, and there are fourteen half-introductory, half-narrative chapters following it. Reading the three prologues in chronological sequence gives the curious sensation that the *man* Tacitus fades away and escapes us. Any account of Tacitus' development from A.D. 98 – when he was about forty-two or forty-three years old – through the first decade of the new century, when he wrote the *Histories*, to the second decade – that of the bulk of the *Annals*, written when he was well on his way to sixty – has to take that into account as one of the major phenomena ...and has to account for it.

Modern books on Tacitus all make the same kind of observation on the *Annals* prologue:

Walker: 'The *Annals* prologue is much more compressed and selective, and also less rhetorical [i.e., less "literary"?] than that of the *Historiae*. But it is quite as effective...observes only the constitutional and other changes which made possible Augustus.'[26] Mendell sees the development as follows: after the *Agricola*, with its wholly rhetorical [?] prologue, highly personal, and detachable from the *narratio*, follows the *Histories* prologue, of conventional character but also with a definite personal note antagonistic to a 'dramatic' representation; the *Annals* prologue goes a step further: the personal address is gone, a unique omission in historical prologues in antiquity. It is on the surface wholly action, only implicitly disclosing Tacitus' own point of view, and even more inseparable from the rest of the work than had been the *Histories* prologue.[27] Syme devotes very little space to the prologues. Of that of the *Histories* he only gives a summary and qualifies it as 'masterly'.[28] He declares of the *Annals* prologue:[29] 'the *Annals* from the opening words go to the limit of brevity and intensity. The prologue falls into two parts, first the vicissitudes of governmental power at Rome, in summary from the kings to Caesar Augustus, next the character of history-writing and the author's design.' He has a footnote to this: 'Editors would have done well to print the first chapter in the form of two paragraphs.' As against the *Histories*, 'the remarks in the *Annales* are ruthlessly depersonalized, and the odious pronoun is restricted to the writer's enunciation of the subject.' That is all.

26. Walker, *Annals of Tacitus*, p. 27.
27. Mendell, *Tacitus, the Man and his Work*, p. 118.
28. Syme, *Tacitus*, pp. 145–6.
29. *Tacitus*, p. 304.

And indeed, in its dry, enumerative presentation the chapter looks unproblematic enough – on the surface.

Let us first look at the relations between the prologue and the *narratio*. In the case of the *Histories*, there could be no doubt about chs. 1, 2–3 and 4–11 being three different parts all belonging to the prologue. The author himself made both the division and the unity clear.

In the *Annals* the case is more complicated. At the end of ch. 1 the author announces that his subject will be '*pauca de Augusto et extrema tradere, mox Tiberii principatum et cetera*'. Now it is clear that the principate of Tiberius starts with ch. 6, beginning with the ominous words *primum facinus novi principatus fuit Postumi Agrippae caedes*. At the same time, however, we can state that in chs. 7–10 the name of Augustus still occurs at least as often as that of Tiberius. The discussions and decisions in the senate on the funeral of Augustus, and the funeral itself are described; then follows the *sermo de Augusto*, divided into *pro* and *contra* opinions (chs. 9–10). Only in chs. 11–14 are the senate's *preces* to induce Tiberius to accept the principate rendered, followed by the relation of some constitutional changes in ch. 15. A clearly-marked new beginning is found in ch. 16, *hic rerum urbanarum status erat, cum Pannonicas legiones seditio incessit*, a transitional formula which is very similar to *Hist.* 1.11 *hic fuit rerum Romanarum status, cum...*

Their function, however, is not wholly the same. In the *Histories*, the formula marks the beginning of the *narratio* after the introductory chapters on the *status rerum Romanarum*, including the provinces; in the *Annals* the transition is from the *status rerum urbanarum* to the *res provinciarum*, the insurrections in Pannonia and Germania (chs. 16–45). At the same time, however, the latter section is a typical *narratio*, whereas the preceding chapters are a *status*-description; within these chapters there seems to be effected a gradual transition from the tone of ch. 6 etc., full of rumours and reflections, and very static, in short similar to that of *Hist.* 1.4–11, to the tone of ch. 15, where the line ends in a veritable anticlimax with an enumeration of *senatusconsulta* of a technical order, which would not have been out of place anywhere in the *narratio*.[30] Thus between chs. 10 and 15 we witness a gradual change in the tone and contents, which effects

30. Koestermann, 'Der Eingang...', pp. 350ff.

a transition from prologue to *narratio* inasmuch as the passage belongs to both. This is remarkable, and different from Tacitus' technique in the *Histories* – to say nothing of the *Agricola*.

Let us now look at chs. 2–5, which must contain the *pauca de Augusto et extrema* (preceding the *Tiberii principatum* beginning in ch. 6) – words translated by Jackson (Loeb) with 'a small part (the concluding one) of Augustus' reign', and Goelzer (Budé) with '*de ne parler d'Auguste que brièvement et de ses derniers jours seulement*', apparently taking *et* as explicative. However, we should observe that only from IV. 2 (*provecta senectus*) and V. 1 (*gravescere valetudo*) onward are the *extrema Augusti* related. Chs. 2–3 do not deal with the *extrema* at all, but give a short survey of the essential facts about Augustus' reign and its foundations; ch. 2 is about his development from *triumvir* in 42 B.C. to *princeps* in 27 B.C., ch. 3 contains the measures taken with regard to the *subsidia dominationis*, the Imperial princes and potential successors from Marcellus (before 23 B.C.) through Agrippa, C. and L. Caesar to Tiberius and Germanicus – measures covering the whole period of Augustus' principate. The chapter ends with the resulting consolidated state of affairs *domi bellique* at the end of his reign (III. 6–7). Thus equal space is devoted to the history of 42 B.C.–A.D. 14 (establishment of the monarchy, dynastical measures), and to the state of affairs and the events at the end of Augustus' reign in A.D. 14.

Apparently we should take the *et* in *pauca de Augusto et extrema* not as explicative, but simply as additive. At the same time we should remember that the next chapters are still full of Augustus. Here again, the technique is transitional rather than 'divisional'.

Working further backwards we must now view the transition between chs. 1 and 2. The first sentence of ch. 2 deserves our attention in this respect. It is one of Tacitus' most elaborate and successful historical periods. Syme comments: 'Tacitus if he wishes can compose a long development, as when, after a prologue cut up into short sentences, he carried the origins of the monarchy at Rome from the battle of Philippi in a vast sweep to the established and accepted power of Caesar Augustus'.[31] The period can be analysed as follows:

31. Syme, *Tacitus*, p. 347; cf. Wimmel, 'Roms Schicksal...', p. 41.

> postquam Bruto et Cassio caesis (42 B.C.) nulla iam publica
> arma, Pompeius apud Siciliam oppressus (36 B.C.) exutoque
> Lepido interfecto Antonio (31 B.C.) ne Iulianis quidem
> partibus nisi Caesar dux reliquus,
> posito...contentum
> ubi...pellexit,
> insurgere...trahere,
>   nullo adversante cum
>   ferocissimi...cecidissent,
>   ceteri...extollerentur
>   ac...mallent.

If we compare the firm structure of this period with the rather hesitant periodic beginnings in the prologue of the *Agricola*, we can measure the distance between the literary man of A.D. 98 and that of A.D. 115. The central part of the period is tripartite (participle, *ubi*-sentence, historical infinitives); it is preceded by a tripartite *postquam*-clause, and followed by a construction, again tripartite, depending on an added ablative absolute in the Tacitean manner from the *Agricola* onward. This formal structure corresponds with three successive aspects, first the historical events leading up to the monarchic position of Octavian, then his own behaviour in consolidating and strengthening that position, and finally the reaction to this development in the circles of society that mattered. Nothing equally elaborate, equally balanced and equally perspicuous could be performed in any modern language. Here Caesar and Livy had paved the way for Tacitus, and Tacitus cannot help resorting to them from time to time instead of to his beloved Sallust. His personal addition is the position of the ablative absolute after the main clause, containing qualifications, reactions, comments or results.[32]

The interesting thing from our point of view – the links between chs. 1 and 2 – are the wordings of the *postquam*-clause, especially *exutoque Lepido interfecto Antonio ne Iulianis quidem partibus nisi Caesar dux reliquus*, which is a slightly expanded version of those in 1. 1 *Lepidi atque Antonii arma in Augustum cessere*, much in the same way as the sequence, *qui cuncta discordiis civilibus fessa nomine*

---

32. On this use see R. Enghofer, *Der Ablativus absolutus bei Tacitus* (Dissertation, Würzburg 1961), pp. 130ff., with references.

principis sub imperium accepit, is taken up in an expanded form by the sequence of our period. This establishes a close relation between chs. 1 and 2. The bird's-eye view of Roman history from the kings onward to Augustus continues in ch. 2 – only the bird has come down to take a closer view. The impression of continuity is further strengthened by the similar syntactical means by which the future *princeps* Tiberius is presented as the remaining dynastic heir in 3. 3 (*at Agrippa*, etc.), to which Koestermann has drawn our attention.[33] It is the 'ten little Indians' story again! I stress this also because it suggests very effectively a strong element of the arbitrary in the course of fate – the *ludibria rerum mortalium*, to which Tacitus alludes in his story of Claudius' inheritance of the throne in *Annals* III. 18.

There is another, yet stronger link of a thematic nature between ch. 1 and chs. 2ff., but for this we have first to take a closer view of the bird's-eye view in ch. 1.

> (1) Urbem Romam a principio reges habuere; (2) libertatem et consulatum L. Brutus instituit. dictaturae ad tempus sumebantur; neque decemviralis potestas ultra biennium neque tribunorum militum consulare ius diu valuit. (3) non Cinnae, non Sullae longa dominatio; (4) et Pompei Crassique potentia cito in Caesarem, Lepidi atque Antonii arma in Augustum cessere, (5) qui cuncta discordiis civilibus fessa nomine principis sub imperium accepit. (6) sed veteris populi Romani prospera vel adversa claris scriptoribus memorata sunt, (7) temporibusque Augusti dicendis non defuere decora ingenia, donec gliscente adulatione deterrerentur: (8) Tiberii Gaique et Claudii ac Neronis res florentibus ipsis ob metum falsae, postquam occiderant recentibus odiis compositae sunt. (9) inde consilium mihi pauca de Augusto et extrema tradere, (10) mox Tiberii principatum et cetera, sine ira et studio, quorum causas procul habeo.

Chapter 1 begins with five asyndetic main-clauses (*Urbem . . . dominatio*), which had best be printed with full stops. *Et Pompei* is the first syndeton and seems to indicate a division of 1. 1–5 into two halves.

33. Koestermann, 'Der Eingang . . .'.

(1) *Urbem...habuere.* Instead of beginning with stating his subject, as he did in the *Histories*, Tacitus goes straight back to the earliest stage of Roman constitutional history. It has been observed for a long time that the sentence reads as a hexameter in the archaic manner. Among others, the commentators Furneaux–Anderson and Koestermann believe this verse-structure to be non-intentional. To me this seems hard to believe in view of the fact that Livy, too, starts with a hexametrical beginning (*facturusne operae pretium sim*). And our credulity is still harder pressed if we take into account that the first sentences of both monographs of Sallust end with a *clausula heroica* (*Cat.* I. 1 *oboedientia finxit*; *Iug.* I. 1 *virtute regatur*). Quintilian tells us *est enim* [*historia*] *proxima poetis et quodammodo carmen solutum* (x. 1. 31) – and indeed I believe that we must take into account that in the ancient tradition, from Herodotus onwards, historiography had something heroic (and tragic), both in style and in representation and interpretation. This character might well be stressed by a verse-like start.

A principio, not *principio* (compare Sall. *Cat.* VI. 1, *urbem Romam ...habuere initio Troiani*) launches the sweeping chronological movement, so characteristic of all Tacitus' prologues. At the same time, Tacitus seems to suggest that the story of *dominatio* in Rome starts already with the earliest beginnings of Roman history. We are reminded of Sall. *Hist.* fr. 11M *dissensiones fuere iam inde a principio* – a revision of his earlier view that these only started after the fatal year 146 B.C.

(2) *libertatem et consulatum* links the Republican constitution and the concept of political liberty. The sentence is parallel to the first one, which emphasizes the inner antithesis. However, instead of enlarging upon the history and conception of *libertas*, as he did in the *Histories*, Tacitus goes on with an enumeration of instances of *dominatio* or absolute power even under the Republic. First he gives a general exception to Republican liberty, the dictatorships, in the form of an imperfect; but they were only temporary and in accordance with the temporary needs of the moment (*ad tempus*). Then follow a number of special phenomena, the *decemviri legibus scribundis* of 451/450 B.C. and the *tribuni militum consulari potestate* of the years around 400 B.C. The phrasing implies that all three were legal resorts (*sumebantur, potestas, ius*) and that they were limited in time (*ad tempus, neque...ultra biennium, neque diu*).

(3) *non...dominatio*: in a new, verb-less colon two instances of real *dominatio* are mentioned, that of the *popularis* Cinna (87–84 B.C.) and that of the *nobilis* Sulla (82–79 B.C.), both lasting three years only (*non...non longa*). In a similar passage, *Hist.* II. 38. 1, Marius is coupled with Sulla: *mox e plebe infima C. Marius et nobilium saevissimus L. Sulla victam armis libertatem in dominationem verterunt.* The whole of that chapter 38 is a close imitation of Sall. *Hist.* fr. 12M *pauci potentes, quorum in gratiam plerique concesserant, sub honesto patrum aut plebis nomine dominationes adfectabant.* This reminds us of the fact that Sallust is always in the background of a passage like our ch. 1, and that the whole idea of such sweeping surveys of Roman history under special viewpoints is Sallustian.

(4) *et Pompei...cessere*: in a clearly distinguished new development the two triumvirates are mentioned. *Potentia* and *arma* mark their illegal and military character. Formally, the statements differ from the preceding ones. What does Tacitus want us to believe: that the six members of the two triumvirates (except Augustus) continue the list of temporary suspensions of *libertas*?[34] That would misrepresent the facts to an unbearable degree: from 60 to 44 B.C. there was a perpetual state of *dominatio* (Crassus and Pompey falling off in 53 and 47 B.C.), and the same holds good for the period after the Ides of March, when there was *dominatio* from the Second Triumvirate in November 43 until 27 B.C. (Lepidus falling off soon after 42, and Mark Antony in 31 B.C.). That would leave just one year of Republican freedom – and what freedom! – namely 44/43 B.C., between 60 B.C. and 27 B.C. Thus, for any Roman reader aware of the facts, the suggestion would rather be that the attacks on *libertas* became chronic by 60 B.C., and that both triumvirates, begun as a shared and thereby tempered *dominatio*, quickly (*cito*) developed into monarchies – not a mere continuation, but an intensification of the process, a new, intermediate (transitional!) stage in the development from republicanism, only temporarily interrupted, to firmly established monarchy. Caesar was a prefiguration of Augustus,[35] but he did not bring the end of all Republican possibilities.

34. Wimmel 'Roms Schicksal...', pp. 35ff.
35. As Schillinger-Häfele, 'Zum Annalenproömium...', points out against Wimmel.

(5) *qui...accepit*: in a kind of ritardando, these words mark
the final stage – the principate. *Cuncta discordiis civilibus fessa* recalls the despair of Horace's *Epodes* 7 and 16, and the atmosphere
of the end of *Georgics* 1. Within the context, however, they rather
suggest that *libertas* had finally lost the battle by exhaustion, not
by conviction. In 2. 1, the process will be described in the terms
dulcedine otii pellexit, words too similar to *Agr.* III. 1 *subit quippe
etiam inertiae dulcedo* to allow the supposition of any warm feeling
on the part of Tacitus. His view seems darkened indeed after
the statement in *Hist.* 1. 1 *pacis interfuit*, and the conclusion at the
end of the *Dialogus*. We are also reminded of Sall. *Iug.* XLI *ita
quod in advorsis rebus optaverant otium, postquam adepti sunt, asperius
acerbiusque fuit...Nomine principis sub imperium* contains an antithetical note. *Princeps* (*senatus*), leader of the deliberative council,
and *imperium*, executive power, were incompatible under the
Republic: 'he called himself *princeps*, but he was an *imperator*'
(comp. Sall. *Hist.* fr. 1. 12M *sub honesto nomine* etc.). Yet *imperium*
was a term for legal power; the real term occurs in 3. 1: *dominatio*.
Ch. 2. 1 (*insurgere, trahere*) may imply a gradual shift from *imperium*
to *dominatio*, comparable to that of Sulla who, according to
Sallust, *Cat.* XI. 4 *armis recepta re publica bonis initiis malos eventus
habuit, rapere omnes, trahere* etc. The conception of gradual transition
seems to be omnipresent in the *Annals* prologue, and also determines
its form. However, there is not only progression, but also return:
Rome had returned to the stage of permanent *dominatio* in its
beginning – *urbem Romam a principio reges habuere*, the 250 years of
kingship. That is what had become of Virgil's *magnus ab integro
saeclorum nascitur ordo*.

(6) *sed...memorata sunt*: *sed* is important, as so often in these
prologues. Is it a mere transitional particle, marking the introduction of a new paragraph in the well-known Sallustian manner?
This seems to be the *communis opinio* among modern scholars. As
far as I can see, however, the instances quoted by Gerber–Greef
do not present a clear case of this use; at any rate, it seems to be
scarce in Tacitus. If we conceive *sed* as 'but', 'however', the
implication would be that the history of Republican *libertas* versus
dominatio is an attractive subject, but already dealt with adequately.
This would be very much in agreement with the ideas in the
prologue of the *Histories* and at the beginning of the digression

in *Ann.* IV. 32, with the rather bitter comparison between his own subject (in *arto et inglorius labor*) with the great works of those *qui veteres populi Romani res composuere* – Sallust and Livy.

(7) *temporibusque...deterrerentur*: the Augustan times are linked with the Republic; historiography of this period was in a state of transition (again!). Livy is probably in Tacitus' mind here. His *Ab urbe condita* went down to 9 B.C. only, but the last part of the work was written towards the end of Augustus' reign. In *Ann.* IV. 34 the comparative freedom of Livy under Augustus is opposed to the position in which Cremutius Cordus found himself under Tiberius. *Glisco* is a favourite word with Tacitus in the *Annals* (twenty-one instances in Gerber–Greef against two for the *Histories*); it expresses beautifully his new conception of the 'graduality' of all things in history. In the *Histories* the judgement on Imperial historiography was much more block-like: *postquam bellatum apud Actium...magna illa ingenia cessere*. There, Livy fell between two chairs; here he gets his proper place on the bench.

(8) *Tiberii...compositae sunt*: in an adversative asyndeton Tacitus proceeds to a condemnation of post-Augustan historiography. However, his manner is less abstract and general than in the *Histories*; distinction is made between adulatory treatment during the emperor's lifetime, and bitter invective immediately after his death. Thus he anticipates and justifies his own declaration at the end of the chapter. The historians concerned (men like Servilius Nonianus, Cluvius Rufus, Fabius Rusticus, Aufidius Bassus) scarcely deserved such wholesale condemnation: but then one is never very just towards one's predecessors in the same field.

(9) *inde...tradere*: at last Tacitus gives his *acte de présence*, which in the *Histories* he did already in the first sentence of the prologue. Syme remarks: 'The excuse for omitting Augustus is literary rather than historical, and, on the author's showing, not wholly valid'.[36] However, in the same way he had suggested in the *Histories* prologue that a history of the Julio-Claudian emperors was less urgent than that of the Flavians. Here, he announces that for the moment he will restrain himself to a few corrections of the traditional image of Augustus (*pauca*); but at the same time he indicates that a renewed full treatment of that emperor is

36. *Tacitus*, p. 364.

still necessary. And indeed he announces his plans, never fulfilled, in this direction explicitly in *Ann.* III. 24. 3.

The meaning of *pauca...et extrema* has already received our attention.

(10) *mox...cetera*: these words summarize in the driest possible manner the list *Tiberii Gaique et Claudii ac Neronis res* – thus establishing a close link with the preceding sentence.

sine...habeo: the same is the case here; that Tacitus had no reasons for personal bias has been prepared by *recentibus* (!) *odiis*. The last emperor to be described had died in A.D. 68, when Tacitus was about fifteen years old. So he did not, as in the *Histories*, have to promise to keep to the *prima lex historiae*, in spite of the *recentia odia* towards Domitian. He wisely does not take into account those *causae* which spring from sympathy or antipathy, from personal convictions, and from resemblances to living persons or actual situations, and the hopes and fears they evoke in the historian's mind. It is such *causae* that may be held responsible for Tacitus' often coloured account of men like Tiberius. *Sine ira et studio* has won the honour of being the definitive formula for historical impartiality – rather than the more sophisticated *neque amore et sine odio* of the *Histories*. Cicero had used the terms *gratia* and *simultas* (*de Or.* II. 62): in fact the idea was so common in historians that Seneca could parody it in the prologue of his *Apocolocyntosis* (1. 1): *quid actum sit in caelo a.d. III Idus Oct. anno novo, initio saeculi felicissimi, volo memoriae tradere. Nihil nec offensae nec gratiae dabitur: haec ita vera!*

Looking back upon ch. 1 as a structural whole as it has become clear to us, I first recall Syme's remark quoted at the beginning: 'editors would have done well to print the first chapter in the form of two paragraphs'.[37] I should think that this rather spoils the whole structure. The chapter is not divided into two parts, the first containing a survey of history, the second a survey of historiography. The whole chapter is dominated and held together by one idea – that of history as a subject for historiography. It is the eagle flying high and surveying the *post conditam urbem octingentos et viginti annos prioris aevi*, in search of his prey and defining it as the monarchic tendencies discernible even under the Republic. The basic theme and the element of constancy

37. *Tacitus*, p. 304.

in this chapter is the same as that of the prologue of the *Histories*. The difference could be expressed with the help of the following paradox: in the *Histories* Tacitus was concerned with *libertas*, even under the Empire; in the *Annals* he is concerned with *dominatio*, even under the Republic. The shift, and its implications, are clear enough. The same theme – *dominatio* gradually crushing *libertas* – is at the basis of the following chapters, sketching the development of Augustus' monarchic *imperium* to *dominatio* (ch. 2), the *subsidia dominationis* (ch. 3), the criminal beginnings of Tiberius' *dominatio* (ch. 6), the *servitium* of *consules, patres, eques*, and the hypocrisy of Tiberius, *tamquam vetere re publica et ambiguus imperandi* (ch. 7. 11). The prologues of Tacitus have often been compared to musical overtures; they are, in so far as they present the basic themes and announce the general tone of the work. In the case of the *Annals* the overture is like those which imperceptibly develop into the action itself. It presents reflection already in the form of action – Roman history as the antagonism of *libertas* and *dominatio*.

Was a synthesis between the two still possible in the present? Tacitus had praised the comparative liberty of the Trajanic era in his earlier works, rather hesitantly in the first stages (*Agricola*), more firmly some years later, in the *Histories*. A comparable statement is lacking in the *Annals*, nor does he announce any plans for the future concerning the present era. This is scarcely due to his more ascetic approach to prologue-writing only; he probably was less sure than ever about the possibility of a satisfactory and stable go-between. Just as *libertas* too easily degenerated into *licentia* under the Republic, monarchs tend to be bad – fascinating but bad – and disastrous to their subjects. To be aware that, in the Rome of the present, monarchy was inevitable, was but a poor consolation. Of course it gave grim satisfaction to scrutinize the monarchic mind, and this was the historian's main duty under the Empire. Tacitus did not do it *sine ira et studio*; but only a bitter mind could have the force and the courage to see through the *species rerum* and the *simulatio hominum*. How glorious, how beautiful, how eternal Rome looked even under the worst emperor! But under the Elysian surface and the dazzling splendour, a dark abyss, a Tartarus opened to the penetrating eye. It was enough to make an honest man choose death; but in order to see and to understand one must live, and even be as near as possible to the emperor.

Tacitus' great predecessor Sallust had been fascinated by the struggle between *optimates* and *populares*. First he believed that the fault was with the *pauci potentes*, and that true *libertas* could be established by a regime of the *populares*. Later on, in the *Histories*, he found that usurpers were recruited from both parties, and that *respublica* and *libertas* were nothing to them. Tacitus, writing some 150 years later, saw what happened: the *dominationes* of the *pauci potentes* soon developed into the *perpetua dominatio* of the principate. Yet *libertas* was not quite dead. It only took a different form — that of dignified personal behaviour, of a firm decision to make the best of the new circumstances, of keeping up the responsibilities of the senators.[38]

Finally, it is our duty to see what has become of the five topical themes of historical prologues in the case of Tacitus' last prologue.

(1) Personal information about the author is minimal here, and considerably less than in the *Histories*. His career is not mentioned, nor are his past experiences and his plans for the future.

(2) The information about the subject is reduced to a minimum, too, if we look at 1. 1 only; and there is nothing in the following to match the great chapters, *Histories* 1. 2–3.

(3) On the other hand, the whole of ch. 1 can be said to be concerned with the author's choice of, and approach to, his subject. Here both the theme of *dominatio* versus *libertas* and the profession of *veritas* fit in. The latter again takes the form of *Auseinandersetzung* with earlier historians of the same period. The link he feels with the *clari auctores* of the Republic is expressed much more implicitly than in the *Histories*; there is not a hint that *veritas* is encouraged by a renewed *libertas* in the political sense. The idea of history as a *documentum virtutis*, so predominant in the *Agricola*, and found only in ch. 3 of the *Histories* prologue, is absent here; but there is, of course, the elliptic statement *praecipuum munus annalium* in *Ann.* III. 65. Tacitus is still basically a moralistic historian, but he apparently does not care any more to make a personal point of it.

(4) And indeed Tacitus' conception of history, at least of Roman history, is that of a perpetual antagonism between

38. Wirszubski, *Libertas*, ch. 5.

libertas and *dominatio* – a purely political idea. And as far as man is concerned, the approach is psychological rather than moral. In short, his conception of history now recalls Thucydides rather than Sallust. Only in the great digression of *Annals* IV. 32–3 does this conception become wholly clear, as we have seen in our discussion of *inscitia rei publicae* (*Hist.* I. I. I). The more aware Tacitus becomes of the fundamental and permanent character of the forces in history and human conduct, the less important the specific choice of a subject becomes. Emphasis and allusion allow the writer to be 'actual' even when treating a remote period.[39] There are no divisions, only transitions, new variations of the same eternal themes: *urbem Romam a principio reges habuere.*

(5) Accordingly, a summary of earlier events is given in the form of a gradual transition from the (already 'historical') *mise-au-point* in ch. I to the *narratio* proper in chs. 16ff. Chs. 2–15: prologos? logos? A purely 'rhetorical' question, and useful only in view of the conclusion that it cannot be answered.

V. ·SOME REMARKS ON THE AGRICOLA PROLOGUE

We have left the prologue of the *Dialogus* outside the picture, as it belongs to a different literary genre – though we duly remarked a similarity with the other prologues in its chronological frame-work. In the case of the *Agricola*, the difference in genre is less marked, but it is there all the same; consequently it cannot be compared without qualification to the two prologues just treated. Basically, it introduces a biography, and thus belongs to a genre which the ancients always considered as distinguished from historiography both in its *ratio rerum* (one protagonist, attention to *mores*, not only in great but also in small things), and in its *ratio verborum*, which dispenses with the grand manner of history. The curious thing about the *Agricola* is, however, that it treats its subject nevertheless in the manner of historiography: the style is scarcely less 'Sallustian' than that of the two great histories, and the insertion of a digression like that on the *situs Britanniae* (chs. 10ff.) seems to show the influence of Sallust's historical mono-graphs. Some aspects, e.g., the prosopopoiia of Agricola at the

39. Leeman, *Orationis Ratio*, pp. 344ff.

end, suggest the influence of the *laudatio funebris*. We could even be tempted to consider it, in a way, as an *oratio pro Agricola* against the charge of collaboration with the monstrous regime of Domitian: for this I refer to the end of ch. 42 with its remarkably vehement rejection of a too principled and stubborn political opposition, seeking death to no avail of the *res publica*.

It is helpful to keep in mind the complex character of the whole *vita Agricolae* as we turn to its prologue.

In the first place, its rhythm is totally different from that of the two historical prologues. It is one continuous unit covering no less than three chapters, not to be divided into more or less independent sub-units, but progressing in three waves, corresponding with the individual chapters.

(Ch. 1) *Clarorum virorum facta moresque posteris tradere* is a clear definition of the task of the biographer. The moral aspect of the biography is indicated at once, whereas in the *Histories* prologue a similar phrase is found only in ch. 3: *bona exempla virtutum... supremae clarorum virorum necessitates*. In the *Agricola*, on the other hand, we have to wait until ch. 2 before the *libertas–veritas* complex turns up. The pivotal words of ch. 1, with its broad periods reflecting the broad movement of the whole prologue, are found at the end of the first period, *vitium parvis magnisque civitatibus commune, ignorantiam recti et invidiam* – a *vitium* common to states, and consequently not only found in the Empire but also present, though apparently to a lesser degree, in the Republic. Commentators like Ogilvie–Richmond (following Furneaux–Anderson) note that the thought is commonplace (referring to Nepos, *Chabr.* III. 3 and Sall. *Iug.* x. 2). But they fail to notice the individual variation in Tacitus, namely the addition of *ignorantia recti* to *invidia*, and thereby explaining the latter.

The idea that *virtus* is in danger of meeting a lack of appreciation because of a widespread *ignorantia recti* is curious indeed. It is somewhat similar to the role of the *inscitia rei publicae*, political ignorance, in the *Histories* prologue. Great *virtus* imposes itself, teaches what *virtus* is and silences criticism. The implication is that such *virtus* is worthy of description and useful for posterity as a moral *documentum*. Another implication is that Tacitus is going to describe an instance of such *virtus*, but anticipates a lack

of understanding in his readers: this will indeed turn out to be
a basic idea of the whole prologue.

Sed (1. 2) again bears the meaning 'but there is a difference',
namely in the extent of *ignorantia recti et invidia* during the Republic
when it was minimal and under the Empire, when it was maximal.
Under the Republic, both *virtus* and the advertising of *virtus*
came naturally and were considered an unselfish moral duty,
bona conscientia. We still move in a wholly moral, even philosophical
atmosphere, recalling, e.g., Cicero *De rep.* VI. 8, but also Sallust
Cat. III. 1 and VIII. 4; the Sallustian note is struck already in
pronum (a very Sallustian word) *magisque in aperto* (cf. *Iug.* V. 3:
illustria magis magisque in aperto).

Even autobiography, i.e. advertising one's own *virtus*, was
accepted by the public. Within the context this statement figures
as a premise for an *a fortiori* conclusion – even autobiography, let
alone biography. But there may be an emphatic allusion besides
this contextual aspect. Tacitus' own career under Domitian had
been rather similar to that of his father-in-law, and there may be
an implied 'autobiographical' aspect in his biography, namely
the defence of a general line of conduct of *obsequium ac modestia*
combined with *industria ac vigor*, as it will be described in the
very emotional ch. XLII.

Chapter 1 ends with two parallel periods (*adeo* || *tam*) contrasting
virtus and its description under the Republic and under the
Empire (*nunc*). The general observation gets a personal point in
at nunc mihi narraturo. His relation to the person described is not
mentioned; *defuncti hominis* is a deliberately general description:
the hero is dead and there can be no suspicion of *gratia* and
ambitio. *Venia opus fuit* also leaves open what kind of *venia* is
meant; this is essential. Misled by the perfect tense, commentators have interpreted this as a real demand for permission
which Tacitus supposedly had addressed to Domitian, after
Agricola's death in 93 but before the emperor's death in 96.
This seems unacceptable because in ch. 1 Tacitus is only
concerned with a general characterization of the moral
conditions under the Empire, *nostra tempora*, as opposed to those
of the Republic. Moreover, it appears from the last words of
the prologue, *professione pietatis aut laudatus erit aut excusatus*[40] that

40. As Büchner, 'Das Proömium...', and others rightly saw.

opus fuit is an 'epistolary' perfect and applies to the moment when Tacitus was writing his prologue (cf. the similar cases *Ann.* III. 65 and IV. 5).

Tacitus adds bitterly that he would not have to ask allowance if he were to write an invective: *obtrectatio et livor pronis auribus accipiuntur* (*Hist.* I. 1. 2)! *Ignorantia recti et invidia* are maximal in these *infesta virtutibus tempora*.

Thus ends the first pericope of the prologue with a strong *sententia*, but leaving two questions unanswered: who is the *defunctus homo*, and what kind of *venia* does Tacitus ask?

(Ch. II) With *legimus* (? ⟨intel⟩*legimus*?) Tacitus turns to the fate of biography and biographers under Domitian, and the purge of A.D. 93 with its *Bücherverbrennung*, execution of Rusticus and Senecio, and expulsion of the philosophers, *nequid usquam honestum* (= *rectum*) *occurreret*. Biographers and philosophers are the teachers of *virtus* and of *scientia recti*. Thus the moral theme of ch. I continues throughout ch. II. On the burning of biographies Tacitus exclaims *quasi illo igne vocem populi Romani et libertatem senatus et conscientiam generis humani aboleri arbitrabantur*. Thus biography is implicitly exalted as the voice of the Roman people, the free utterance of the senators (the four people mentioned were all senators, as were Agricola and Tacitus himself), and thirdly as a manifestation of human moral consciousness. *Vox* takes up the thread of *posteris tradere, memorare, prodere memoriam, narrare, narraturo mihi* in ch. I, and of *laudare, monumenta* in ch. II; *conscientia* that of *virtus* (occurring four times in ch. I), *mores, rectum, bona conscientia, fiducia morum*, to be continued by *honestum* in ch. II. *Libertas*, on the other hand, which plays such a predominant part in the prologues of the *Histories* and the *Annals*, appears here for the first time – but not for the last. There is a gradual shift from the purely moral to a more political sphere. The thematic structure of the *Agricola* prologue is well-designed, though somewhat looser than in the other prologues.

The sentence (II. 3) beginning with *dedimus* and ending with *commercio* is the third in succession with an elaborate ablative absolute attached at its end. It is followed by a shorter epigrammatic sentence, almost a *sententia*, with the same concluding force as the last sentence of ch. I.

Dedimus profecto grande patientiae documentum has a very effective double meaning, *patientia* having a negative sense of slavish meekness, but also, especially in a Stoic philosophical context as here, the more heroic sense of endurance, καρτερία. The latter would be more in the spirit of the forty-second chapter (*obsequium ac modestiam*, but with *industria ac vigor*). *Ultimum in libertate* during the Republic (*licentia quam stulti libertatem vocant* says Maternus in a boutade, *Dial.* XL. 2) and *ultimum in servitute*, extreme *dominatio* under the Empire, are again contrasted; and in the attached ablative absolute, *loquendi audiendique* take up the *vox* theme again, continued in the paroxysm of the last *sententia*. Under Domitian, people were stunned into lethargy; not only was their *vox* silenced, but they even wished to lose the faculty of memory. However, now that all is over, the historian has to take up his task and fulfil the bitter duty, *memoriam prioris servitutis* (III. 3). Yet Tacitus hesitates, and his hesitations are reflected in the next chapter.

(Ch. III) *Nunc*, as contrasted to the past Domitian era of ch. II, here represents the present *beatissimum saeculum* of Nerva and Trajan. In *beatissimum saeculum, felicitas temporum* (*Hist.* I. I. 3), *securitas publica* Tacitus uses the slogans of the new era; some of them were already worn out under earlier emperors (Sen. *Epist.* LXXIII. 2 on *securitas publica* under Nero, of all emperors!). This suggests some scepticism on the part of Tacitus as to their real applicability and validity in the post-Domitian era, also expressed in the strangely involved phrase *nec spem modo ac votum securitas publica, sed ipsius voti fiduciam ac robur assumpserit* – something somewhere between hope and fulfilment.

The whole chapter moves in this uncertain sphere of transition – of beginning convalescence. This medical metaphor is exactly that of Tacitus himself, for *nunc demum redit animus* does not mean 'now at last the heart comes back', 'now we dare to speak again', nor even 'now at last we begin to breathe', but 'now we are regaining consciousness', 'now we are coming back to our senses', after the *defectio animi* suggested at the end of ch. II. Striking instances of this literal, medical meaning are Plautus, *Truc.* 365ff., esp. *ah, aspersisti aquam: iam redit animus*, and Ovid, *Her.* XIII. 21ff., esp. *vix mater gelida maesta refecit aqua... ut rediit animus, pariter rediere dolores* (cf. Plaut. *Epid.* 569; Q. Curtius IX. 5. 11; Seneca, *Troad.* 623, *Oed.* 595; Plin. *HN* XXX. 48 and

xx. 152). In *Agricola* xxvi the same words return, indicating the sleepy soldiers coming to their senses.

The metaphor of the patient in a state of beginning convalescence pervades the whole chapter, e.g. in the words *tardiora sunt remedia quam mala,* and the ensuing parallel between the body and the mind. Livy had made use of a similar metaphor in his preface in a diagnosis of the agony of the Roman state – *haec tempora quibus nec vitia nostra nec remedia pati possumus (praef.* 9). *Ipsius inertiae dulcedo* suggests the lethargic euphoria of the ill patient. Similarly, the words *revocaveris, extinguuntur, securitas, votum, robur, infirmitate* have medical overtones.

This metaphor effectively expresses how Tacitus feels about the new era – certainly not 'optimistic',[41] but not without hope, and realizing that the last two years have only brought the first symptoms of recovery of a still very weak patient, who has just been on the brink of death. The specious slogans only stress how far he still feels from their fulfilment. Have *principatus ac libertas, res olim dissociabiles,* really overcome their traditional incompatibility? Does a new, limited form of *libertas* provide possibilities for a revival of intellectual activity, *ingenia studiaque,* and of the art of biography especially?

In the next sentence, *quid si...venimus,* the antithesis between illness and reconvalescence is hardened into one between life and death. The fifteen years of Domitian had not only brought actual death to many excellent men, but even the survivors had not only survived the dead, but their own spiritual death. The enforced *silentium* of their *vox* had killed them as human beings, recalling those sub-human beings who, according to Sallust, *vitam silentio transeunt sicuti animalia (Cat.* I. I). Spiritual life is real life, and in this sense Tacitus can say at the very end of the *Agricola* (XLVI. 4), *Agricola posteritati narratus et traditus superstes erit.*

After his general analysis of the pathology of the present generation, Tacitus turns to the purely personal statements at the end of the whole prologue. These are introduced by the words *non tamen pigebit,* which are difficult to grasp in their tone. Ogilvie–Richmond paraphrase 'yet (in spite of the difficulties which beset me) it will not be an unpleasant task, = iuvabit'; this is in my

41. Ogilvie and Richmond, p. 131.

opinion beside the mark. Tacitus has not enumerated a number of difficulties, but given an almost obsessive picture of past tyranny and present beginning recovery from the all-but-mortal blows. I would rather suggest something like '[sigh] nevertheless I believe it will be a good thing.'

Vel incondita ac rudi voce is revealing. Ogilvie's remark, 'such self-depreciation was conventional', is less happy than another remark, 'T. refers to the neglect of his own literary powers during the last fifteen years.' However, the direct connection is with *silentium*, the dreadful silence under Domitian's reign of terror. After such a stunned silence one can only speak in rough and incoherent language without polish or refinement. Tacitus seems to explain his style, full of *inconcinnitas*, from his experiences in life: *qualis oratio talis vita* (Sen. *Epist.* 114. 1). Tacitus' style is not just an artistic nicety, a Sallustian mannerism, or an assumed attitude. After *silentium*, the words take up again the *vox–memoria* theme, combined with the *servitus–libertas* theme in the ensuing words: *prioris servitutis* carries all the heavy load of II, and *praesentium bonorum* points to the limited *libertas* and the general convalescence of III.

The present biography is finally announced, but only as an 'interim'-publication on Tacitus' way to history. Apparently the prologue has a wider application than to the present *opusculum*: it introduces Tacitus the historian.

In *honori Agricolae soceri mei destinatus*, *honori* takes up the *virtus* motif (*honor* is *praemium virtutis*, Cic. *TD* 1. 4; *ad Fam.* v. 20), *soceri mei* prepares for *professione pietatis*: his deed is an act of *pietas* towards his father-in-law, and may be praised or excused accordingly. This is extremely important, and should not be misunderstood as a declaration of modesty. The main point in chs. I and II was that biography was best appreciated in olden (Republican) times, but became suspect and sometimes even dangerous under the Empire, *infesta virtutibus tempora*. In a very general phrase Tacitus had adduced these dangers (*narraturo mihi venia opus fuit* (1. 4)) as an instance of a very general evil. As an *argumentum veniae* he now alleges *pietas*. Büchner has rightly referred to *Dial.* x,[42] where Aper blames Maternus, writer of a tragedy, *Cato*, full of political allusions (6) *nec pro amico aliquo,*

42. Büchner, 'Das Proömium...'.

sed quod periculosius est, pro Catone offendit; nec excusatur (!) *offensa necessitudine officii...aut...*(8)*...si quando necesse sit pro periclitante amico potentiorum aures offendere, et probata sit fides et libertas excusata*(!). I also draw the attention to Quintilian's prescriptions on the oratorical prologue, where in IV. 1. 7 he speaks about the way the defender may win the *benevolentia* of the jury. The most important thing is to make believe that he is a *vir bonus*:

> sic enim continget, ut non studium advocati videatur afferre, sed paene testis fidem. Quare imprimis existimetur venisse ad agendum ductus officio vel cognationis (!) vel amicitiae, maximeque, si fieri poterit, rei publicae aut alicuius certe non mediocris exempli.

This is interesting, because it reveals something of the rhetorical background of this '*oratio pro Agricola*', and of the meaning of *professione pietatis aut laudatus erit aut excusatus*.

'Either praised or (at least) excused' seems to take up the antithesis between republican biography, which found a willing ear – *fides* and no *obtrectatio* (1. 3) – and imperial biography which had to overcome high barriers of *ignorantia recti et invidia*, and incurred even mortal danger under Domitian. The new era of comparative *libertas* still suffered from the symptoms of previous illness. Has society recovered far enough to give praise to Tacitus' act of *pietas*, or will it not yet go further than to excuse it? That, I think, is the suggestion contained in the alternative within the structure of the prologue, especially after the diagnosis of ch. III. Thus the theme of *libertas* is in the background again, together with those of *virtus* and *vox*. The prologue ends in a mood similar to that of the end of the *Histories* prologue; only, in the latter Tacitus is entitled to be more confident with regard to the new *libertas*, after some more years of experience with the government of Trajan. Then, the problem of objective, political *libertas* will be less acute than that of subjective *libertas* – the use a historian could and should make of his new possibilities.

If we compare the *Agricola* prologue with the two historical prologues, the most obvious differences are in the *vox–memoria* theme, so functional in the *Agricola* with its metaphor of the unconscious and speechless patient coming back to his senses, and the stress laid on the moral function of his writing right from the beginning. As all good prose composition is teleological and perpetually works towards an end, we should look at the end of the prologue and put the question as follows: why does Tacitus want to do *honor* to the *virtus* of Agricola? That *virtus* could scarcely be said, at first sight, to be of the quality of *magna aliqua ac nobilis virtus* which imposes itself on anybody (I. I). Nor could it be said to be of the quality of the four Stoics, whose unhappy end is mentioned in II. On the contrary, ch. XLII. 3–4 contrasts Agricola's *virtus* with that of those over-principled men who sought glory *inani iactatione libertatis*, and by an ambitious, but useless, self-inflicted death. Agricola's *virtus* is that of *obsequium ac modestia*. In his philosophical training, related in ch. IV. 3, *retinuit...quod est difficillimum, ex sapientia modum* – apparently enabling him to make his career under Domitian in *modestia*.

The case of Agricola proves what seems to be Tacitus' thesis from the prologue onward, *posse etiam sub malis principibus bonos viros esse* (XLII. 4) – an idea on which the author returns with a curious insistence in his later work (cf. *Annals* IV. 20. 4–5 on Lepidus, and *Ann.* VI. 10. 3–5 on L. Piso).

At the same time, however, Tacitus stresses that there were rumours that Agricola had nevertheless been poisoned by Domitian (XLII. 2). Thus Agricola acquires something of a hero's nimbus after all. Had his *modestia* failed after all under the *infestus virtutibus princeps*? Or does Tacitus want to add the glory of a heroic death to that of an unheroic life? Thus we are left with incongruities, even contradictions, which seem to point to a fundamental embarrassment of Tacitus himself. Was Agricola right? Had Tacitus himself been right? What is a *bonus vir*? What is *virtus* under the Empire? Tacitus had not solved his problem.[43]

There is still a last question we have to answer – a question springing from our initial observations on the *Agricola* prologue. We started by rejecting the idea that it could be expected to present the same traditional elements as the historical prologues proper, because the *Agricola* is not historiography in the proper sense, but a variation of the biographical genre. We also stated that the prologue is at the same time the prologue of the *Agricola* itself, and in a way a prologue of the announced historical *œuvre* of Tacitus, an introduction of the historian himself.

43. Syme, *Tacitus*, p. 540.

We have now to qualify these remarks in the light of our findings with regard to the prologue and its structure. If we recall the five traditional elements of historical prologues, we see that the first, information about the author, is presented at the very end, where Tacitus says that he is the *gener* of Agricola, and announces his plans for the future. On the other hand, after an ephemerical *mihi* (at the end of I. 1) II. 1 and II. 3 present a collective *legimus* and *dedimus*, and III. 2 a collective *sumus* and *venimus*. The focus is on Tacitus' generation and its experiences rather than on the author himself, who as a member of this generation came to the writing of history and biography.

The second, the subject, is indicated in III. 3; but more important is the way in which Tacitus came to his subject and saw the use of it: and this can be said to be the underlying theme of all three chapters. Here, as in the other prologues, he has a keen sense of his own historicity, his choice being determined by his own historical situation. All this, however, is well within our third theme. Not *veritas*, but *libertas* is what he desires, hopes for and promises, and his aim is not to present *veritas* but *virtutis documenta*.

After a long time it seems possible again to present such *documenta virtutis*, though they cannot be hoped to meet with the same approval and appreciation as they did under the Republic. Just as in the prologue of the *Histories*, this is implied in the sketch of the development of biography and its background in the political realities, from the Republic, via the Empire and Domitian, to the present age. At the same time the atmosphere of ch. II functions as the general background of the life of Agricola which is to be described. He too was comprised in the collective nominatives of that chapter. In this respect, it functions within the second theme, characterization of the subject.

All in all, I venture to conclude that the *Agricola* prologue, too, presents most of the traditional themes, but in a very personal, adapted, variation. And herewith I would like to take leave of this extremely rich, full, yet enigmatic prologue, more complex, less balanced, more human, less aloof than the later ones.

The Tacitean Germanicus

D. O. ROSS, JR.

THE FIGURE of Germanicus in Tacitus' *Annals* has long been interpreted with exceptional unanimity. Only one recent scholar has questioned the validity of the usual version:[1] that Tacitus knew a Germanicus whose actual career was often open to the criticism of failure, blundering, and weakness, but that the historian did the best he could with the facts to make the popular hero a foil to the villain Tiberius and a shining exemplar of political virtue.

M. P. Charlesworth, for instance: 'Young, handsome and courageous, he was reputed to possess his father's Republican and democratic sentiments, and since A.D. 13 he had been in command of the armies of the Rhine. It may be suspected that the tradition, so uniformly favourable to him and kindly to his memory [*n.*: The portrait in Tacitus should be compared with the shorter eulogies that are to be found in Suetonius, *Calig.* 3 and Josephus, *Ant.* XVIII, [6], 207ff.], rests on writers who were glad to find in his gracious figure a foil to the dourness of Tiberius, but it is obvious that he had much to attract.'[2] E. Koestermann can speak of Tacitus' partiality for the illustrious figure of Germanicus as self-evident.[3] B. Walker is representative: 'The greater length of the account of the German mutiny is then explained by the appearance there of Tacitus' political hero Germanicus (who does not, when one reads carefully, acquit himself particularly well; but certainly the facts were against Tacitus here, and he did what he could for Germanicus, with

---

1. D. C. A. Shotter, 'Tacitus, Tiberius and Germanicus', *Historia* 17 (1968), 194–214. Shotter's article appeared after a version of the present paper had been read to the Yale Classical Club (February 1968). The subject seems important enough to justify another examination on different grounds, and a further plea that the figure of Germanicus as hero not be taken for granted.
2. *CAH* x, 610 and n. 2.
3. *Annalen, Band I, Buch 1–3* (Heidelberg 1963), 39: 'Dass er eine Vorliebe für die lichte Gestalt des Germanicus besessen hat, liegt natürlich auf der Hand.'

difficult material)'; and, 'The memory of Drusus, his German
campaigns, and his loyal though somewhat operatic handling
of the German mutiny, combine to build up for Germanicus an
heroic stature.'[4] C. W. Mendell speaks of a 'tragedy of Germanicus', and even calls Germanicus' handling of the German mutiny
a 'success'.[5] And finally Syme: 'From first to last, Germanicus
Caesar is adorned and enhanced, although there were grounds
for construing not all at favourably his conduct, whether during
the mutiny, as a general in Germany, or as deputy for the emperor
in the eastern lands. The historian, had he so chosen, might have
questioned the tradition.'[6]

D. C. A. Shotter's correction of these assumptions[7] deserves
attention, and may be given further support in two ways. First,
by a more detailed analysis of Tacitus' portrayal of Germanicus;
then, if the historian seems not to present Germanicus always
in the best possible light, by asking why he did not. The first
major portion of the *Annals* devoted to Germanicus (the German
mutiny) will here serve to demonstrate the historian's method

4. *The 'Annals' of Tacitus* (Manchester 1952), pp. 9 and 118.

5. *Tacitus, The Man and his Work* (New Haven 1957), p. 130: 'The Pannonian fracas, with its weak handling on the part of young Drusus, serves to
enhance the glory of Germanicus' success with the revolt of the German
armies.'

6. *Tacitus* (Oxford 1958), p. 418, with n. 7 ('The encomiastic nature of
the tradition is patent in Suetonius, *Cal.* 1–6. It owed much to historians
writing under the son and the brother of Germanicus, but had begun early.
Note also Dio's enhancement of the exploits of Germanicus in Illyricum in
A.D. 7–9'). See also p. 492.

Modern echoes of the ancient tradition may be extended indefinitely.
S. G. Daitz ('Tacitus' Technique of Character Portrayal', *AJP* 81 (1960),
37), for instance, inflates the Tacitean Germanicus to 'a hero of almost epic
quality. Certainly, according to the later descriptions of Tacitus, no mythical
hero could have been more universally mourned upon his death than was
Germanicus.' And see now D. R. Dudley, *The World of Tacitus* (London 1968),
p. 100: 'The dark figure of Tiberius is contrasted at the beginning of his reign
with the heroic and radiant Germanicus...Germanicus is indeed the one
truly virtuous figure in the pages of Tacitus – the only one, that is to say, who
is both good and great.'

The use of the word 'hero' in this paper may seem to some unfairly strong,
even though the consensus of modern opinion does find a heroic Germanicus
in the *Annals*. The term may be regarded as a convenience for such awkward
alternatives as 'sympathetic figure', 'admirable protagonist', or whatever.

7. 'Tacitus, Tiberius and Germanicus'. Shotter reviews Germanicus' entire
career in the *Annals*, and is particularly concerned with his relationship with
Tiberius.

and intentions. The second question demands an appeal to certain general principles of Tacitus' view of history (his views of character, of family politics in the imperial house, and of Republic and Principate), principles too broad and debatable to be argued fully here, but which may suggest that Tacitus would have had difficulty fitting Germanicus the hero into the larger philosophical and historical structure of his work.

The mutiny of the armies in Germany is presented as an exact parallel to the Pannonian mutiny. If a structural syntax of Tacitus could be conceived and written, substituting chapters for words, a structural style and movement as abrupt and dramatic as Tacitus' verbal syntax would be described. The mutiny of the Pannonian legions is covered in fifteen chapters (*Ann.* 1. 16–30), with Drusus the subject; this account is followed by twenty-two chapters (*Ann.* 1. 31–52) devoted to the German mutiny, Germanicus the subject. Obviously the two accounts are paratactic, and obviously the central focus for the contrast will be the figures of the two 'sons' of Tiberius.

Hic rerum urbanarum status erat, cum Pannonicas legiones seditio incessit, nullis novis causis, nisi quod mutatus princeps licentiam turbarum et ex civili bello spem praemiorum ostendebat (1. 16. 1).[8] Two causes for the Pannonian mutiny are expressly stated: the change of emperor gave opportunity for (1) license in the ranks and (2) expectation of rewards from civil war. These are the real causes (not the superficial demands of the troops detailed only later) stressed by Tacitus, and are his own. *Licentia* will be significant, and the immediate emphasis on civil war is remarkable and should be kept in mind.

Isdem ferme diebus isdem causis Germanicae legiones turbatae, quanto plures, tanto violentius, et magna spe fore ut Germanicus Caesar imperium alterius pati nequiret daretque se legionibus vi sua cuncta tracturis (1. 31. 1). Exactly the same causes are seen behind the revolt in Germany. *quanto plures, tanto violentius* is a gloss on *licentia turbarum*. *ex civili bello spes praemiorum* is paraphrased and made more specific in the connection with Germanicus (*et magna spe fore ut Germanicus Caesar...*). The two causes will serve the historian as a focus for the handling

8. Citations throughout are from the Teubner text of E. Koestermann (revised 1965).

of each mutiny: the winner will be the leader most successful in recognizing and controlling these forces.

First, Drusus. Three legions in summer quarters begin the mutiny in Pannonia, led on by the histrionic Percennius (1. 16–17). Their commander, Junius Blaesus, arrives as they are building a tribunal, and proclaims his own loyalty with the words, '*mea potius caede imbuite manus: leviore flagitio legatum interficietis quam ab imperatore desciscitis. aut incolumis fidem legionum retinebo, aut iugulatus paenitentiam adcelerabo*' (1. 18. 3). It works; that is, it works as Tacitus reports it. Blaesus' words, directly quoted for special emphasis, are successful in Tacitus' dramatic context; it matters not that some concessions have been made, that Blaesus' own son is to serve the troops by carrying their demands as a legate to Rome, that only *modicum otium* has been restored.

New life is given the mutiny by the troops stationed at Nauportus and by Vibulenus, another *gregarius miles* (1. 20–3), and the news reaches Tiberius, *quamquam abstrusum et tristissima quaeque maxime occultantem* (1. 24. 1). Drusus is sent, with Sejanus, *nullis satis certis mandatis, ex re consulturum*. He reads a letter from his father, in which the emperor had promised to take their demands to the Senate, and that meanwhile Drusus would grant what he could on the spot. Demands are then presented which Drusus denies he can grant. The situation becomes ugly once again, Gnaeus Lentulus barely escapes stoning, and Drusus and his staff withdraw (1. 25–7).

That night, with violence expected at any moment to erupt, an eclipse of the moon occurs: *noctem minacem et in scelus erupturam fors lenivit* (1. 28. 1). As Blaesus' words had quieted the first uprising, *fors* quiets the second; the superstitious soldiers liken their own cause to the failing of the moon, and lament that eternal labor is portended, that the gods oppose their misdeeds. *fors* may be translated as 'a lucky break', and, were it Tacitus' intention to minimize Drusus' effectiveness, would have been left as such. But the historian's purpose is otherwise: *utendum inclinatione ea Caesar et quae casus obtulerat in sapientiam vertenda ratus circumiri tentoria iubet* (1. 28. 3). Drusus turns what chance had offered to strategic advantage. Clearly it is an over-simplification to assume that Tacitus is in the process of building a picture of a weak and ineffectual Drusus, saved only by chance, *fors*. The centurian Clemens and a few others make the rounds of the tents, playing on the soldiers' panic: *tum redire paulatim amor obsequii* (1. 28. 6).

The following morning Drusus speaks to the troops again, and legates are sent again to Rome. A debate among Drusus' staff follows in which two alternatives are presented: *cum alii opperiendos legatos atque interim comitate permulcendum militem censerent, alii fortioribus remediis agendum* (1. 29. 3). Then Tacitus notes, *promptum ad asperiora ingenium Druso erat*; and follows this generalization with the fact that only the two ringleaders are executed (*vocatos Vibulenum et Percennium interfici iubet*). Others were killed, it is true, but without Tacitean dramatic fanfare, and only *quisque praecipuus turbator* (1. 30. 1). The difficulty is obvious: can this remedy be characterized so simply as '*asperiora*'?

The facts of Drusus' handling of the mutiny (to which we will return) are clear and simple: a difficult situation was met with confidence, an assist from nature was skillfully turned *in sapientiam*, to shrewd advantage. Of the two possibilities for remedial action presented by his staff, Drusus chose firm action and settled the sedition by the quiet execution of a few ringleaders. Tacitus has but one comment that seems discordant with the facts, '*promptum ad asperiora ingenium Druso erat*', but the relevance of this will be made clear later.

After Tacitus' statement that the very same causes lay behind the mutiny of the German legions (the differences are of degree), the scene is vividly and violently set (1. 31–2). No one leader, *sed pariter ardescerent, pariter silerent, tanta aequalitate et constantia, ut regi crederes* (1. 32. 3). The beatings of the centurions dramatically present the fury of the first uprising of the Lower army.

With this scene of violence set, Tacitus turns his attention suddenly to Germanicus: chapter 33 is devoted to his 'biography'. 'Meanwhile, word of the death of Augustus reached Germanicus as he was taking the census in Gaul, as we have mentioned. *neptem eius Agrippinam in matrimonio pluresque ex ea liberos habebat.*' Nothing could be more pointed, because unexpected, than the emphasis on Agrippina here at the beginning of Germanicus' biography, and on her as the grand-daughter of Augustus – *neptem eius Agrippinam*; and then their children (*pluresque ex ea liberos habebat*), in the same familial line. Why this focus on Augustus,

Agrippina, and her children, rather than on Germanicus? Simply
to emphasize Germanicus' alliance with the Julian side. The
biography continues only then with the lineage of Germanicus
himself: *ipse Druso fratre Tiberii genitus, Augustae nepos, sed anxius
occultis in se patrui aviaeque odiis, quorum causae acriores quia iniquae.*
Germanicus' actual line of descent is, in effect, denied, and the
political alliance is substituted as the real and important one.
Then Tacitus mentions Germanicus' father Drusus, whose memory
is still great among the Roman people, since it was believed that
he would have restored the Republic, had he become emperor
(*credebaturque, si rerum potitus foret, libertatem redditurus*), and hence
there was the same favor and expectation for Germanicus (*unde
in Germanicum favor et spes eadem*). Thus, Tacitus stresses two aspects
of Germanicus, succinctly and emphatically: his intimate connection with the Julian branch of the imperial house, and his
position as a representative, through his father Drusus, of the
old Republic and *libertas*. To these aspects we must return later,
and to the question of what they meant for Tacitus.

Then, as expected in the tradition of biography, Germanicus'
character is touched upon: *nam iuveni civile ingenium, mira comitas
et · diversa ab Tiberii sermone vultu, adrogantibus et obscuris. mira
comitas* is the key – wonderful affability, congeniality – and this
in marked contrast to Tiberius. For the moment we will grant
the obvious, that Germanicus is a foil to Tiberius, with only the
warning that this opposition will not remain so deceptively
simple. Then another sudden shift of attention, to the hostility
between Livia and Agrippina: as it had begun, so the biography
closes, with Agrippina. We may expect Tacitus to have written
no word of this biography unconsidered, and may fairly demand
to know what will come of its main elements as the mutiny
proceeds.

The assumption that Germanicus is a foil to Tiberius – an
assumption which would have been immediately made by the
ancient reader even without suggestion by Tacitus – is straightway
undercut; the next chapter (34) begins with a rather startling
statement that Germanicus did not act his expected role: *sed
Germanicus quanto summae spei propior, tanto impensius pro Tiberio
niti.* Clearly Tacitus advises us that his Germanicus is not the
same man the Roman people had expected. Germanicus opposes

the troops finally on the same grounds invoked successfully before by Blaesus: *at ille moriturum potius quam fidem exueret clamitans* (1. 35. 4). There the parallel ends. Germanicus' actions are theatrical in the extreme: his suicide play brings only encouragement from the troops (*vix credibile dictu*, comments Tacitus) and the offer of a sharper sword from a certain Calusidius[9] – the action which, because so shocking even to the enraged soldiers, allowed a safe escape in the stunned silence which followed.

Such is Germanicus' first attempt to quiet the mutiny. Both in its position in the narrative and by its content it parallels Blaesus' success in Pannonia.[10] At first in command, Germanicus then becomes, through an action so ludicrous that even the mob cannot take it seriously, a figure of almost comic failure. We may now propose an obvious question, though one seldom asked in this context: is this the way such a subtle master of innuendo and suggestion as Tacitus would go about creating a hero, even given the facts he had to work with? Surely the parallel with Blaesus is an intentional feature, and surely Calusidius could have been suppressed entirely. The scene requires only one reaction: that we wonder whether the hero of the people is to be a hero for the historian.

The next scene too has a parallel in the account of the Pannonian mutiny. Germanicus meets with his staff, and three alternatives are presented. First, to arm the *auxilia* and *socii* against the mutineers, the result of which, however, would be civil war: *at si auxilia et socii adversum abscedentis legiones armarentur, civile bellum suscipi* (1. 36. 2). Then, *periculosa severitas, flagitiosa largitio: seu nihil militi sive omnia concederentur, in ancipiti res publica.* The second alternative is severity, with resultant danger; the third is compliance with the soldiers' demands, with resultant disgrace. At Drusus' staff meeting, Tacitus had presented two simple (unqualified) alternatives; here in Germany the hero faces a

9. Dio (LVII. 5. 2) does not report the soldier's name, a definite indication that Tacitus is purposely stressing the incident.

10. Shotter calls this 'an interesting comparison' (p. 198): 'To Blaesus, however, unlike Germanicus, this was a logically considered step which was designed to appeal both to logic and to emotion...We see here very clearly the difference between the seasoned professional and the youthful amateur; for by contrast, Germanicus' action is seen for what it really was – an impulsive and desperate act of bravado.'

choice not of remedies, but of results: civil war, or danger or disgrace.

Germanicus first chooses *flagitiosa largitio*, and does so in a way which only seems to emphasize his *flagitium*. He forges a letter from Tiberius granting the soldiers' demands, and Tacitus again seems to go out of his way to emphasize the folly of the forgery: *sensit miles in tempus conficta statimque flagitavit* (1. 37. 1). If Germanicus' failure with the letter seems again almost comic, worse is to follow. The *largitio* consists in part of payment to be made then and there from Germanicus' official travel funds, and a scene results far more terrible for the Roman reader than for us: Caecina leads the first and twentieth legions away, *turpi agmine, cum fisci de imperatore rapti inter signa interque aquilas veherentur* (1. 37. 2). The powerful symbols of Roman military might are made to accompany the purses looted from the general. Are these details added to portray a hero?[11]

The *flagitium* of *largitio* is emphasized finally when Germanicus, having set out for the Upper army, and having received the oath from three of the legions, met a little hesitation from the fourth: *quartadecumani paulum dubitaverant; pecunia et missio quamvis non flagitantibus oblata est* (1. 37. 3). These very concessions, it is remembered, Drusus himself had refused to grant when his mutiny was at its worst (1. 26. 1).

Then follows a terrible night in which Munatius Plancus, a consular, is nearly killed – 'a rare thing, even in action against the enemy, that a legate of the Roman people stain the altars of the gods in Roman camps with his own blood'. The next morning brought relief, and a realization of their failure: *satis superque missione et pecunia et mollibus consultis peccatum* (1. 40. 1), Germanicus' friends advise; the folly, and the disgrace, of *largitio* is clear to all. Plan One (the third alternative) ends in abysmal failure. Agrippina is to be sent away, as if to clear the stage for *periculosa severitas*, but she refuses (*cum se divo Augusto ortam neque degenerem ad pericula testaretur*, 1. 40. 3). But Germanicus and Italian sentimentality prevail, and the disgraceful procession prepares to flee the general's camp: *incedebat muliebre et miserabile agmen, profuga ducis uxor, parvulum sinu filium gerens* (1. 40. 4). The disgrace is emphasized, and the responsibility for it laid by Tacitus by

11. These details too are omitted by Dio (LVII. 5. 3–4).

implication on Germanicus: *non florentis Caesaris neque suis in castris, sed velut in urbe victa facies*, begins the next chapter. Again, is it with such words that one purposefully portrays a hero?

At the sounds of lamentation from this wretched procession the troops begin to come out of their tents. *quis ille flebilis sonus? quod tam triste?* Remorse sets in, *pudor et miseratio*, at the thought of her father Agrippa, her grandfather Augustus, her father-in-law Drusus – and finally of the *infans* Caligula. Remorse allows Germanicus a long, and emotional, speech, one which promises nothing and settles nothing, but merely attends on the fact of the soldiers' contrition. But then a rude form of justice is set up. The most seditious of the soldiers are led bound to the tribunal and are forced to mount it one by one. If the legions below, standing with drawn swords, call him guilty, he is thrown down to them and slaughtered. Tacitus' comments on this spectacle are reserved and pointed: *et gaudebat caedibus miles, tamquam semet absolveret; nec Caesar arcebat, quando nullo ipsius iussu penes eosdem saevitia facti et invidia erat* (I. 44. 3). Modern historians have been shocked, no less than Tacitus himself: but might not he easily have avoided such a direct condemnation of Germanicus, had he wanted to? The veterans are then sent out, ostensibly, says Tacitus, against the Suebi, but, in fact, *ut avellerentur castris trucibus adhuc non minus asperitate remedii quam sceleris memoria* (I. 44. 4): for the historian, a *scelus* has been committed. The second alternative, *severitas*, has been tried, and the result is butchery by mob rule. Drusus' *fortiora remedia* come to mind: two of the ringleaders killed, plus a few others – firm, quick action. Germanicus, by contrast, has done nothing but avoid all responsibility, and let *saevitia* run its course.

Perhaps we can now understand the one discordant note in the account of Drusus: *promptum ad asperiora ingenium Druso erat* (I. 29. 4), a comment by the historian directly contradicted by the facts. Tacitus has commented on Germanicus equally simply, *civile ingenium, mira comitas* (I. 33. 2), a characterization he neither contradicts nor allows us to forget – except by the presentation of facts that are obviously contradictory. (These 'facts', of course, do not speak for themselves: it is easily seen how Tacitus makes them eloquent.) The historian repeats as his own what was generally known and accepted, that Drusus was a harsh and violent man by nature, and Germanicus a friend to all; then, by the presentation of factual information which demonstrates the opposite, the accepted clichés are effectively denied and the popular tradition overturned.

Two of the three alternatives have been tried, *largitio* and *severitas*, and each with disastrous results. But the mutiny has not yet been quelled: the fifth and twenty-first legions remain unrepentant, unsubdued, and the situation there is the worst and most dangerous yet. One alternative remains, and is pointedly introduced by the historian: *igitur Caesar arma classem socios demittere Rheno parat, si imperium detrectetur, bello certaturus* (1. 45. 2). The reference to the first alternative proposed at Germanicus' staff meeting is clear: *at si auxilia et socii adversum abscedentis legiones armarentur, civile bellum suscipi* (1. 36. 2). But before the obvious conclusion, civil war, is reached, the scene changes.

At Rome Tiberius is accused by the citizens of inaction and delay, but the emperor has his reasons for not visiting the mutinous legions – *maior a longinquo reverentia.* This dramatic change of scene contributes more than suspense: Germanicus and Tiberius are directly contrasted. But is Germanicus simply a foil to Tiberius? The question may now be answered. Rome is anxious that the emperor go himself, thinking that the sight of him will be enough to quiet the rebellion, *ubi principem longa experientia eundemque severitatis et munificentiae summum vidissent* (1. 46. 2). Not a word of contrast is even implied in these two chapters. Tiberius' two sons are to act as his representatives, while Tiberius keeps himself and his *maiestas* safe and in reserve at Rome. If Drusus and Germanicus both fail, then the emperor remains as a final line of defense, but on the same grounds and by the same means that we have seen so vividly in action thus far: *severitas* and *munificentia.* It is in the people's mind alone that Germanicus, with his *mira comitas*, is Tiberius' foil: for the historian Germanicus is merely a lower representative of the supreme power, exercising the imperial virtues *severitas* and *largitio.*

At Germanicus... But even now Germanicus is not ready to take firm action. (Tiberius, we note, has just been accused by the *trepida civitas* of 'feigned delay', *cunctatio ficta.*) Thinking that a space of time must be offered for the mutinous fifth and twenty-first legions to consider the *exemplum* of *severitas* so recently afforded them, Germanicus sends a letter on to the commander Caecina, saying that he was on his way with a force and, unless they themselves punished the guilty, he would employ indiscriminate slaughter (*usurum promisca caede*, I. 48. 1). Once again, Tacitus reports evasion of responsibility on Germanicus' part (and is this not a special Tiberian virtue?). Caecina takes the hint, organizes the loyal non-coms, and, at an agreed time, the slaughter begins: *trucidant ignaros, nullo nisi consciis noscente quod caedis initium, quis finis* (I. 48. 3).

Diversa omnium, quae umquam accidere, civilium armorum facies: so begins the final scene of the German mutinies, with a clear reference to the *civile bellum* predicted at the beginning. The absolute horror felt by the Romans for civil war we can barely begin to realize; and this is the spectre that Tacitus has devised as the ultimate result of Germanicus' handling of the German mutiny (it could hardly have been in his sources).[12] The statement of this climax may be read in two ways (the ambiguity seems purposeful): first, it may be read as a specific reference to the actual situation – 'the aspect of *this* civil war was different from all (civil wars) which have ever taken place' – and so it is usually and properly taken; but the word-order and the plural *civilia arma* suggest that, when the sentence is read for the first time, quickly and before its context develops, it was intended to give the impression of a general proposition – 'different from all (things) which have ever happened is the aspect of civil wars'.[13] The latter reading emphasizes the horror of the third alternative, now realized. *clamor vulnera sanguis palam, causa in occulto; cetera fors regit* (I. 49. 1): *fors*, it is remembered, had settled Drusus' mutiny, but chance turned with a firm sure hand *in sapientiam*. It does not require an over-subtle reading of the two panels to

---

12. Dio, of course, has no such interpretation of the event.

13. Translators usually add the demonstrative (e.g., Jackson in the Loeb ed., 'No civil war of any period has presented the features of this'), and commentators (e.g., Furneaux and Koestermann) confine themselves to the question of whether the genitive *omnium* is a Grecism with *diversa* ('different *from* all') or a subjective genitive. Taken out of context, the sentence is a general statement, with *omnium* suitably construed as a substantive = 'all things'. So, I am sure, Tacitus intended it, emphasizing his own interpretation of the event; the following sentence effects the change from a generalization about civil wars to this particular scene, and only then can this first sentence be re-read as a specific comment.

realize the significance, and the obvious difference, in the appearance of *fors* at the conclusion of each. *neque legatus aut tribunus moderator adfuit: permissa vulgo licentia atque ultio et satietas* (I. 49. 2 – *licentia* will concern us shortly). The very next sentence brings Germanicus (the general, with his *proconsulare imperium*) finally to the camp, *non medicinam illud plurimis cum lacrimis, sed cladem appellans, cremari corpora iubet*. Once again abdication of responsibility, of the very *imperium* he has just before commanded the troops to recognize, has led to indiscriminate carnage. Is this an unavoidable historical fact, or an emphatic Tacitean suggestion? Surely the latter: the historian has so worked his material that it is impossible to avoid the conclusion that Germanicus alone is responsible. It is not the first time, nor will it be the last, that the hero's plans leave him reduced to tears.

Our question, 'Is this the way a master of suggestive innuendo would set about portraying a hero?', might have been asked at many more points in Tacitus' narrative of the German mutiny, and can now be answered with an emphatic negative. The paratactic panels of the two mutinies have been analyzed and the steps taken by Drusus and Germanicus shown to be parallel in their important elements, and compared to the discredit of the latter. Tacitus has taken the popular hero, who, in the mind of the people, represents the clearest alternative to Tiberius, and, by continually suggesting this popular image only to undermine it by subtle artistic re-creation of selected facts, has reduced this hero to an entirely weak and destructive impotence, more a counterpart, rather than a foil or alternative, to Tiberius.

I would like now to suggest three general considerations which make it entirely unlikely that Tacitus could have considered Germanicus either a hero or an acceptable alternative to Tiberius, all three based on fundamental principles of his view of history.

My first suggestion concerns Tacitus' view of character. D. M. Pippidi[14] has advanced a view of the Tacitean theory of Tiberius' character (accepted and amplified by Balsdon),[15] which, for our purposes, is very suggestive, and should be studied in greater

14. 'Tacite et Tibère', *Ephemeris Dacoromana* 8 (1938), 233–97.
15. See his review of Pippidi, *JRS* 36 (1946), 168–71; the summary of Pippidi given here is basically Balsdon's.

detail as a general theory of Tacitus' concept of character. Briefly, soon after Tiberius' death his reign was divided into a good part and a bad part (the dividing line being variously placed). Why this change? One could claim a curse on Tiberius (Dio), or accept the explanation of L. Arruntius (*Ann.* vi. 48) that power corrupted the emperor (*vi dominationis convulsus et mutatus*), or lay the blame on the company he kept (as Tacitus suggests at the beginning of Sejanus' influence, *Ann.* iv. 1). Madness was rejected as an explanation by all. Suetonius generally avoided the question. Dio claimed that Tiberius' character was good but deteriorated. For Tacitus none of these explanations was sufficient or acceptable: he saw Tiberius' character as fundamentally evil, but the evil was checked at first by his own self-control, then by fear or respect for Augustus, Germanicus, Drusus, his mother Livia, and finally Sejanus: on this theory *simulatio* and *dissimulatio* supply the key. Thus Pippidi; Balsdon, in his important review, makes the theory not original with Tacitus, but suggested earlier in the tradition, with specific traces in Suetonius and Dio. How fundamental this theory of unchangeable character is for Tacitus can easily be seen from a review of his life of Tiberius; Tacitean innuendo then has a real purpose in his account of the early years, the good part of the rule – Tiberius had always been, observably, evil.

What concerns us here, however, is how inevitable this view of Tiberius was for Tacitus, for whom character was not something subject to change and development, but fixed and immutable. The fullest exposition of Tacitus' idea of the immutability of character is that of W. H. Alexander.[16] Modern character, according to Alexander, 'is not a thing of fixed nature, whatever at its first appearance, or when we first take cognizance of it, it may appear to be, but a developmental result, definable *at any given time* as being a certain something, and again *at the next point of review* perhaps capable of being exhibited as a certain quite different something.'[17] For Tacitus, character was very different:

16. 'The Tacitean "Non Liquet" on Seneca', *University of California Publications in Classical Philology* 14, no. 8 (1952), esp. pp. 352–77. Students of comparative literature will be inspired by Alexander's comments on Agatha Christie and Lytton Strachey.

17. P. 355.

Far easier is it to assume in the individual a character born
within him, as definitely, permanently, and inescapably
attached to him as the impression of the mint die upon the
coin, something which is actually in its main features constant throughout his life, although for a time, perhaps long,
perhaps short, not revealed in full. It is nonetheless always
there, always fundamentally the same, but the luck of the
run of events, or skilled hypocrisy, or some quirk of circumstances conceals it. The late Professor F. B. Marsh, one of
the acutest students in recent years of Tacitus as man and
as historian, says, and I think justly, of Tacitus that 'he
conceived character as a wholly static and immutable
thing'.[18]

This theory of Tacitus' view of character can, and should, be
further tested, and if possible, expanded, but I can only suggest
here one possibility. Given Tacitus' theory of an immutable
character, so important for the historian, and applying it to
Germanicus' family, is it likely that the blood nephew of Tiberius,
the father of Caligula, the brother of Claudius, the grandfather
of Nero, could have been an acceptable hero?[19] One specific
illustration: it may be noted that Caligula, the only one of these
emperors of whom no one, ancient or modern, found anything
at all good to say, is pointedly called *Germanici filius* when he is
chosen to succeed Tiberius (*Ann.* vi. 46). For Tacitus, I think,
the basically Roman idea of moral degeneration became a controlling concept in his view of character: the list of emperors
directly related to Germanicus could hardly have allowed the
historian to feel any confidence in the basic character of Germanicus. The seeds of dissolution had to be there.

My second consideration is somewhat related to the first.
Roman party politics were essentially family politics, and Tacitus
did not lose sight of the fact that the transition from Republic

18. Pp. 355–6; see Marsh, *The Reign of Tiberius* (Oxford 1931), p. 14.
19. S. G. Daitz (*AJP* 81 (1960), 34–5) considers lineage one of Tacitus'
chief means of character portrayal, but does not develop the idea: 'In the
case of the major characters, there are certain things which Tacitus almost
always describes. Tacitus, as did most ancients, attached great importance
to the lineage of the character, and will usually mention it, often with an
appropriate comment. Thus he speaks of Tiberius as *vetere atque insita Claudiae
familiae superbia*.' (Daitz gives other similar examples.)

to Empire did not change the functioning of power politics: within the imperial house the struggle for power continued along family lines – the Julian and the Claudian. We observed earlier that Germanicus' marriage placed him securely on the Julian side, a fact insisted upon by Tacitus in the 'biography'. When, in the second book of the *Annals*, Piso is introduced and the *occulta mandata* are mentioned, the two covert factions of the court are outlined – the supporters of Drusus and of Germanicus:

> divisa namque et discors aula erat tacitis in Drusum aut Germanicum studiis. Tiberius ut proprium et sui sanguinis Drusum fovebat; Germanico alienatio patrui amorem apud ceteros auxerat, et quia claritudine materni generis anteibat, avum M. Antonium, avunculum Augustum ferens. contra Druso proavus eques Romanus Pomponius Atticus dedecere Claudiorum imagines videbatur. et coniunx Germanici Agrippina fecunditate ac fama Liviam, uxorem Drusi, praecellebat. sed fratres, egregie concordes et proximorum certaminibus inconcussi. (*Ann.* II. 43. 5–6)

This description is an accurate reflection of both family politics and Tacitus' purpose. But two significant distortions are to be noted: first, it is Germanicus' maternal lineage that is stressed, connecting him by birth as well as by marriage ultimately with Augustus (the fact that Germanicus' father was Tiberius' brother is conveniently ignored); and secondly, the amazing twist of logic that makes Germanicus' own sister Livia, the wife of Drusus, appear inferior to Agrippina, solely in order to glorify Germanicus!

The conflict, then, is Julian versus Claudian, but are we justified in simply concluding that, for Tacitus, Germanicus and the Julian faction[20] are so clearly on the side of right, while Tiberius and his son Drusus represent all things villainous? An answer can only be suggested here by reference to a similar situation where Tacitus' method has been brilliantly revealed. In two illuminating

20. What follows is based on the assumption that there was in fact such a 'faction', but it should be remembered (as G. W. Bowersock has reminded me) that it is difficult to populate any such faction. Tacitus, however, *does* view imperial politics in such a way, quite clearly, and we are justified in following him, whether or not the actual situation was ever so simple.

articles, the first by Charlesworth in 1927[21] and the second by
R. H. Martin in 1955,[22] it has been demonstrated that Tacitus
drew his unique and unrealistic portrait of the evil Livia (in all
other writers the proper *matrona Romana*, innocent and steadfast)
from Agrippina the younger, an acknowledged horror. Propaganda
issued by the Julian party, culminating in the younger Agrippina's
own memoirs, had produced a sympathetic picture of an abused,
but noble and long-suffering, line: Agrippina the younger had
based her public case for the accession of her own son Nero on
the grounds that Nero was more closely related to Augustus than
was Britannicus (the son of Claudius and Messalina), and that
thus the rule would be restored to the line of Augustus. But what
had become of the line of Augustus? Tacitus stresses the degeneration of Nero by constant reminders of Germanicus. B.
Walker, who makes a great deal of the fact that Caligula is only
once referred to as 'the son of Germanicus' (forgetting the first
book of the *Annals* and the fact that all the books dealing with
the reign of Caligula are lost), finds the continual references to
Nero's descent from Germanicus especially significant:

> Agrippina bases her claim to marry Claudius on her possession
> of a son who is 'Germanici nepos'; the people support him
> 'ex memoria Germanici, cuius illa reliqua suboles virilis'.
> Octavia, in her despair, appeals to the ancestor she shared
> with Nero, and Agrippina finds her last hope in his memory
> – 'praetorianos toti Caesarum domui obstrictos memoresque
> Germanici nihil adversus progeniem eius atrox ausuros'.
> This devotion extends also to Nero and frequently protects
> him from the consequences of his crimes. The emphasis
> cannot be accidental, for in the struggle for power we see
> clearly that dynastic considerations no longer counted
> for very much, except when the name of Germanicus was
> invoked...Nero 'parricida matris et uxoris, auriga et
> histrio et incendarius' is also the last 'stirps Germanici'. The
> reader is intended to appreciate the humiliation of that fact.
> The people looked to the house of Germanicus for deliverance,
> and they found Nero.[23]

21. 'Livia and Tanaquil', *CR* 41 (1927), 55–7.
22. 'Tacitus and the Death of Augustus', *CQ* 49 (1955), 123–8.
23. *The 'Annals' of Tacitus*, 127–8.

I would argue that the younger Agrippina's own campaign for her son Nero was based on the figure of Augustus, but that the emphasis on Nero's descent from Germanicus is Tacitus'. I would also argue that the disparagement must work both ways: that the object of the comparison is not only to point out the people's disappointment and frustration in finding Nero when they looked to the house of Germanicus for deliverance, but also to darken the figure of Germanicus, and that this *is* done through dynastic considerations which *were* still very important indeed. For Tacitus, neither the Julian nor the Claudian side had anything to recommend it; it is thus that he can create a false Livia on the analogy of the younger Agrippina, and in the same way he can suggest the impossibility, and futility, of the popular image of Germanicus – the hero. I need only refer to one other question: does anyone still suppose that Augustus – the beginning of the Julian line as far as the *Annals* is concerned, the line in which Tacitus so repeatedly and emphatically inserts Germanicus – is, for Tacitus, a figure of hope and the representative of the ideal state?

My third suggestion follows from this, but it too can only be outlined here, and concerns a Tacitean view as disputable as it is fundamental. In Tacitus' biography of Germanicus, his father Drusus, the brother of Tiberius, received this notice: *credebaturque, si rerum potitus foret, libertatem redditurus; unde in Germanicum favor et spes eadem* (1. 33. 2); followed by the virtues of Germanicus' character, *civile ingenium, mira comitas*. In this of course Germanicus is presented as the foil to Tiberius: the hope of *libertas* against the reality of *dominatio*. On other occasions too Tacitus stresses *libertas* in connection with Drusus and Germanicus – as, for instance, at Germanicus' triumph in A.D. 17: *sed suberat occulta formido, reputantibus haud prosperum in Druso patre eius favorem vulgi, avunculum eiusdem Marcellum flagrantibus plebis studiis intra iuventam ereptum, breves et infaustos populi Romani amores* (II. 41. 3). What Tacitus means to suggest is clear: Germanicus, as his father before him, was a representative of the Republic, and more specifically of *libertas* and the popular party. *Libertas* had long been the slogan of the *populares*.[24]

24. See, for instance, D. C. Earl, *The Political Thought of Sallust* (Cambridge 1961), pp. 54–7. '*Libertas*, in fact, became a political catchword, employed especially by the *populares* in assailing the *dignitas* of the *optimates*' (p. 55). The

But, once again, is it right to conclude that Tacitus favored Republican *libertas*, and therefore Germanicus? To argue the question here, of course, is impossible. I will only refer to Maternus' summation in the *Dialogus*. It had been argued earlier in that work that true *eloquentia* can exist only in a republic, only at a time of flourishing *libertas*; but *eloquentia*, says Maternus, is the offspring of license, which fools call liberty, and worse: *magna illa et notabilis eloquentia alumna licentiae, quam stulti libertatem vocant, comes seditionum, effrenati populi incitamentum, sine obsequio, sine severitate, contumax, temeraria, arrogans, quae in bene constitutis civitatibus non oritur (Dial..* XL. 2).[25] Maternus' eloquent condemnation of *libertas* and the Republic is so moving and climactic that it would seem impossible to doubt that he speaks for Tacitus himself.[26] One final point remains to be made. When Tacitus noted that *licentia* is what fools call *libertas*, he was far from being original: in Roman political terminology, *libertas* gone wrong is often *licentia*.[27] The mutinies begin and end with *licentia*, a word easily associated in the Roman mind with *libertas* and therefore with Germanicus. The two causes of the mutinies were that the change of emperor gave opportunity for the *licentiam turbarum* and for hope of gain from *civile bellum*: the final scene of the mutinies presents both – *civilium armorum facies*, and *permissa vulgo*

term, of course, was not restricted to the *populares* (see, for instance, R. Syme, *The Roman Revolution* (Oxford 1939), pp. 154–5; and C. Wirszubski, *Libertas as a Political Idea at Rome during the late Republic and early Principate* (Cambridge 1960), *passim*).

25. One should note how closely the vocabulary of Maternus' description parallels the language of the actual mutinies in *Ann.* I. This, of course, is hardly intentional, but does indicate how intricately bound in Tacitus' mind are the two concepts *libertas* and *seditio*. Perhaps the inordinate length and importance given the mutinies in *Ann.* I is due to Tacitus' fascinated realization of the close relationship of the two concepts – and to the fact that Germanicus, the popular representative of *libertas*, found himself so helplessly involved in *seditio*. Once this connection was made, it was almost necessary that a further step would be taken by the historian, to make the mutiny, inevitably, a *civile bellum*.

26. That Tacitus is speaking through Maternus is obvious from the importance of this profession as anti-Ciceronian: *Brut.* XLV, *pacis est comes otique socia et iam bene constitutae civitatis quasi alumna quaedam eloquentia.*

27. See Wirszubski, *Libertas*, p. 7: 'In fact, it is the notion of restraint and moderation that distinguishes libertas from licentia, whose salient feature is arbitrariness; and libertas untempered by moderation degenerates into licentia'; see the examples given in n. 3. (Cf. A. D. Leeman, above p. 181.)

licentia. Tacitus, by stressing Germanicus' popular support and his association with *libertas*, allows the Roman reader to make the Roman association with *licentia* and to follow the progress of this *licentia* until it leads to the final scene of destruction and futility. If Tacitus is not a lover of *dominatio*, neither is he a wistful advocate of *libertas*, which must degenerate into *licentia*, nor of the Republic, which resulted, as Maternus so eloquently argued, only in civil war.

I have interpreted the Tacitean Germanicus, as he appears in the first major episode of the *Annals*, as a figure of failure and futility. To present such a figure Tacitus had sketched its outlines in recognizable, traditional terms – the *mira comitas*, the *favor populi*, the popular hero and general, the final tragic end. Everyone could recognize, and still does recognize, these outlines for what they are – anti-Tiberian, Republican, Julian. But the colors and details, the shading and the total effect, are Tacitus' own, and the final impression so contradicts the outlines that a new and very different Germanicus is the result. On one level Tacitus does preserve the traditional opposition, the popular contrast between emperor and rival: this can still serve the historian as one means by which to darken the figure of Tiberius. But on another level (one more subtle, but actually supported by fact rather than by popular tradition) the heroic Germanicus is continually undermined, the 'lichte Gestalt' grows grayer, and opposites begin to merge and diverse paths to approach the same undesirable ends. Why Tacitus had to portray Germanicus in such a way I have tried to suggest, with reference to the historian's concept of character, to his view of the reality of imperial family politics, and to his idea of the impossibility of both unrestrained Republic and uncontrolled Principate. Tacitus was above all a realist, and for this reason the Tacitean Germanicus is a realistic, and unique, figure.

Juvenal's 'Patchwork' Satires: 4 and 7

ROSS S. KILPATRICK

The charge of 'loose construction' is frequently leveled at Juvenal. This is a largely defensible point of view, but it should not be permitted to obscure instances where the satirist may be aiming at a higher degree of cohesion between the parts of a satire, nor preclude our seeking them out. The clearest instances of this kind of·criticism of Juvenal are directed against *Satires* 4 and 7, the two most frequently cited for lack of unity and coherence. *Sat.* 4, it is true, has had a number of defenders since Nägelsbach (1848),[1] including most recently Helmbold and O'Neil,[2] and Anderson[3] who have suggested new approaches to its thematic unity. But the pessimistic estimate of Kenney[4] finds support from Coffey: 'the fourth satire remains obstinately in two parts.'[5]

·The most useful approach now remaining to a clearer view of these particular poems is to try to determine what the poet's intentions were with regard to their basic designs. If this is possible, it should eventually give perspective to the detailed thematic studies already done; for the purposes of this paper, however, discussion of these other studies will be omitted except where obviously pertinent.

1. C. Fr. Nägelsbach, 'Über die Composition der vierten und sechsten Satire Juvenals', *Phil.* iii (1848), 469–82. For a later defense, see W. Stegemann, *De Iuvenalis dispositione* (Weyda 1913), pp. 30–6. Highet's survey of the literature is very useful (*Juvenal the Satirist* (Oxford 1954), pp. 256f.).

2. W. C. Helmbold and E. N. O'Neil, 'The Structure of Juvenal iv', *AJP*, 77 (1956), 68–73.

3. W. S. Anderson, 'Studies in Juvenal', *YCS* 15 (1957), 68–80. This contains a highly satisfying analysis of the blend of poetry and rhetoric in the satire. The most recent discussion of *Sat.* 4 and Book i is that of W. Heilman ('Zur Komposition der vierten Satire und des ersten Satirenbuches Juvenals', *Rh. Mus.* 110 (1967), 358–70), who sees Crispinus as a kind of Domitian in miniature; so the introduction of *Sat.* 4 would refer as much to the latter as to the Egyptian.

4. E. J. Kenney, 'The First Satire of Juvenal', *PCPS* 8 (1962), 30–1.

5. M. Coffey, 'Juvenal Report for the Years 1941–1961', *Lustrum* 8 (1963), 206. Also (*inter al.*) Highet, *Juvenal*, pp. 76–7.

SAT. 4

The two generally acknowledged weaknesses of *Sat.* 4 invite
answers to two questions: (1) how did Juvenal conceive of the
poem's relationship to the rest of Book 1? and (2) what did he
intend us to see as its own design? The crux of the first question
immediately appears in vv. 1–3:

> Ecce iterum Crispinus, et est mihi saepe vocandus
> ad partes, monstrum nulla virtute redemptum
> a vitiis.

Here the *apparent* problem may be summarized as follows: 'Juvenal
says, "Here's Crispinus again – and I mean to summon him often
to play a part. He's a monster without one redeeming virtue!"
But after that he has the gall to break his promise: Crispinus is
given only a walk-on part later (4. 108f.) and never appears in
another place in the collection after that! Even his role in *Sat.* 1
(*whenever* that poem was composed), is not impressive enough to
qualify, although *iterum* (4. 1) is appropriate enough. How could
Juvenal have failed to repair all this before publishing Book 1?'[6]

Since Crispinus does not in fact reappear in Juvenal beyond
this brief 'inopportune entry',[7] perhaps we should consider
whether 'I *must* summon him often' is de facto too strong a
translation for *est mihi vocandus*. One obvious recourse is to give
it a slightly different interpretation: 'I *should* call him.' Juvenal
must be saying, 'Look, Crispinus again. What's more I *should*
really call him often to play a role – a monster without a redeeming
virtue!' Or else, taking *mihi* as an ethical dative, 'In my view
he is one to be called often.'[8] This interpretation painlessly dis-
poses of any desperate theories about lost satires attacking

---

6. A. Gercke's sensible comments upon Friedländer's chronological specu-
lations are worth reading (*GGA* 12 (1896), 981f.).

7. Kenney, 'First Satire', p. 30.

8. This is a suggestion made to me by E. D. Francis. See Roby's *Latin
Grammar* IV (London and New York, 1896), ch. 14, p. 168 for examples of the
gerund used as an epithet, rather than a predication. Cf. perhaps *Sat.* 4. 153f.,
postquam cerdonibus esse timendus coeperat. The translations of Green ('and I shall
have frequent occasion to parade him before you') and Humphries ('I shall
have to summon him often onto our stage') are typical. See also Highet,
Juvenal, p. 258.

Crispinus.[9] Likewise it allows more flexibility in accounting for
Crispinus' bit-part in the tale of the turbot. When he does show
up again we may be somewhat surprised at his walk-on – *et
matutino sudans Crispinus amomo | quantum vix redolent duo funera* (108f.)
– but surprise is not a rare element in this satire. He is only third
in succession, after Rubrius and Montanus, and by no means
even the most vicious of the group: *saevior illo | Pompeius tenui
iugulos aperire susurro* (109f.)! What's more, he contributes nothing
to the debate, leaving the real honors to others: blind Catullus
(best astonished gape), *prudens* Veiento (interpretation of the
omen), and the fat and waddling Montanus (the perfect solution).
It is no less surprising that such a well-attested connoisseur of
sea food as Crispinus would have no active part in this decision-
making. Only one object of lampoon is mentioned – his extrava-
gant use of perfume (a special scent for the morning);[10] but we
cannot forget the vicious crimes linked to him that were seasoned
with selfish gluttony in the introduction. Similarly the caricatures
of the councillors, even their *nugae*, reflect vicious characters.
Juvenal achieves economy, effect, and proportion in his sketches
of the privy councillors by his two-sided advance attack on
Crispinus. His vicious crimes go hand in hand with venial ones,
gluttony and extravagance. This lends the same extra dimension
to the description of his peers when he accompanies them into
the chamber. Nor should we be surprised when we are reminded
of the realities of Domitian's character and reign (150–4).

Juvenal begins *Sat.* 4 by apologizing rhetorically for dragging
Crispinus in again (*iterum* very definitely refers to *Sat.* 1. 26–9), on
the grounds of the man's utter degeneracy, which he then
elaborates in grand style (3–15). Of course the standard rhetorical
topos allows at least one redeeming virtue to a foe (if only to
enhance his vices); but even this is denied to Crispinus.[11] When
the attack is concluded, the epic tale of Domitian, the turbot,
and the council meeting begins and consumes the remainder of
the poem, leading to the satirist's final observations (150–4).

The problem remaining to be discussed is how Juvenal intended

9. See Friedländer, p. 7; and Highet, *Juvenal*, p. 258.
10. With his morning perfume cf. his summer ring (*Sat.* 1. 28).
11. Friedländer (ad loc.) cites Sen. *Q.N.* 1. 17. 4; Sen. Rh. *Exc. Contr.
praef.* 11 for this topos.

the two parts of the poem to fit. A re-examination of vv. 28–35 may suggest an answer. This section falls into two parts: (1) an apparently rhetorical question (28–33), 'What sort of sumptuous fare do we suppose our Valiant Lord devoured, when Crispinus ...?', and (2) the formulaic invocation to the Muse (34–6) that begins (the jarring abruptness was acknowledged even by Nägelsbach)[12] an epic parody, possibly of Statius' *de bello Germanico*.[13] This rhetorical argument from probability is quite apt, logically, but the suture does seem harsh.

But suppose we move the beginning of the mock epic invocation right back to v. 28. Then the entire question beginning *Qualis tunc...putamus* should be taken in close conjunction with *incipe Calliope* (34):[14]

> Qualis tunc epulas ipsum glutisse putamus
> induperatorem (cum tot sestertia, partem
> exiguam et modicae sumptam de margine cenae,
> purpureus magni ructarit scurra Palati,
> iam princeps equitum, magna qui voce solebat
> vendere municipes fracta de merce siluros)?
> incipe, Calliope. licet hic considere; non est
> cantandum, res vera agitur. narrate puellae
> Pierides. prosit mihi vos dixisse puellas. (28–36)

12. 'Über die Composition...', p. 472. 'Will man sich den Zusammenhang prosaisch vermitteln, so genügt ein einziges *sed* vor *incipe*.'

13. Valla's note on 4. 94, based on ancient scholia now lost; and Highet, *Juvenal*, p. 256.

14. Similarly, for the right relationship of the Muse's invocation to Hor. *Carm.* I. 24 see A. Khan, 'Horace's Ode to Vergil on the Death of Quintilius', *Latomus* 26 (1967), 107–17. A parallel for this *order* (i.e. question followed by imperative and vocative) can be found in Stat. *Silv.* III. 1. 49–50: *Sed quaenam subiti, veneranda, exordia templi,* | *dic age, Calliope*. At *Theb.* x. 628–31 Statius sandwiches the question between two injunctions: *Nunc age, quis stimulos...* | *addiderit iuveni...* | *...memor incipe Clio*. Cf. Val. Fl. VI. 33–4: *Hinc age Rhipaeo quos videris orbe furoris* | *Musa mone*. (My thanks to A. T. Cole for these references.) Perhaps Verg. *Aen.* VII. 641–5 is relevant, too. Juvenal's *qualis...putamus* is printed in the text as a direct question, but it could also be, as the parallels from Statius and Valerius would suggest, indirect. The *indicative* of the question, whether indirect or paratactic in intent, is common enough, especially in early Latin with *dic, responde*, etc. Cf. also Luc. I. 126: *quis iustius induit arma,* | *scire nefas*. If the problem of dating Sulpicia's fragment does not vitiate a parallel from there, it may be the best (34): *Dic mihi, Calliope, quidnam pater ille deorum* | cogitat? an terras et patria saecula mutat?' Whether Juvenal intended the question to be direct or indirect does not, however, affect the essential cohesion of vv. 28–36.

What kind of sumptuous fare, then, do we suppose our
Valiant Lord devoured when so many sesterces, just part
of the trimmings of a modest meal, were belched up by that
ermined palace sponge? Now foremost of the Knights, he
used to hawk with bellowing voice his compatriot sprats,
just odds and ends. The tale begin, Calliope. Sit you may
for this: no need to *sing* – the truth is wanted! Tell the tale,
Maids of Pieria. (Success be mine – for calling you *Maids*!)

The particle *tunc* (28) serves as the connective between the main
attack on Crispinus and the invocation, and points to the logic
Juvenal intends. After a parting shot at Crispinus, in which he
is reduced to an entirely ludicrous figure, the poet proceeds to
the main business of the satire, the tale. *Induperator*, a word going
back to Ennius (four occurrences) and Lucretius (two occurrences)
but not appearing in any extant poetry before Juvenal,[15] is most
appropriate within the formal framework of the actual epic
parody, as part of the invocation.[16]

The beginning of the narrative (37) fits much more smoothly
with what precedes if the invocation is seen to comprise all of
vv. 28–36 and the tale that follows is the Muse's response to
this request. *Tunc* (28) looks back logically at what has been
said already about Crispinus and forward to the parenthetic
cum-clause (29–33).

One may still be left with the suspicion that vv. 1–38 were
composed after the story of Domitian and the fish. Nevertheless,
if we accept the premise that we have *Sat.* 4 in the form in which
Juvenal left it, we can see what he has tried to do. He has begun
the satire as if he fully intended to devote *all* of it to the worst
vices of Crispinus, but then departs abruptly (11) from a discussion
of the sublimely wicked Crispinus to the ridiculously wicked one.
Even in the mullet episode, the 'real' sin is presented in terms of
an absurd anticlimax: *emit sibi* (22)! The change of attack away
from Crispinus' gluttonous extravagance is certainly less abrupt

15. See *TLL* vii. 554. 5ff. A very rare word in extant Latin literature; but
Statius may have used it in his lost epic as a compliment to Domitian.

16. The parody is of an invocation such as Ov. *Met.* v. 338ff. (also to
Calliope). There Ceres is *canenda mihi* (344) and *carmine digna* (345), and
Calliope rises to perform. It is tempting to wonder if Statius had something
like this.

than the shift at v. 11, and is handled not through a *sed nunc de epulis regiis* link but rather a shift to the mock epic-style by means of the invocation, which presents the handbook argument from probability as the means of blackening Domitian's character. The Muses are invited to relate a tale of what surely has to be the acme of gluttony – imperial gluttony – and enjoined to do it in the soberest of fashions. But the Muses betray us (as we might by this time have anticipated) with a tale in *grand* style which includes the catching of the turbot (37–56), its triumphal procession to the emperor's palace (57–71), the privy council meeting (72–149), and the satirist's jaundiced judgement on the affair (150–end) – everything but *epulas glutisse!*[17] Yet is should be remembered that in spite of the use of detour and anticlimax, there actually is a sort of chiastic design informing the two parts. The vices of Crispinus move from the ghastly (a hint) to the contemptible (in detail), while those of Domitian are treated in the opposite direction: the humiliating and sadistic waste of time (in detail) to a cryptic reference to the genocide attempted by Domitian against the Roman nobility.[18]

This three-part division of the prefatory section (1–36), especially considering the deliberate break in thought at v. 11 and the Muses' perversity, makes the transition at v. 37 tolerably smooth: 1–10 (Crispinus the monster), 11–27 (Crispinus the gluttonous fool), 28–36 (invocation to the Muses to go on to a real story of prodigal gluttony – about Domitian himself). It is important to try to arrive at the kind of standards of formal unity and coherence Juvenal sets for himself in this satire, and judge both their appropriateness and his compliance with them. He makes no claim that he will deal extensively with Crispinus, either in this work or elsewhere. His lesser vices lead naturally into the story of one of Domitian's lesser vices (mullet – gluttony: turbot – cynical caprice) but also to a clearer picture of the

17. Kenney's remarks ('First Satire') about the analysis of this satire by Helmbold and O'Neil are important. He points out that the second part is not about gluttony nor about Domitian's trivial crimes. (Indeed Suetonius does *not* make Domitian out to be a glutton.) His judgement on the unity and coherence of the piece is certainly as harsh as any: 'Verses 28–33 are a declaimer's transition of the most palpable kind, an obvious and awkward device to conceal patchwork.'

18. Stegemann (*De Iuvenalis dispositione*) had spotted this chiasmus.

really monstrous nature of the men who came to the meeting, the emperor included. The last five lines of the satire serve to make sure that there is no misunderstanding on this account.

SAT. 7

The most extreme 'analyst' view of *Sat.* 7 is again that of Friedländer, who suggested that the introduction (1–21) was written after the accession of Hadrian and then attached to the main body of the poem (written during the principate of Trajan) by the transitional passage vv. 22–35. The identification of Caesar (1) has occasioned considerable speculation, with Trajan, Hadrian, and even Domitian as candidates.[19]

Juvenal *appears* to begin with a dedication to the emperor, in which the distinction of being the only real patron of contemporary *studia*[20] is bestowed upon him (1–21); this is followed by a transitional section addressed to Telesinus which continues the attack on miserly patrons (22–35).The bulk of the poem (36–243) depicts the sad financial plight of writers (36–105), barristers (106–49), rhetors (150–214), and grammatici (215–43). In spite of the canonical view that Juvenal's structure is generally loose, a reinterpretation of *Sat.* 7 that is simple and convincing and suggests that Juvenal was striving for a greater degree of unity and coherence than has been recognized up to this point might be worth considering.[21]

One important and clear fact is that most of the poem (36–end) comprises an attack on the miserly rich who cheat writers, pleaders,

19. See Friedländer's notes (ad loc.), as well as Highet (*Juvenal*, pp. 269ff.), for nineteenth-century opinions. Hermann, Ribbeck, and Teuffel favored Trajan as the *Caesar* referred to. Hardy and Highet support Hadrian, while Nettleship and more recently Helmbold and O'Neil (*CP* 54 (1959), 100–8) believe Domitian to be the one. According to Helmbold and O'Neil the preface is an *attack* upon Domitian, but both Anderson and Kenney have effectively countered this proposal (see Coffey, 'Juvenal Report', pp. 207–8).

20. There is no need to restrict these *studia* to poetry, although poets are cited as the first example (*enim*), and are discussed all the way to v. 97. In the context of the whole poem it is better to take the word generically, as it is used in Plin. *Pan.* XLVII.

21. 'The theme of the poem may be described as the relationship between cash and culture, but a structural unity cannot be found in what is in fact an impossibly wide interpretation of the meaning of *disertos* (31) nor in the other arguments of Helmbold and O'Neil' (Coffey, 'Juvenal Report', p. 208).

and teachers of their due – financial security – while they take
advantage of them and their services. Actually, this attack begins
as early as v. 30 (in the 'transitional' section) and recalls even
the 'introduction'. Once under way, the tone and momentum of
the attack continue (except for vv. 17–21) unabated to the end.

In the light of this fact, it seems curious that a poem dedicated
to Caesar for his generosity contains so little by way of specific
examples of his largess. That is actually referred to as something
to come *posthac* (18), and resulting from a present attitude. It is
possible, I suppose, to see here a mild protreptic tone like that of
Pliny's *Panegyricus*, meant to encourage future benefactions by
praising past ones. But other than this there is no hint of any
attempt to prod the emperor into greater efforts at patronage.
No, the whole burden of the satire and its individual parts is
unquestionably an *attack*. The question we should ask, then, is
why Caesar is mentioned at *all*, since his compliment is so under-
played. The reason that Juvenal does not plunge into a comprehensive indictment of patronage is not far to seek. An emperor
interested even superficially in the arts could have been offended.
Suppose then the opening of *Sat.* 7 is not a real dedication to
the emperor at all. It becomes a clear statement of the theme,
combined with a careful and tactful exclusion of the emperor
from the ranks of those he is going to attack: wealthy patrons.[22]
The opening reference to him serves two purposes: (1) a tactful
and complimentary exclusion of him and (2) a glance at the
reverse of the coin before a detailed account of the obverse. It
parallels the rhetorical topos of pointing out an enemy's one
virtue as a contrast to his manifold vices. The enemy in *Sat.* 7
is the system of patronage in Rome.

By the placing of the emperor's patronage in this perspective
another fact becomes clear. *Sat.* 7 emerges as a *suasoria* addressed
to one Telesinus (25).[23] Whether real or imaginary, this person is

22. De Decker's comment (*Juvenalis declamans* (Gand 1913), p. 77), 'Au
début du poème, v. 1–21, Juvénal nous avertit que l'empereur régnant ne
mérite pas les reproches qu'il va adresser aux riches indifférents', is right on
target. Kenney's reminder of the worth of De Decker's book in studying
Juvenal is timely (*Latomus* 20 (1963), 707).

23. We are not to be surprised when Telesinus appears to be forgotten later
(as Postumus is forgotten in *Sat.* 6), at least after v. 97, when the survey moves
away from poetry and poets. On the other hand, the examples of historians,

carefully characterized as a good poet, determined to make a success of his calling through fond hopes for support from some contemporary Chesterfield. Whether the *studia* (1) refer to letters in general or poetry in particular, the topic for discussion is in fact narrowed down to the financial difficulties of poets, and are for Telesinus' benefit.

> Et spes et ratio studiorum in Caesare tantum;
> solus enim tristes hac tempestate Camenas
> respexit, cum iam celebres notique poetae
> balneolum Gabiis, Romae conducere furnos
> temptarent, nec foedum alii nec turpe putarent
> praecones fieri, cum desertis Aganippes
> vallibus esuriens migraret in atria Clio. (1–7)

Tantum (1) and *solus* (2) shift the whole focus of the satire upon the following indictment of *ceteri patroni studiorum*. Also the syntax of *hac tempestate respexit…cum…temptarent* can be approached more objectively if we discount reference to the accession of a *new* emperor:[24]

> he alone, *in the recent past*, has shown interest in our native Muses, a time when really popular and noted poets were trying their hand at contracting (a small bath-house at Gabii – some bake-shops at Rome) and others were coming to the opinion that there was nothing sordid or disgraceful in becoming auctioneers; where hunger was making Clio desert the vale of Aganippe and move to the auction hall.

lawyers, and teachers do serve to reinforce the argument of the *suasoria* to Telesinus: that he should be realistic in his own hopes for support.

24. Helmbold and O'Neil's arguments that *respexit* (3) is a preterite, with which the *cum*-clause is in sequence, are attacked by Kenney ('First Satire', p. 31) with examples of secondary sequence after true perfects. But the syntax of this passage is best explained by taking *hac tempestate* to refer to the period of time comprising the recent past up to the present, a usage common enough with *tempus, dies, anni, biduum*, etc. (e.g. Nep. *Att.* XXI. 5–6). For a discussion of 'characterizing' *cum*-clauses (common in Juvenal) see B. L. Ullman (*The Classical Tradition: Studies in Honor of Harry Caplan* (Ithaca 1966), pp. 274f.), and Woodcock (*A New Latin Syntax* (Cambridge 1959), p. 234). Woodcock cites Caes. *B.G.* VI. 24, and Cic. *S. Rosc.* XXXIII: *accepit enim agrum temporibus eis cum iacerent pretia praediorum.* He comments: 'The subjunctive does more than indicate the time when the action took place; it describes it as well.'

The point of this state of affairs is brought home to Telesinus personally (8–11):

> nam si Pieria quadrans tibi nullus in umbra
> ostendatur, ames nomen victumque Machaerae
> et vendas potius commissa quod auctio vendit
> stantibus.

If *you* discovered there wasn't a sou to be found in the shade of Pieria, *you* would be content with the title and livelihood of Machaera, and switch to selling the wares the standing crowd buys at auction.

Such a mean occupation would be far less degrading than being a professional perjuror like the parvenu knights of the east (13–16).

Juvenal then elaborates on the contrast that royal patronage makes with the rest. It would be reasonable to suppose that there was an official position on patronage by this time, as an outgrowth of a past tendency on Caesar's part to be a patron of the arts (18–22):

> nemo tamen studiis indignum ferre laborem
> cogetur posthac, nectit quicumque canoris
> eloquium vocale modis laurumque momordit.
> hoc agite, o iuvenes: circumspicit et stimulat vos
> materiamque sibi ducis indulgentia quaerit.

But henceforth no one will be forced to endure toil unworthy of his interests – no one of those who weave vocal utterance or have chewed the laurel. Lay on, Lads! He is on the look-out for you, and prods you, and his bounty searches for scope for itself.

But it is also clear that Juvenal's optimism about Caesar's patronage, significant in the past and growing in scope, pertains only to true and gifted poets, as vv. 17–21 imply. In view of the promise of sure bounty for talented writers in the future, Telesinus (the object of the *suasoria*) would have to be out of his mind to look elsewhere for it (22–9)! That the satirist does consider him worthy is suggested by his very urging, and is confirmed by vv. 28–9:

> qui facis in parva sublimia carmina cella
> ut dignus venias hederis et imagine macra.

In v. 30 the two opposite styles of patronage confront:

> spes nulla ulterior; didicit iam dives avarus
> tantum admirari, tantum laudare disertos,
> ut pueri Iunonis avem.

'There's no other hope. The rich miser has by now learned only to *admire*, only to *praise* eloquence, as boys do Juno's bird.'

So the real foe has been named: *dives avarus*. Telesinus' Chesterfield has learned that praise is cheap, and serves to enhance his own prestige. But while the poet pays his fruitless court to a cheapskate patron, time passes by, along with his prime and any likelihood of finding a more profitable occupation (32–3). The section concludes with a gloomy picture of the old age of a starveling poet (34–5):

> taedia tunc subeunt animos, tunc seque suamque
> Terpsichoren odit facunda et nuda senectus.

Then malaise creeps over your spirit. *Then* old age, prolific (and bare) loathes itself and its own sprightly Muse.

Vv. 1–35 are in fact one whole section, the introductory *suasoria* to the poet Telesinus to break with his miserly patron, who (like his peers) has not a shred of sincere generosity. There is a gleam of hope in the darkness, though: the emperor, who has of late begun to show himself a generous patron of superior talent, promises to continue as such *posthac*. But this light, which flares most brightly in the apostrophe to the poets of the future (20–1), serves the satirist chiefly to curse the darkness around it. Even poets of talent, without Caesar's help, will continue to lead wretched lives.

The rest of the satire (36–end) consists of melancholy but brilliant *evidentia*: the plight of those who depend on writing, pleading, and teaching for their livelihood; i.e. the *studia* of v. 1. These *studia* were focused immediately upon poetry, and a warning issued to Telesinus not to put his trust in a *dives avarus* when he can go to Caesar.

If this is the unity of theme that Juvenal intended, it remains to see whether the two *parts* present a coherently-linked design. The longer section begins (36): *accipe nunc artes*. This is usually translated 'Now listen to their *methods*,' which suggests a kind of makeshift bridge to a topic only loosely related to what has preceded. But if *nunc* is antithetical to *tunc...tunc* (34), it must be the emphatic word of the injunction: 'Give heed *now* to their ways (– while there's time)!' Specific reference to Telesinus' patron (real or potential) and his ruses to avoid a cash outlay follow (36–44). The plight of poets is then described in wider terms, culminating in the incident of Statius and Paris (82–9). The case against the contemporary patrons of poetry at Rome is wound up in vv. 90–7 by the satirist as *laudator temporis acti*. Once again, the *tu...tu* at whom the moral is pointed may still be Telesinus; for it is with respect to genuine talent that their case is made:

> tum par ingenio pretium, tunc utile multis
> pallere et vinum toto nescire Decembri.

The logic of the progression to the plight of the historians, by way of direct address, is perhaps the most tenuous of the whole satire. It is under the guise of an *incrementum* in the *evidentia* (98–9):

> vester porro labor fecundior, historiarum
> scriptores? perit hic plus temporis atque olei plus.

Once again the *indignatio* their plight arouses comes as a result of meager financial rewards for prodigious efforts (103–4):

> quae tamen inde seges? terrae quis fructus apertae?
> quis dabit historico quantum daret acta legenti?[25]

Once the satirist has made the break from poetry to history he contrives a dramatic means to proceed to the other exploited professions. It is not unlikely that the objection *sed genus ignavum, quod lecto gaudet et umbra* (105) should be assigned to Telesinus.[26] The point of the interruption is perhaps, 'Of course historians don't get support – they don't contribute anything!' If it is

---

25. Cf. the last two lines of this satire, in which the rewards of the grammaticus are outlined: '*haec*' inquit '*cura. Sed cum se verterit annus, | accipe victori populus quod postulat aurum.*'

26. Or else the *dives avarus* himself (30) defending his peers' reluctance to pay. It is curious that of all the professions mentioned in the poem the historians get both the briefest and most satirical treatment. No attempt is made to refute the charge, which adds to the humor. Are we to infer that historians were exceptionally well-off? See Highet, *Juvenal*, pp. 270f.

Telesinus speaking, the remark would be motivated by his desire to convince himself, at least, that there is some rationale behind the attitude of Roman patrons: 'Just because historians are (predictably and with some justification) starving doesn't mean that poets are being exploited!' In any case the brief remark is mechanically the dramatic motivation for the abundant *evidentia* that consumes the rest of the poem.

In *Sat.* 7 Juvenal has set out to expose and attack the cruel and stingy patrons at Rome. His plan develops through these stages: (1) The general grim picture, with Caesar placed prominently as the one hopeful exception – for poets of talent (1–21). (2) The *suasoria* proper to Telesinus to forget his cheapskate patron and rely on Caesar, where there is *some* hope. (3) A didactic account of the ruses poets' patrons use to avoid paying (36–97). (4) A brief excursus on the similar plight of historians – humorously rejected by someone, perhaps Telesinus himself (98–105). (5) A tacit concession that historians are drones, leading to a change of subject – those who plead in court (106–49), teach rhetoric (150–214), and literature (215–end). The occupational hazards of each are aggravated by meager financial rewards.

The satire begins as a hypothesis addressed to Telesinus' predicament, which, while never becoming irrelevant to him, becomes a thesis bearing on the depressed state of arts and letters at Rome.